Lecture Notes
in Business Information Processing
471

Series Editors

Wil van der Aalst, *RWTH Aachen University, Aachen, Germany*

Sudha Ram, *University of Arizona, Tucson, AZ, USA*

Michael Rosemann, *Queensland University of Technology, Brisbane, QLD, Australia*

Clemens Szyperski, *Microsoft Research, Redmond, WA, USA*

Giancarlo Guizzardi, *University of Twente, Enschede, The Netherlands*

LNBIP reports state-of-the-art results in areas related to business information systems and industrial application software development – timely, at a high level, and in both printed and electronic form.

The type of material published includes

- Proceedings (published in time for the respective event)
- Postproceedings (consisting of thoroughly revised and/or extended final papers)
- Other edited monographs (such as, for example, project reports or invited volumes)
- Tutorials (coherently integrated collections of lectures given at advanced courses, seminars, schools, etc.)
- Award-winning or exceptional theses

LNBIP is abstracted/indexed in DBLP, EI and Scopus. LNBIP volumes are also submitted for the inclusion in ISI Proceedings.

Ewa Ziemba · Witold Chmielarz ·
Jarosław Wątróbski
Editors

Information Technology
for Management

Approaches to Improving Business
and Society

AIST 2022 Track and 17th Conference, ISM 2022
Held as Part of FedCSIS 2022
Sofia, Bulgaria, September 4–7, 2022
Extended and Revised Selected Papers

 Springer

Editors
Ewa Ziemba 🆔
University of Economics in Katowice
Katowice, Poland

Witold Chmielarz 🆔
University of Warsaw
Warsaw, Poland

Jarosław Wątróbski 🆔
University of Szczecin
Szczecin, Poland

ISSN 1865-1348   ISSN 1865-1356 (electronic)
Lecture Notes in Business Information Processing
ISBN 978-3-031-29569-0   ISBN 978-3-031-29570-6 (eBook)
https://doi.org/10.1007/978-3-031-29570-6

This Springer imprint is published by the registered company Springer Nature Switzerland AG
The registered company address is: Gewerbestrasse 11, 6330 Cham, Switzerland

Preface

Seven volumes in this series appeared in the last seven years:

- *Information Technology for Management* in 2016 (LNBIP 243);
- *Information Technology for Management:* New Ideas and Real Solutions in 2017 (LNBIP 277);
- *Information Technology for Management:* Ongoing Research and Development in 2018 (LNBIP 311);
- *Information Technology for Management:* Emerging Research and Applications in 2019 (LNBIP 346);
- *Information Technology for Management:* Current Research and Future Directions in 2020 (LNBIP 380);
- *Information Technology for Management:* Towards Business Excellence in 2021 (LNBIP 413);
- *Information Technology for Management:* Business and Social Issues in 2022 (LNBIP 442).

Given the rapid developments in information systems and technologies and the related new opportunities and threats for businesses, governments, and societies' development, there was a clear need for the next publication in this series.

The present book includes extended and revised versions of a set of selected papers submitted to the Advances in Information Systems and Technologies conference track (AIST 2022) organized within the 17th Conference on Computer Science and Intelligence Systems (FedCSIS 2022), held in Sofia, Bulgaria, during September 4–7, 2022.

FedCSIS provides a reputable forum for presentation, discussion, and publication in computer science and intelligence systems. It invites researchers and practitioners from around the world to contribute their research results focused on emerging topics related to computer science and intelligence systems. Since 2012, Proceedings of FedCSIS are indexed in the Thomson Reuters Web of Science, Scopus, IEEE Xplore Digital Library, and DBLP Computer Science Bibliography.

AIST covers a broad spectrum of topics that integrate information technologies and systems sciences and social sciences, i.e., economics, management, business, finance, and education. This edition consisted of the following four scientific sessions: Advances in Information Systems and Technologies (AIST 2022), 4th Workshop on Data Science in Health, Ecology and Commerce (DSH 2022), 17th Conference on Information Systems Management (ISM 2022), and 28th Conference on Knowledge Acquisition and Management (KAM 2022).

AIST addresses the most recent innovations, current trends, professional experiences, and new challenges in designing, implementing, and using information systems and technologies for business, government, education, healthcare, smart cities, and sustainable development.

The topic of DSH includes data analysis, data economics, information systems, and data science research, focusing on the interaction of the three fields, i.e., health, ecology, and commerce.

ISM concentrates on various issues of planning, organizing, resourcing, coordinating, controlling, and leading management functions to ensure the smooth, effective, and high-quality operation of information systems in organizations.

KAM discusses approaches, techniques, and tools in knowledge acquisition and other knowledge management areas with a focus on the contribution of artificial intelligence to improving human-machine intelligence and facing the challenges of this century.

At the same time, they show the breadth of the issues discussed every year within AIST; thanks to this diversity, everyone interested in this subject can find something interesting for themselves.

For AIST 2022, we received 54 papers from 29 countries in all continents. The quality of the papers was carefully evaluated by the members of the Program Committee by taking into account the criteria for papers, relevance to conference topics, originality, and novelty. After extensive reviews, only 11 papers (20%) were accepted as full papers and 10 (18%) as short papers, yielding an acceptance rate of 38%. Finally, 11 papers (20%) of the highest quality were carefully reviewed and chosen by the Chairs of the AIST track, and the authors were invited to extend their research and submit the new extended papers for consideration for this LNBIP publication. Our guiding criteria for including a paper in the book were the excellence of the submission as indicated by the reviewers, the relevance of the subject matter for improving management by adopting information technology, as well as the promise of the scientific contributions and the implications for practitioners. The selected papers reflect state-of-art research work that is often oriented toward real-world applications and highlight the benefits of information systems and technologies for business and public administration, thus forming a bridge between theory and practice.

The papers selected to be included in this book contribute to understanding relevant trends of current research on and future directions of information systems and technologies for improving and developing business and society. The book's first part focuses on approaches to improving business, the second part presents approaches to improving society, and the third part explores methods for improving business and society.

Finally, we and the authors hope readers will find the content of this book useful and interesting for their own research activities. In this spirit and conviction, we offer our monograph, which is the result of the authors' intellectual effort, for the readers' final judgment. We are open to discussing the issues raised in this book and looking forward to critical or even polemical voices as to the content and form. The final evaluation of this publication is up to you - our Readers.

February 2023

Ewa Ziemba
Witold Chmielarz
Jarosław Wątróbski

Organization

FedCSIS-AIST 2022

Track Chairs

Ewa Ziemba	University of Economics in Katowice, Poland
Witold Chmielarz	University of Warsaw, Poland
Alberto Cano	Virginia Commonwealth University, USA

Program Chairs

Witold Chmielarz	University of Warsaw, Poland
Gloria Miller	Maxmetrics, Germany
Jarosław Wątróbski	University of Szczecin, Poland
Ewa Ziemba	University of Economics in Katowice, Poland

Program Committee

Ofir Ben-Assuli	Ono Academic College, Israel
Andrzej Białas	Instytut Technik Innowacyjnych EMAG, Poland
Alexander Byrski	AGH University of Science and Technology, Poland
Dimitar Christozov	American University in Bulgaria, Bulgaria
Tuan Dang	Posts and Telecommunications Institute of Technology, Vietnam
Gonçalo Dias	University of Aveiro, Portugal
Rafal Drezewski	AGH University of Science and Technology, Poland
Dariusz Grabara	University of Economics in Katowice, Poland
Leila Halawi	Embry-Riddle Aeronautical University, USA
Krzysztof Kania	University of Economics in Katowice, Poland
Adrian Kapczyński	Silesian University of Technology, Poland
Krzysztof Kluza	AGH University of Science and Technology, Poland
Eugenia Kovatcheva	University of Library Studies and Information Technologies, Bulgaria
Jan Kozak	University of Economics in Katowice, Poland

Antoni Ligeza	AGH University of Science and Technology, Poland
Andre Ludwig	Kühne Logistics University, Germany
Jose Maria Luna	University of Cordoba, Spain
Krzysztof Michalik	University of Economics in Katowice, Poland
Maurizio Naldi	LUMSA University, Italy
Thi Anh Thu Nguyen	University of Da Nang, Vietnam
Van Tuan Pham	Da Nang University of Science and Technology, Vietnam
Amit Rechavi	Ruppin Academic Center, Israel
Nina Rizun	Gdansk University of Technology, Poland
Federica Rollo	University of Modena and Reggio Emilia, Italy
Yonit Rusho	Shenkar College of Engineering and Design, Israel
Wojciech Sałabun	West Pomeranian University of Technology in Szczecin, Poland
Joanna Santiago	ISEG - University of Lisbon, Portugal
Marcin Sikorski	Gdansk University of Technology, Poland
Vijender Kumar Solanki	CMR Institute of Technology, India
Francesco Taglino	IASI-CNR, Italy
Łukasz Tomczyk	Pedagogical University of Cracow, Poland
Julian Webber	Osaka University, Japan
Paweł Ziemba	University of Szczecin, Poland

DSH 2022

Chairs

Bogdan Franczyk	University of Leipzig, Germany
Carsta Militzer-Horstmann	WIG2 Institute for Health Economics and Health Service Research, Germany
Dennis Häckl	University of Leipzig, Germany and WIG2 Institute for Health Economics and Health Service Research, Germany
Jan Bumberger	Helmholtz-Centre for Environmental Research – UFZ, Germany
Olaf Reinhold	University of Leipzig/Social CRM Research Center, Germany

Program Committee

Adil Alpkoçak	Dokuz Eylul University, Turkey
Alireza Ansari	Leipzig University, Germany and IORA Regional Center for Science and Technology Transfer, Iran
Emílio José Montero Arruda Filho	Universidad Federal do Para and University of Amazonas, Brazil
Nilanjan Dey	Techno International New Town, India
Eric Fass	WIG2 Institute for Health Economics and Health Service Research, Germany
Marcin Hernes	Wroclaw University of Economics and Business, Poland
Karol Kozak	Fraunhofer and Uniklinikum Dresden, Germany
Marco Müller	WIG2 Institute for Health Economics and Health Service Research, Germany
Piotr Popowski	Medical University of Gdańsk, Poland
Artur Rot	Wroclaw University of Economics and Business, Poland
Shelly Sachdeva	National Institute of Technology Delhi, India
Agnieszka Siennicka	Wroclaw Medical University, Poland
Patrick Timpel	WIG2 Institute for Health Economics and Health Service Research, Germany and Technical University Dresden, Germany
Katarzyna Wasielewska-Michniewska	Systems Research Institute of the Polish Academy of Sciences, Poland

ISM 2022

Chairs

Bernard Arogyaswami	Le Moyne University, USA
Witold Chmielarz	University of Warsaw, Poland
Jarosław Wątróbski	University of Szczecin, Poland
Jerzy Kisielnicki	University of Warsaw, Poland
Ewa Ziemba	University of Economics in Katowice, Poland

Program Committee

Zane Bicevska	University of Latvia, Latvia
Janis Bicevskis	University of Latvia, Latvia

Vincenza Carchiolo	Università di Catania, Italy
Beata Czarnacka-Chrobot	Warsaw School of Economics, Poland
Susana de Juana Espinosa	Universidad de Alicante, Spain
Yanqing Duan	University of Bedfordshire, UK
Monika Eisenbardt	University of Economics Katowice, Poland
Renata Gabryelczyk	University of Warsaw, Poland
Nitza Geri	The Open University of Israel, Israel
Christian Leyh	Dresden University of Technology, Germany
Michele Malgeri	Università degli Studi di Catania, Italy
Karolina Muszyńska	University of Szczecin, Poland
Anastasija Nikiforova	University of Tartu, Estonia
Nina Rizun	Gdansk University of Technology, Poland
Uldis Rozevskis	University of Latvia, Latvia
Andrzej Sobczak	Warsaw School of Economics, Poland
Jakub Swacha	University of Szczecin, Poland
Symeon Symeonidis	Democritus University of Thrace, Greece
Edward Szczerbicki	Newcastle University, Australia
Oskar Szumski	University of Warsaw, Poland
Janusz Wielki	Opole University of Technology, Poland
Jarosław Wątróbski	University of Szczecin, Poland
Marek Zborowski	University of Warsaw, Poland

KAM 2022

Chairs

Krzysztof Hauke	Wroclaw University of Economics, Poland
Małgorzata Nycz	Wroclaw University of Economics, Poland
Mieczysław Owoc	Wroclaw University of Economics, Poland
Maciej Pondel	Wroclaw University of Economics, Poland

Program Committee

Frederic Andres	National Institute of Informatics, Japan
Petr Berka	Prague University of Economics and Business, Czech Republic
Yevgeniy Bodyanskiy	Kharkiv National University of Radio Electronics, Ukraine
Iwona Chomiak-Orsa	Wroclaw University of Economics and Business, Poland

Dimitar Christozov	American University in Bulgaria, Bulgaria
David Chudán	Prague University of Economics and Business, Czech Republic
Marcin Hermes	Wrocław University of Economics and Business, Poland
Tomáš Kliegr	Prague University of Economics and Business, Czech Republic
Krzysztof Kluza	AGH University of Science and Technology, Poland
Antoni Ligęza	AGH University of Science and Technology, Poland
Eunika Mercier-Laurent	Jean Moulin Lyon 3 University, France
Kazimierz Perechuda	Wroclaw University of Economics and Business, Poland
Jeanne Schreurs	Hasselt University, Belgium
Pradeep Singth	KIET Group of Institutions, India
Yashwant Singth	Jaypee University of Information Technology, India
Małgorzata Sobińska	Wroclaw University of Economics, Poland
Michael Stankosky	University of Scranton, USA
Sudeep Tanwar	Nirma University, India
Sudhanshu Tyagi	Thapar Institute of Engineering & Technology, India
Jan Vanthienen	Katholike Universiteit Leuven, Belgium
Julian Vasiliev	University of Economics, Varna, Bulgaria
Yungang Zhu	Jilin University, China

Acknowledgment

We would like to express our thanks to everyone who made the FedCSIS AIST track successful. First of all, our authors for offering very interesting research and submitting new findings for publication in LNBIP. We express our appreciation to the members of the Program Committees for taking the time and effort necessary to help us with their expertise and diligence in reviewing the papers and providing valuable insights for the authors. The high standards followed by them enabled the authors to ensure the high quality of the papers. The excellent work of the Program Committee members and the authors enabled us to ensure the high quality of the conference sessions and valuable scientific discussion. We acknowledge the Chairs of FedCSIS 2022, i.e., Maria Ganzha, Marcin Paprzycki, Dominik Ślęzak, and Leszek A. Maciaszek, for building an active international community around the FedCSIS conference. Last but not least, we are indebted to the team of Springer-Verlag, mainly Ralf Gerstner without whom this book would not have been possible. Many thanks also to Christine Reiss for handling the production of this book.

We cordially invite you to visit the FedCSIS website at https://fedcsis.org and join us in future at the Information Technology for Business and Society (ITBS 2023) track that replaces AIST track in 2023.

Contents

Approaches to Improving Business

Configuration Approach of User Requirements for Analytical Applications - Challenges, State of the Art and Evaluation

Christian Hrach[1](✉) ⓘ, Rainer Alt[2] ⓘ, and Stefan Sackmann[3] ⓘ

[1] Institute for Applied Informatics, Goerdelerring 9, 04109 Leipzig, Germany
hrach@infai.org
[2] Leipzig University, Grimmaische Str. 12, 04109 Leipzig, Germany
rainer.alt@uni-leipzig.de
[3] Martin Luther University Halle-Wittenberg, Universitätsring 3, 06108 Halle, Germany
stefan.sackmann@wiwi.uni-halle.de

Abstract. The integration of process orientation and the use of analytical applications to provide process-related analytical information in operational process activities (e.g., Operational BI) has become increasingly widespread. But at the same time, the insufficient involvement of analytical end users with their process context and the resulting unclear requirements/expected analytical software functions are still one of the main reasons for analytical project failure. This paper is based on a previous conference publication [26] and extends the detailed presentation of failure causes as well as shows the shortcomings of existing approaches, tools and models (1. BPMN process model extensions, 2. Configurators in analytical applications, 3. Models used in analytical development projects) for the documentation/conceptual configuration of analytical requirements. In addition, this paper presents the evaluation results of a process-oriented and service-based configuration approach for analytical applications, whose practicability, usefulness and acceptance were evaluated in expert reviews and were tested in a Population Forecast scenario.

Keyword: Requirements configuration · Analytical service · Service configuration

1 Introduction

The approach of process orientation has established itself in corporate practice since the 1990s as a primary procedure to structure corporate organizations and as a basis for the (re)organization of operational value-adding activities. Systems of insight [2] and analytical applications have long been used for retrospective analysis of corporate activities for the management in terms of Business Intelligence (BI). Due to a wider dissemination of analytical information in operational processes [38], original focus and functional range of analytical application/BI design have widened as well [50]. Additional aspects include 1. the trend to a modular analytical application structure

© The Author(s), under exclusive license to Springer Nature Switzerland AG 2023
E. Ziemba et al. (Eds.): FedCSIS-AIST 2022/ISM 2022, LNBIP 471, pp. 3–22, 2023.
https://doi.org/10.1007/978-3-031-29570-6_1

[12], 2. the consideration of analytical self-services [23] and 3. the implementation of real-time monitoring and automatic actions [22, 56].

The insufficient inclusion of users with their process context and the resulting unclear requirements/expected deliverables are repeatedly cited in literature as the main causes for project failure or for the development of analytical applications that does not meet user expectations [1, 4]. This hypothesis was confirmed by interviews and an online survey with analytical requirements experts: five of the experts surveyed find inadequately communicated/documented requirements very frequent, four experts find them rather frequent and two experts find them less frequent as a main reason for delayed or insufficient implementations of analytical applications.

In addition, practice-oriented literature as well as the above-mentioned interviews and the online survey with experts in analytical requirements management provide evidence for a number of detailed causes for delays or failure of analytical development projects. They point out important aspects that must be better taken into account in the design of future user- and process-oriented conceptual analytical application configuration in terms of requirements documentation. These include:

1. **Unclear ideas on the users' side about goals, functionalities and detailed system specifications** due to insufficiently elaborated and planned project scopes, information needs and use cases [1, 41]. Three out of four analytical experts surveyed in interviews regard incomplete requirements as one of the main problems in analytical development projects. Experts who participated in the online survey confirmed this aspect, according to which the majority of important requirements are very often (two mentions) and rather often (four mentions) identified or explicitly named only at a belated point in the development process. In this context, unclear ideas regarding goals, functionalities and detailed specifications occur very often (four mentions) and rather often (two mentions) on the side of the analytical users.

2. **Requirements formulated by users in an unclear and/or misleading manner** and the resulting misunderstandings among technical developers [4, 33]. The experts participating in the online survey reported that misunderstandings occur very often (four mentions) and rather often (two mentions) in user requirements handling. The main reason for this is that users often have a different perspective and a different mindset than developers and communicate in a different language or with different terms [16]. Three out of four experts surveyed in interviews consider it to be a major problem in the development of analytical applications. The weakly structured natural language documents (e.g., in the form of continuous text or bullet points) most commonly used in practice for requirements documentation [34] generally contain only few to no requirements design guidelines and thus offer users little support for technically correct and unambiguous requirements formulation [35, 40]. Three out of four of the analytical experts interviewed rated the text-based tools used in their companies for requirements documentation (e.g., Word, ticket systems) as only good to less good in terms of completeness of content/depth of detail and in terms of an intersubjectively unambiguous description.

3. **Changing user requirements often lead to increased efforts and project delays** [1, 33], since on the one hand the natural-language-based tools often used for requirements documentation have to be searched protractedly in order to find the relevant

text passages for the requirements changes, and the text changes have to be formulated in natural language each time again. On the other hand, when different requirements documents and/or requirements models are used in practice (according to the online survey very often (two mentions), rather often (two mentions) and less often (three mentions)), they must be adapted individually and must be coordinated afterwards again with one another. In contrast, a single integrated configuration approach for requirements documentation that (pre-)structures the planned analytical application as a modular system (e.g., based on a service-oriented architecture approach) can respond much more easily and flexibly to requirements changes by adapting or replacing individual modules/services, and can leverage synergies by reusing modularly encapsulated requirements content to a much greater extent.

4. **Uncoordinated planning and implementation of individual data analyses within processes** [55] lead to fragmented and insufficiently integrated analytical application landscapes and impede a data-driven process design. Among the experts participating in the online survey, insufficient integration of analytical applications into operational processes occurs rather often (three mentions) and less often (four mentions) in their own projects. This manifests itself in the use of different and sometimes incompatible data sources and inhomogeneous analytical applications in the same process, and in a lack of (automated) data interfaces for the transfer of analytical data/information between process steps.

5. **Data privacy risks known to the process users and not considered right from the start throughout requirements elicitation and documentation** [4, 16] lead to extensive subsequent adjustments [16] up to the (partial) removal of already implemented data analyses. In this context, the consideration of data protection requirements concerns not only the successive design and adaptation of the technical analytical components, but also the upstream selection of analytical applications and system components available on the market.

6. **Unclear requirements regarding the desired customizability of analytical applications by users in terms of insufficient consideration of analytical self-service features.** In recent years, the provision of easy-to-use analytical self-service functions for all user groups has become increasingly important in practice (as part of the general spread of approaches to enable software users to independently adapt and further develop software applications [36]). However, when developing analytical applications, the inherently desired analytical self-service functions often take a back seat in favor of the (initially) required concrete data analyses and information visualization.

These aspects suggest that models, configurators and other tools used in the documentation of requirements for process-related analytical applications in development projects are apparently insufficient. To proof this hypothesis, it is necessary to carefully analyze the current state of the art concerning the following tools and models for configuration and conceptual modeling of analytical applications (as an extension of an earlier literature review in [25]):

- Applicability of process modeling languages to present information requirements;

- Availability of models for requirements documentation/conceptual configuration provided with analytical application products;
- Use of tools for requirements documentation in analytical development projects.

In addition, the authors conducted expert reviews to proof the completeness and usefulness of an approach for the conceptual configuration of analytical applications based on analytical services (initially presented in [25]) and its practicability in the context of process-related analytical requirements documentation. This led to the following two research questions:

RQ1: What support do models and tools from science and practice provide regarding documentation/configuration of process user requirements for analytical applications?

RQ2: To what extent is a configuration approach for analytical services suitable to be used in analytical development projects and to solve the identified challenges regarding documentation/configuration of process user requirements for analytical applications?

After the introduction in Sect. 1, Sect. 2 shows the relevant configuration characteristics for analytical requirements and their specific distribution/consideration in previous requirements configuration models in scientific literature. Section 3 presents the research method. Section 4 provides the current state of the art regarding additional tools and models for documenting conceptual requirements for analytical process support in science and practice. Section 5 shows the practical relevance of the new process-oriented configuration approach for analytical applications based on evaluation results. A discussion in Sect. 6 concludes the paper.

2   Literature Review Regarding the Configuration of Analytical Requirements

Analytical/BI applications that can be successfully used in practice are characterized by the fact that they provide 1. the right **information** at 2. the right **time** in 3. a suitable **presentation form** and generated with 4. the right **analysis methods** to 5. the right **users** [50]. In addition to these five content-related aspects, the following necessary design aspects (identified in a literature review) for tools and models supporting the configuration of analytical applications address the denoted detailed causes for delays or failure of analytical development projects mentioned in Sect. 1:

6. **Models utilized by business users** (causes 1 + 2): Requirements documentation tools should be designed for users [28] with their specific abilities and knowledge to get them more involved in the analytical design process.
7. **Configuration alternatives** (causes 1 + 2): Providing configuration alternatives in analytical requirements models [32] ensures acceleration of selection decisions and reduces the risk of misleading requirements descriptions.
8. **Graphical modeling notation** (cause 2): Graphical models for requirements documentation [35] provide a more intuitive access to conceptual models [17].
9. **Service-oriented design** (cause 3): To support the adjustment of analytical applications due to changing processes [12], the modularized provision of subcomponents of analytical applications as reusable analytical services in terms of service-oriented

architectures (SOA) [38, 48] enables customer-centric service provision [46] as well as the (re)combination of analytical components from different providers [57].

10. **Process-relation** (cause 4): A strong link to process design in the phase of requirements elicitation and requirements documentation [47] has a positive effect on an analytical information provision that is coordinated between process activities.

11. **Data privacy** (cause 5): An examination of the planned analytical use cases from a data privacy perspective is important within the requirements analysis to prevent extensive adjustments during the development of analytical applications [52].

12. **Self-services** (cause 6): To enable rapid customization of analytical applications [23] due to changes in process information demand, analytical self-service applications should enable process staff to independently adapt or create analytical reports/dashboards, to integrate new data, to check and/or improve data quality and to adjust analytical data models [3].

To stress the deep integration of operational processes with analytical applications (accompanied and pushed, e.g., by the dissemination of approaches such as "Business Process Intelligence", "Business Activity Monitoring", "Operational BI" [20] in research and practice), another important requirements aspect regarding analytical application design (identified in a literature review) must be added:

13. **Automatic actions**: The proliferation of IoT assets and their integration into operational process controls [49], the acceleration of operational applications (e.g., faster data storage structures) and direct interconnections between systems of data origination and data use are drivers for "real-time enterprises" with the ability to react immediately to occurring events [7]. Business Activity Monitoring (BAM) applications [56] monitor process executions to identify threshold violations or error events and support the automated/rule-based execution of actions.

The structured literature review (presented in more detail in [25]) used to search and analyze scientific models for analytical requirements documentation and configuration regarding the aforementioned 13 design aspects included a broad search space ("requirements" AND "analytical software" OR "information systems") in order to obtain results without restrictions in the perspectives of observation (e.g., business engineering) and business domains (e.g., production). The analysis of 13 finally identified requirements and configuration approaches [10, 11, 15, 18, 19, 24, 27, 31, 32, 44, 51, 53, 54] aimed to find out to what extent these approaches comprehensively, partially, or do not address the mentioned requirement aspects. The results of this analysis showed that none of these approaches even comes close to addressing all aspects, with major deficits in the areas "periodicity", "presentation", „configuration alternatives", "service-oriented design", "process-relation", "data privacy", "self-services" and "automatic actions" [25].

3 Research Methodology

The research results presented in this article have been elaborated as parts of a wider research project following the six-step Design Science Research Methodology Process

(DSRMP) [39], whose aim was to develop a configuration approach to specify conceptual process user requirements for analytical applications (for further details see [25]). In order to identify the specific problems in practice and to substantiate the situation of currently insufficient scientific and practice-oriented solutions (first DSRMP phase), the following research methods were used:

- Identification of causes for the insufficient specification of user requirements in analytical projects (Sect. 1) together with an analysis regarding the quality of different models, notations and documents used in practice to document analytical user requirements (Sect. 4.3) was based on a search in practice-oriented literature, on four interviews with BI project/requirements managers (2015 - 2020), and on an online survey in August 2021 with seven experts in the field of BI requirements management (about 125 participants of a BI experts talk were invited).
- Analysis of process modeling notations to find suitable process representations to configure analytical process requirements (Sect. 4.1) encompassed all previously elaborated extensions of the process modeling language Business Process Model and Notation (BPMN) collocated and surveyed by Zarour et al. [58].
- Analysis of analytical products to determine whether they provide pre-built models/configurators for documenting business user requirements (Sect. 4.2) comprised all 13 analytical products in the quadrants "Leaders", "Visionaries" and "Challengers" of "Gartner Magic Quadrant for Analytics and BI Platforms 2021" [42]. Investigation techniques included both interviews with software providers and the analysis of written product information.

To evaluate the previously elaborated configuration approach for analytic services [25] as part of the fifth DSRMP phase, the following research methods were used:

- Expert reviews with 13 experts in the field of analytics (project/requirements managers, data scientists) generated a quality feedback regarding the defined structure and content of the configuration approach to assess the usefulness/practical value (proof of value) [21] of the configuration approach and its acceptance by the model users (proof of acceptance) [14, 21] (Sect. 5.2).
- The configuration approach has been tested in two analytical development projects (proof of use) to specify requirements regarding both an analytical dashboard and an analytical report. Section 5.3 focuses on presenting the elaborated configuration models regarding a Population Forecasting dashboard for a healthcare company.

4   State of the Art Regarding the Configuration of Analytical Process Support

4.1   Representation of Information Requirements in Process Modeling Languages

Generic process-modeling languages are suitable to describe process-related information requirements. The BPMN notation (as a widespread and standardized process modeling language (ISO/IEC 19510)) provides data objects to represent informational inputs in or outputs from process activities. But in the standard version of BPMN, data objects are only black-box objects containing no further details (e.g., without content specification, the origin of information or the way of information provision). With these standard data objects, it is not possible to provide a comprehensive specification of desired information requirements within processes [37].

For BPMN notation, a large number of notational extensions have emerged (surveyed by Zarour et al. [58]). But, most of them support the representation of technical and data-oriented content which is not included in this research (e.g., the representation of technical data models (e.g., [9]) and the representation of backend data flows, data changes and technical interactions with data stores (e.g., [9, 29])). A minor set of these modeling extensions focus on individual domain-specific requirements aspects, but they predominantly do not address the specification of analytical requirements in favor of specific application domains/industries such as disaster management [6]. The only modeling extension linked to analytical applications is provided by D'Ambrogio et al. [13], but this approach considers just a very small part of the user-oriented requirement spectrum of analytical applications with the specification of threshold values for specific key figures to support simulation runs (addressing analytical requirements regarding the aspects "data/information" and "automatic actions").

4.2 Conceptual Configurators for Analytical Application Products

The conceptual configuration of analytical products is a kind of product configuration to specify the quality and structure of product-relevant characteristics [8]. For the development of configuration systems in the special context of software configuration, configurators/configuration models can emerge in different forms [43]: 1. software reference models to analyze the potentials of a software product including the description of data structures, operational transactions (functions) and supported processes, 2. checklists for the interactive and systematic reduction of the configuration area regarding a (standard) software product by a question and answer dialogue between user and system, and 3. preconfigured systems as exemplary preselected configuration variants for a homogeneous target group or operational context. The focus in this current work lies on conceptual configuration models in the form of checklists/requirements catalogs to allow flexible conceptual analytical application configuration by the users themselves or in direct interaction with the users.

The analysis of analytical products to identify pre-built models/configurators for documenting business requirements (e.g., as a support function for implementation projects) comprised all analytical software suites except products of niche players in the "Gartner Magic Quadrant for Analytics and BI Platforms 2021" [20]: Microsoft, Tableau and Qlik in the "Leaders" quadrant; MicroStrategy, Domo and Google (Looker) in the "Challengers" quadrant; and Sisense, ThoughtSpot, Oracle, SAS, SAP, Yellowfin and TIBCO Software in the "Visionaries" quadrant. As a main result, all examined analytical software products have no specific models/configurators to collect user requirements. Taking the example of Microsoft Power BI, limited support addresses the specification of textual change requests for dashboards and reports using a comment function with unstructured plain text. Other tools provide interfaces to external software development applications (e.g., Github) to maintain requirements. Some analytical vendors conduct community areas to support collaborative development and to collect and discuss ideas for further developments/adaptations of the standard functions of their tools. However, these functions are not suitable to specify/configure concrete requirements for individual analytical use cases. As an example, TIBCO Software explicitly stated that the provision of models for product-specific application configuration or for user requirements documentation is deliberately no part of their own range of tools. To sum up, software vendors avoid the effort to provide configuration models that are adapted to the specific functional conditions of their software, and pass the responsibility and the choice of suitable requirements configurators and documentation models to the external implementation partners.

4.3 Requirements Documentation in the Context of Analytical Development Projects

According to an online survey, Table 1 shows the prevalence of tools and models used in analytical development projects for requirements documentation in practice (column "Sum"). Textual and unstructured/less structured use case descriptions are by far the most widespread tool for requirements documentation. At the same time, the users with their usage and operating requirements in form of textual user stories are an important information source, whereas formats which were popular in previous times (e.g., requirements specification sheets) seem to play a less important role. The leading textual user stories are followed at some distance by both the content-structured requirements catalogs (checklists) and the data models.

Table 1. Assessment of the completeness of content

Models/documents	Very good	Good	Less good	Bad	Sum
Textual user story	1	3	2	-	6
Requirements catalog	1	2	-	-	3
Data model	3	-	-	-	3
Requirements specification sheet	-	-	2	-	2
Backlog	-	1	-	-	1
Process description	-	1	-	-	1
Mockup/PoC	1	-	-	-	1

Data models have a technical-oriented focus and they are not able to provide even a complete picture of the various analytical requirement facets (e.g., with respect to structural and graphical design of user interfaces, access and distribution paths of information). Besides the technical-oriented data models and the mockups (belonging rather to the technical development area), requirements catalogs perform best in terms of achievable completeness of requirements content (Table 1).

Requirements catalogs provide a set of various design alternatives of an analytical application, which can thus be considered or deliberately excluded to be a part of a

Table 2. Assessment of the comprehensibility of content for all stakeholders

Models/documents	Very good	Good	Less good	Bad
Textual user story	-	2	3	1
Requirements catalog	2	1	-	-
Data model	2	1	-	-
Requirements specification sheet	-	-	2	-
Backlog	-	1	-	-
Process description	-	-	1	-
Mockup/PoC	1	-	-	-

planned analytical application. Furthermore, the use of formulation rules also supports a uniform specification of requirements that takes into account the essential requirements content elements. Requirements catalogs also provide requirements documentation that is understandable both for business users and developers (Table 2), since here structural relationships and terminologies are already defined [45] to facilitate a common understanding.

Table 3. Assessment of the frequency of inconsistencies with other models/documents used for requirements documentation

Models/documents	Very often	Often	Rather often	Less often	Rarely
Textual user story	2	2	1	1	-
Requirements catalog	-	-	-	-	3
Data model	-	-	-	-	3
Requirements specification sheet	1	-	-	1	-
Backlog	-	-	1	-	-
Process description	-	1	-	-	-
Mockup/PoC	-	-	-	-	1

Regarding the frequency of inconsistencies (Table 3), requirements catalogs reach a positive result because the clear requirements structure in catalogs can be recognized and compared more easily than content in unstructured continuous texts (e.g., use case descriptions). Focusing on the consideration of data privacy risks in requirements documentation (Table 4), text-based documents were rated worse, while requirement catalogs at least received a better rating. But, actually no model or document achieved a very good rating here, what again substantiates the still inadequate consideration of data privacy risks in requirements documentation.

Only one expert provided detailed information about the requirements catalog model used in projects of his company: The cross-domain requirements templates according to

Table 4. Assessment of the consideration of data privacy risks

Models/documents	Very good	Good	Less good	Bad
Textual user story	-	2	3	1
Requirements catalog	-	2	1	-
Data model	-	1	-	2
Requirements specification sheet	-	-	1	1
Backlog	-	-	-	1
Process description	-	1	-	-
Mockup/PoC	-	1	-	-

Rupp [45] structure requirements in a uniform way in form of sentences with specific content placeholders in a particular order. However, these predefined placeholders provide no information about the structure and the design of analytical or other domain-specific applications and about relevant requirements aspects and variants.

To sum up, requirements catalogs seem to be best suited for documenting requirements with regard to analytical applications from a practical point of view in terms of a complete, consistent and unambiguous provision of content. In addition, a requirements catalog for analytical applications should encompass and complement the specific functional and non-functional properties of this software domain, and should actively consider the other design aspects for analytical requirements (Sect. 2).

5   Evaluation of an Approach for the Conceptual Configuration of Analytical Applications

5.1   Presentation of the Modeling Approach

The configuration approach previously presented in more detail [25] enables the configuration of analytical services to document requirements regarding analytical process support. The use of services in the sense of encapsulated functions connected via standardized interfaces [2] allows the flexible conceptual (re-)configuration of analytical applications. This configuration approach can be used in different analytical use cases and business domains and in combination with different data formats as well as analysis methods. It can be classified as a customer-inherent product configuration [8] in order to permit a modular orchestration of analytical components/services, whereat the generation of the instantiated service models should be done in direct interaction between technical developer and user. The configuration approach contains a set of analytical service types [25]. Figure 1 shows the interconnected service types to describe reports/dashboards, their diagrams and the related key figures as well as the underlying basic data (Use Case Specific Configuration Content), each of which can be configured in more detail using different modeling objects ([25], Fig. 3, 4, 5, 6 and 7).

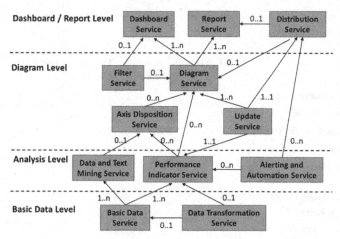

Fig. 1. Analytical service types and their interconnections in the configuration area Use Case-Specific Configuration Content [25]

In order to be able to represent the interconnection of the analytical services needed to configure a specific analytical use case (in terms of a specific dashboard or report) in connection with the related process activity, the analytical service types are represented as data objects (Fig. 2) in BPMN process models [25].

5.2 Results of the Expert Reviews

Within the review of the configuration approach, the analytical experts got an overview about the analytical service types of the three analytical service type networks [25] addressing the three different configuration areas [25], and about the numerous service type-specific graphical service feature configurations (e.g., Fig. 3, 4, 5, 6 and 7). As a main result, the experts confirmed that the configuration approach has a predominantly high and increased potential benefit for practice (Table 5). The benefits address in particular the areas of unambiguity and completeness of content, modularization of requirements and the possibility of reuse, the identification of new design options, obtaining an overview about analytical process support and using the instantiated models as a starting point for deriving a technical concept. It is remarkable that this approach was rated with a predominantly higher added value compared to models previously used in these companies.

Table 5. Assessment of the potential benefits of the analytical service configuration approach for requirements documentation

	High benefit	Increased benefit	Less high benefit	Low benefit	No benefit
Unambiguity of content	9	3	1	-	-
Completeness of content	9	4	-	-	-
Provision of selectable design variants	4	2	2	1	-
Saving of effort in practical projects	3	7	1	2	-
Modular and simple (re-)combination of requirement contents / services	5	4	-	-	-
Recording data privacy-specific conditions of basic data	2	3	2	2	-
Specification of requirements for analytical self-service functions	4	2	1	-	-
Starting point for deriving a technical concept	9	4	-	-	-
Identification of design options not yet considered through proposed configuration content	5	2	-	-	-
Starting point for subsequent adaptations of the analytical software at the same customer	6	5	2	-	-
Starting point for similar future projects with other customers	6	7	-	-	-
Obtaining an overview of the analytical process support	7	6	-	-	-
Representing the sequence of analytical content in processes	5	5	3	-	-
Representing relationships between the individual analytical services via associated BPMN data objects	7	5	1	-	-
	High added value	Increased added value	Less high added value	Low added value	No added value
Added value of the configuration approach to requirements documentation compared to the previous approach in the company	3	7	2	1	-
Added value of the coupled representation of analytical support and user processes compared to the previous requirements documentation in the company	2	8	2	-	-

5.3 Presentation of Evaluation Use Cases

The configuration approach was tested in a healthcare project to configure a dashboard presenting annual **Population Forecast** information for different counties in the federal state of Saxony. In this analytical project, some planning for the dashboard design and a first mockup had already been done before. Based on this, all analytical services needed to describe the entire analytical use case were configured together with three development team members (project manager, data analyst, analytical developer). Due to the numerous design features and design variants considered in the different analytical services, some facets and features of the dashboard that had not yet been considered in the previous development process were identified.

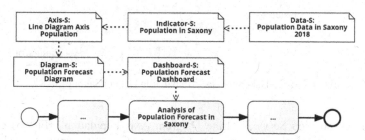

Fig. 2. Process model of the use case Population Forecast

To obtain an overview, Fig. 2 shows the process model for this use case with the inter-connections of all instantiated analytical services. In this context, the "Performance Indicator Service" (Indicator-S) (Fig. 3) plays a central role in analytical use cases and therefore configuration activities should start here, because this is the core information required by an analytical user.

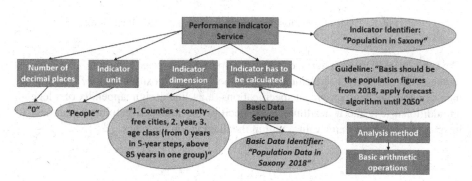

Fig. 3. "Performance Indicator Service" "Population in Saxony"

The calculation of the indicator "Population in Saxony" considers three indicator dimensions and is based on data provided by the "Basic Data Service" (Data-S) "Population Data in Saxony 2018" (Fig. 4). These data are supplied by the State Statistical Office of Saxony in form of persistent xls-files.

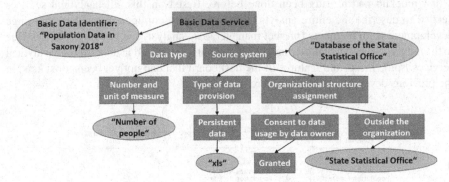

Fig. 4. "Basic Data Services" "Population Data in Saxony 2018"

The "Axis Disposition Service" "Line Diagram Axis Population" (Fig. 5) contains detailed specifications about the graphical representation of the indicator values and the temporal indicator dimension values in the intended line diagram.

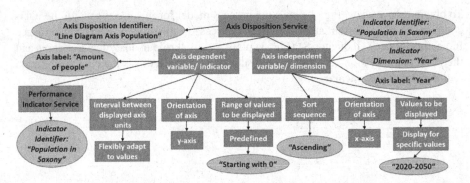

Fig. 5. "Axis Disposition Service" "Line Diagram Axis Population"

The subsequent "Diagram Service" named "Population Forecast Diagram" (Fig. 6) takes up the configured indicator elements within the "Axis Disposition Service". It complements on the one hand graphical specifications (e.g., line design, appendix of a legend, an additional text and a headline), and specifies the intended graphical treatment of incorrect/missing indicator values within the diagram on the other.

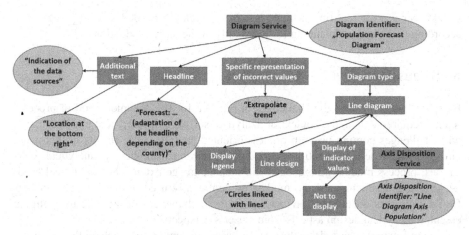

Fig. 6. "Diagram Service" "Population Forecast Diagram"

Finally, the "Dashboard Service" "Population Forecast Dashboard" (Fig. 7) provides information about the intended dashboard access (e.g. about the foreseen user hardware, the work mode, the user role and the maximum amount of parallel access), the ability to hide dashboard elements and the placement of the dashboard within the navigation structure of the overall analytical application.

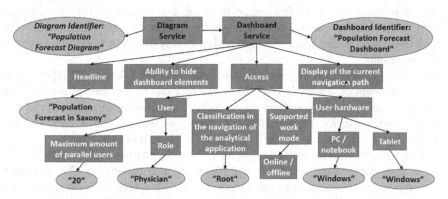

Fig. 7. "Dashboard Service" "Population Forecast Dashboard"

The instantiated analytical service models in the Population Forecast scenario served as the conceptual basis for further dashboard development. The positive feedback from the three experts involved (high benefit: 16 times; increased benefit: 16 times; less high benefit: 3 times; low benefit: 1 time; willingness to use the configuration approach in future projects: 3 out of 3) was clear evidence of the usefulness, acceptance and, in particular, practicability of the configuration approach.

In a second case study, the configuration approach was used to configure a **Machining Daily Demand** report in an industrial enterprise (for more details see [26]). This case study was developed at the beginning of the requirements elicitation process together with a requirements provider from business department. This report should inform a storekeeper in near real time which parts from stock are needed in which quantities, according to the current planning for the supply of the daily production.

6 Discussion

First, this work presents the challenges in practice for the documentation of process-related requirements in the context of analytical software development in combination with challenges coming up with process-oriented analytics. The results in this paper have shown that neither scientific approaches (requirements models for analytical applications; process modeling languages and their language extensions), analytical products nor textual documents and models predominantly used in development projects for requirements documentation can satisfy these challenges or are able to configure essential analytical design aspects from a user's perspective.

Second, experts attested that the service-based conceptual approach for the customer-inherent [8] configuration of analytical services [25] has a predominantly increased to high benefit for analytical development projects. With regard to the existing scientific models, the configuration approach represents significant enhancements in the identified configuration aspects (Sect. 2) regarding analytical applications:

- The elaborated configuration approach does not address a technical perspective on the configuration of needed analytical data and information as most other approaches do, but provides a user-oriented perspective similar to Strauch [53] and Rosenkranz et al. [44]. However, the new approach goes beyond the two approaches mentioned with its detailed feature specification of basic data, key figures as well as data and text mining results.
- Periodicity is only implicitly considered in Strauch [53], and Goeken [2004] mentions the requirement of "timeliness" in data collection just by the way. In contrast, the configuration approach considers the temporal component with a separate service type ("Update Service") for specifications regarding the updating of diagrams, the triggering of information distributions, and the recalculation of key figures.
- For the design of user interfaces, Mayer et al. [32] address only headings, additional texts, links to other analyses, and sliders for filter parameters. The configuration approach allows extensive specifications for the graphical, content-related, and functional design of dashboards/reports ("Dashboard Service", "Report Service") and enables the configuration of "Filter Services" both for individual diagrams and for complex dashboards. Furthermore, this approach includes the configuration of target systems for analytical information or alerting messages ("Distribution Service") and offers extensive setting options for visual, audible and text-based alerts ("Alerting and Automation Service"). In addition and in contrast to all other existing approaches, there is the option to configure alert-based automatic controls.
- In extension of previous research approaches (e.g., [5, 30]), the service-oriented model structure used in the configuration approach comprises newly defined service types that are clearly delineated in terms of content, and arranges them with their dependencies in a service network using newly introduced structuring levels.
- Until now, only Teruel et al. [54] have allowed to indicate associated business processes in their specifications of analytical applications. In addition, the new configuration

approach enables direct graphical input and output links of instantiated analytical "Dashboard Services"/"Report Services" and their associated analytical services in connection with activities in BPMN process models.

- Only Goeken [19] mentions the necessity to consider data protection-specific circumstances of the basic data intended for analyses. In contrast, the "Basic Data Service" of the new configuration approach allows a detailed recording of extensive data protection-related metadata for the assessment of data protection risks.
- Requirements regarding the availability of analytical self-service functions, which are not supported by any previous model approach, are implemented by this configuration approach by providing five independent analytical self-service types in the area of Configuration Content for Analysis Preparation [25].

The applied research design leaves opportunities for further research. A deeper and more comprehensive search of configuration models used in analytical development projects and a more extensive investigation of their particular structural and content-related details could yield additional and new design aspects for the further development of the configuration approach. This could also be complemented with an explicit procedure for periodically checking the validity of service features and for a structured search for new service features in current analytical products. As a second point, this approach uses data objects with a label of the service type and a unique identifier to represent analytical services in the process models. Future research could identify essential service features from the detailed service models appropriate to expand the content of the data objects (using extension mechanisms for type definitions available in BPMN) to visualize more detailed information about analytical process support directly within the process models.

References

1. AEP AG: Warum scheitern viele BI-Projekte? (2020). https://www.aep-ag.com/2-uncategor ised/211-warum-scheitern-viele-bi-projekte
2. Alpar, P., Alt, R., Bensberg, F., Weimann, P.: Anwendungsorientierte Wirtschaftsinformatik. Strategische Planung, Entwicklung und Nutzung von Informationssystemen. Springer, Wiesbaden (2019). https://doi.org/10.1007/978-3-658-25581-7
3. Alpar, P., Schulz, M.: Self-Service Business Intelligence. Bus. Inf. Syst. Eng. **58**(2), 151–155 (2016). https://doi.org/10.1007/s12599-016-0424-6
4. Begerow, M.: Ziele von Business Intelligence (2020). https://datenbanken-verstehen.de/bus iness-intelligence/business-intelligence-grundlagen/business-intelligence-ziele/
5. Besemer, D.: Getting started now on SOA for BI. DM Rev. **17**(5), 26–37 (2007)
6. Betke, H., Seifert, M.: BPMN for disaster response processes. In: Eibl, M., Gaedke, M. (eds.) INFORMATIK 2017, pp. 1311–1324. Gesellschaft für Informatik, Bonn (2017). https://doi.org/10.18420/in2017_132
7. Beverungen, D., et al.: Seven paradoxes of business process management in a hyper-connected world. Bus. Inf. Syst. Eng. **63**(2), 145–156 (2020). https://doi.org/10.1007/s12599-020-006 46-z
8. Blecker, T., Dullnig, H., Malle, F.: Kundenkohärente und kundeninhärente Produktkonfiguration in der Mass Customization. Ind. Manage. **19**(1), 21–24 (2003)
9. Bocciarelli, P., D'Ambrogio, A., Paglia, E., Giglio, A.: An HLA-based BPMN extension for the specification of business process collaborations. In: 2017 IEEE/ACM 21st International

Symposium on Distributed Simulation and Real Time Applications (DS-RT), pp. 1–8. IEEE (2017). https://doi.org/10.1109/DISTRA.2017.8167668

10. Bonifati, A., Cattaneo, F., Ceri, S., Fuggetta, A., Paraboschi, S., Di Milano, P.: Designing data marts for data warehouses. ACM Trans. Software Eng. Methodol. **10**, 452–483 (2001). https://doi.org/10.1145/384189.384190

11. Calvanese, D., Dragone, L., Nardi, D., Rosati, R., Trisolini, S.M.: Enterprise modeling and data warehousing in Telecom Italia. Inf. Syst. **31**(1), 1–32 (2006). https://doi.org/10.1016/j.is.2004.07.002

12. Colangelo, E., Bauernhansl, T.: Usage of analytical services in industry today and tomorrow. Procedia CIRP **57**, 276–280 (2016). https://doi.org/10.1016/j.procir.2016.11.048

13. D'Ambrogio, A., Paglia, E., Bocciarelli, P., Giglio, A.: Towards performance-oriented perfective evolution of BPMN models. In: 2016 Symposium on Theory of Modeling and Simulation (TMS-DEVS), pp. 1–8. IEEE (2016). https://doi.org/10.22360/SpringSim.2016.TMSDEVS.032

14. Davis, G.B.: Advising and Supervising. In: Avison, D.E., Pries-Heje, J. (eds.) Research in information systems. A handbook for research supervisors and their students. Butterworth-Heinemann information systems series, pp. 1–33. Elsevier Butterworth-Heinemann, Amsterdam (2005)

15. Ferrández, A., Maté, A., Peral, J., Trujillo, J., De Gregorio, E., Aufaure, M.-A.: A framework for enriching Data Warehouse analysis with Question Answering systems. J. Intell. Inf. Syst. **46**(1), 61–82 (2014). https://doi.org/10.1007/s10844-014-0351-2

16. Fleming, O., Fountaine, T., Henke, N., Saleh, T.: Ten red flags signaling your analytics program will fail (2018). https://www.mckinsey.com/business-functions/mckinsey-analytics/our-insights/ten-red-flags-signaling-your-analytics-program-will-fail

17. Frank, U.: Domain-specific modeling languages: requirements analysis and design guidelines. In: Reinhartz-Berger, I., Sturm, A., Clark, T., Cohen, S., Bettin, J. (eds.) Domain engineering. Product Lines, Languages, and Conceptual Models, pp. 133–157. Springer, Heidelberg (2013). https://doi.org/10.1007/978-3-642-36654-3_6

18. Giorgini, P., Rizzi, S., Garzetti, M.: GRAnD: A goal-oriented approach to requirement analysis in data warehouses. Decis. Support Syst. **45**(1), 4–21 (2008). https://doi.org/10.1016/j.dss.2006.12.001

19. Goeken, M.: Anforderungsmanagement bei der Entwicklung von Data Warehouse-Systemen. In: Schelp, J., Winter, R. (eds.) Auf dem Weg zur Integration Factory - Proceedings der DW2004, pp. 167–186. Physica, Heidelberg (2004). https://doi.org/10.1007/3-7908-1612-4_9

20. Graupner, E., Berner, M., Mädche, A., Jegadeesan, H.: Business intelligence & analytics for processes - a visibility requirements evaluation. In: Kundisch, D., Suhl, L., Beckmann, L. (eds.) MKWI 2014 - Multikonferenz Wirtschaftsinformatik, pp. 154–166. Universität Paderborn, Paderborn (2014)

21. Gregor, S., Hevner, A.R.: Positioning and presenting design science research for maximum impact. MISQ **37**(2), 337–355 (2013). https://doi.org/10.25300/MISQ/2013/37.2.01

22. Hänel, T., Felden, C.: Operational Business Intelligence im Zukunftsszenario der Industrie 4.0. In: Gluchowski, P., Chamoni, P. (eds.) Analytische Informationssysteme, pp. 259–281. Springer, Heidelberg (2016). https://doi.org/10.1007/978-3-662-47763-2_13

23. Hoffjan, A., Rohe, M.: Konzeptionelle Analyse von Self-Service Business Intelligence und deren Gestaltungsmöglichkeiten. In: Kißler, M., Wiesehahn, A. (eds.) Erfolgreiches Controlling, pp. 99–112. Nomos Verlagsgesellschaft mbH & Co. KG, Baden-Baden (2018). https://doi.org/10.5771/9783845288741-99

24. Horkoff, J., et al.: Strategic business modeling: representation and reasoning. Softw. Syst. Model. **13**(3), 1015–1041 (2012). https://doi.org/10.1007/s10270-012-0290-8

25. Hrach, C., Alt, R.: Configuration approach for analytical service models – development and evaluation. In: 2020 IEEE 22nd Conference on Business Informatics (CBI), pp. 260–269. IEEE (2020). https://doi.org/10.1109/CBI49978.2020.00035

26. Hrach, C., Alt, R., Sackmann, S.: Process-oriented documentation of user requirements for analytical applications - challenges, state of the art and evaluation of a service-based configuration approach. In: Ganzha, M., Maciaszek, L., Paprzycki, M., Ślęzak, D. (eds.) Proceedings of the 17th Conference on Computer Science and Intelligent Systems (ACSIS), vol. 30, pp. 773–782 (2022). https://doi.org/10.15439/2022F181

27. Jovanovic, P., Romero, O., Simitsis, A., Abelló, A., Mayorova, D.: A requirement-driven approach to the design and evolution of data warehouses. Inf. Syst. **44**, 94–119 (2014). https://doi.org/10.1016/j.is.2014.01.004

28. Liskin, O.: How artifacts support and impede requirements communication. In: Fricker, S.A., Schneider, K. (eds.) REFSQ 2015. LNCS, vol. 9013, pp. 132–147. Springer, Cham (2015). https://doi.org/10.1007/978-3-319-16101-3_9

29. Magnani, M., Montesi, D.: BPDMN: A Conservative Extension of BPMN with Enhanced Data Representation Capabilities (2009). https://doi.org/10.48550/arXiv.0907.1978

30. Martin, W.: Analytics meets Enterprise SOA. S.A.R.L. Martin (2006)

31. Maté, A., Trujillo, J.: A trace metamodel proposal based on the model driven architecture framework for the traceability of user requirements in data warehouses. Inf. Syst. **37**(8), 753–766 (2012). https://doi.org/10.1016/j.is.2012.05.003

32. Mayer, J.H., Winter, R., Mohr, T.: Situational Management Support Systems. Bus Inf Syst Eng **4**(6), 331–345 (2012). https://doi.org/10.1007/s12599-012-0233-5

33. Meister, D.: Woran scheitern Data Science Projekte? Datahouse AG (2019)

34. Meth, H., Mueller, B., Maedche, A.: Designing a requirement mining system. J. Assoc. Inf. Syst. **16**(9), 799–837 (2015). https://doi.org/10.17705/1jais.00408

35. Misra, J., Sengupta, S., Podder, S.: Topic cohesion preserving requirements clustering. In: Minku, L., Miransky, A., Turhan, B. (eds.) Proceedings of the 5th International Workshop on Realizing Artificial Intelligence Synergies in Software Engineering - RAISE '16, pp. 22–28. ACM Press, New York (2016). https://doi.org/10.1145/2896995.2896998

36. Neumann, G., Human, S., Alt, R.: Introduction to the minitrack on end-user empowerment in the digital age. In: Proceedings 53. Hawaii International Conference on System Sciences, pp. 4099–4101 (2020). https://doi.org/10.24251/HICSS.2020.501

37. O'Shea, M., Pawellek, G., Schramm, A.: Durch maßgeschneiderte Informationsversorgung zu mehr Usability. Wirtschaftsinformatik & Management **5**(6), 104–114 (2013). https://doi.org/10.1365/s35764-013-0370-8

38. Panian, Z.: How to Make business intelligence actionable through service-oriented architectures. In: 2nd WSEAS International Conference on Computer Engineering and Applications, pp. 210–221 (2008)

39. Peffers, K., Tuunanen, T., Rothenberger, M.A., Chatterjee, S.: A design science research methodology for information systems research. J. Manag. Inf. Syst. **24**(3), 45–77 (2007). https://doi.org/10.2753/MIS0742-1222240302

40. Pohl, K., Rupp, C.: Requirements engineering fundamentals. A study guide for the certified professional for requirements engineering exam, foundation level - REB compliant. Rocky Nook, Santa Barbara (2015)

41. Prisma Informatik GmbH: Die sechs häufigsten Fehler in Business Intelligence Projekten (2020). https://www.prisma-informatik.de/erp-blog/2016/06/die-sechs-haeufigsten-fehler-in-business-intelligence-projekten/

42. Richardson, J., Schlegel, K., Sallam, R., Kronz, A., Sun, J.: Magic Quadrant for Analytics and Business Intelligence Platforms 2021. Gartner Inc. (2021)

43. Ritter, J.: Prozessorientierte Konfiguration komponentenbasierter Anwendungssysteme. Dissertation, Universität Oldenburg (2000)

44. Rosenkranz, C., Holten, R., Räkers, M., Behrmann, W.: Supporting the design of data integration requirements during the development of data warehouses: a communication theory-based approach. Eur. J. Inf. Syst. **26**(1), 84–115 (2017). https://doi.org/10.1057/ejis.2015.22
45. Rupp, C.: Requirements-Engineering und -Management. Das Handbuch für Anforderungen in jeder Situation. Hanser, München (2021). https://doi.org/10.3139/9783446464308
46. Sachse, S.: Customer-centric Service Management - Conceptualization and Evaluation of Consumer-induced Service Composition. Dissertation, Universität Leipzig (2018)
47. Sarma, A.D.N.: A generic functional architecture for operational BI system. Int. J. Bus. Intell. Res. **9**(1), 64–77 (2018). https://doi.org/10.4018/IJBIR.2018010105
48. Schiefer, J., Seufert, A.: Towards a service-oriented architecture for operational BI. In: Schumann, M., Kolbe, L.M., Breitner, M.H., Frerichs, A. (eds.) Multikonferenz Wirtschaftsinformatik 2010, pp. 1137–1149. Universitätsverlag Göttingen, Göttingen (2010). https://doi.org/10.17875/gup2010-1573
49. Schönig, S., Jablonski, S., Ermer, A.: IoT-basiertes Prozessmanagement. Informatik Spektrum **42**(2), 130–137 (2019). https://doi.org/10.1007/s00287-019-01140-x
50. Schulze, K.D., Dittmar, C.: Business Intelligence Reifegradmodelle. In: Chamoni, P., Gluchowski, P. (eds.) Analytische Informationssysteme: Business Intelligence-Technologien und -Anwendungen, pp. 72–87. Springer Verlag, Berlin (2006). https://doi.org/10.1007/3-540-33752-0_4
51. Shanks, G., Darke, P.: Understanding corporate data models. Inf. Manage. **35**(1), 19–30 (1999). https://doi.org/10.1016/S0378-7206(98)00078-0
52. Sharma, S., Chen, K., Sheth, A.: Towards practical privacy-preserving analytics for IoT and cloud-based healthcare systems. IEEE Internet Comput. **22**(2), 42–51 (2018). https://doi.org/10.1109/MIC.2018.112102519
53. Strauch, B.: Entwicklung einer Methode für die Informationsbedarfsanalyse im Data Warehousing. Dissertation, Universität St. Gallen (2002)
54. Teruel, M.A., Maté, A., Navarro, E., González, P., Trujillo, J.C.: The new era of business intelligence applications: building from a collaborative point of view. Bus. Inf. Syst. Eng. **61**(5), 615–634 (2019). https://doi.org/10.1007/s12599-019-00578-3
55. Uria-Recio, P.: Top 25 Mistakes Corporates Make in their Advanced Analytics Programs (2018). https://towardsdatascience.com/top-25-mistakes-corporates-make-in-their-advanced-analytics-programs-c51e76218e20
56. Vera-Baquero, A., Colomo-Palacios, R., Molloy, O.: Real-time business activity monitoring and analysis of process performance on big-data domains. Telematics Inform. **33**(3), 793–807 (2016). https://doi.org/10.1016/j.tele.2015.12.005
57. Wu, L., Barash, G., Bartolini, C.: A Service-oriented architecture for business intelligence. In: IEEE International Conference on Service-Oriented Computing and Applications (SOCA 2007), pp. 279–285 (2007). https://doi.org/10.1109/SOCA.2007.6
58. Zarour, K., Benmerzoug, D., Guermouche, N., Drira, K.: A systematic literature review on BPMN extensions. BPMJ **26**(6), 1473–1503 (2019). https://doi.org/10.1108/BPMJ-01-2019-0040

Human Performance Management: A Humanist and Supportive Model for IT Professionals

Marcus Vinicius Alencar Terra$^{(\boxtimes)}$ [ID], Vanessa Tavares de Oliveira Barros [ID], and Rodolfo Miranda de Barros [ID]

Computing Department, State University of Londrina,
P.O. Box 10.011, Londrina, Paraná, Brazil
secretaria.dc@uel.br
http://www.uel.br/cce/dc/

Abstract. Society and its organizations have transformed performance related issues into situations that are merely focused on goals and competitiveness. Especially in the Information Technology (IT) area, this approach causes the general feeling of being under constant pressure due to the need for immediate delivery of results. The main purpose of this article is to contribute to overcome this scenario, where IT employees are seen, essentially, as replaceable production resources, proposing, for this cultural change, a human performance management (HPM) model specific for IT professionals, linked to the philosophical current of Humanism and based on social support theory, addressing aspects such as equality, respect, collaboration and personal development. For this research, the design science paradigm was chosen, since this study focused on the development of valid and reliable knowledge. In addition to the performance management model proposed, this study can also be considered as a starting point for an organizational culture change, establishing good practices and incorporating humanism and social support concepts to produce a positive and sustainable work environment. Considering that the presented model is generic and flexible and its adoption may require adaptations and additional research, this study should be extended to produce new ways to improve HPM.

Keywords: Performance management · Performance appraisal · IT professional · Model · Humanism · Social Support

1 Introduction

Human performance management (HPM) is an essential and beneficial process inside organizations. The main objective of this type of management is to provide a performance measure for activities carried out by employees, while promotes the improvement of productivity, motivation and satisfaction. Therefore, this process can be considered a structuring basis for developing organizational culture and relationship between organization and its employees [5, 21].

© The Author(s), under exclusive license to Springer Nature Switzerland AG 2023
E. Ziemba et al. (Eds.): FedCSIS-AIST 2022/ISM 2022, LNBIP 471, pp. 23–47, 2023.
https://doi.org/10.1007/978-3-031-29570-6_2

The benefits of an effective performance management are even more evident in areas such as Information Technology (IT) where complexity, dynamism and innovation are ever-present factors, requiring professionals to have high levels of knowledge and creativity [9,16,17].

Evaluate IT professionals performance and define the skills needed for the job are not recent concerns [3,6,12,23,38], however, nowadays society, as a result of economic globalization, has transformed issues related to performance into situations merely focused on goals and competitiveness, which generates, on IT employees, the feeling of being under constant pressure due to the need for immediate delivery of results.

Given this scenario, several initiatives have emerged seeking to humanize and improve the relationship between employees and organizations [14,31,52]. But there are same gaps on these studies, since, current and past research, listed in this article, address the topics presented here in a disassociated way, often disregarding the concepts of humanism and social support or the particularities relevant to Information Technology professionals. In addition, the performance management models proposed by the researchers [5] are, for the most part, generic and difficult to adapt to reflect the needs and expectations of IT professionals, becoming a constant source of stress, demotivation and frustration.

The high turnover of professionals in Information Technology area [42,43,46] and occupational diseases, like stress and burnout [40], are just some of the problems related to performance management on IT, specially, when the adopted management model is primarily focused on impersonal treatment, competitiveness, productivity and value delivery.

Thus, the main motivation for this study comes from the opportunity to develop an analysis regarding performance management and satisfaction of IT professionals inside organizations, proposing, as a result, a management model composed by a set of guidelines based on the principles of Humanism and social support. In addition, there is the real possibility of contributing to the improvement of the quality of life and well-being of IT professionals at work, by understanding their particularities, expectations and needs, reconciling professional performance and personal fulfillment.

Following the same line of thought, the purpose of the present research is to define a performance management model for IT professionals based on social support and linked to the philosophical stance of Humanism, considering, therefore, the issues related to a human centered management and addressing aspects of human nature, such as dignity, limits, aspirations, capabilities and potential.

Other important contributions of this study are focused on: detailing organizational culture, social support and human performance management concepts; analysing humanistic ethics in corporate environment; knowledge structuring for developing more effective methods of appraisal. Such contributions aims to be adherent to the current and future reality of IT professionals.

This research is believed to be scientifically original, since it proposes, as far as is known, a unique model for human performance management, based on the perspective of IT profile singularities together with extremely important concepts for society, like organizational culture, humanism, social support and ethics.

It also can be justified by the proposition of a management model potentially capable of improve people and organizations, representing an extremely relevant artifact in a context full of uncertainties, challenges and constant transformations. In addition, the results obtained by this research are expected to server as groundwork for future studies focused on producing new knowledge, frameworks and methodologies related to HPM.

The rest of this article is structured as follows: Sect. 2 sets out the theoretical foundation and related works considered for the research; Sect. 3 describes the scientific methodology employed; Sect. 4 describes the proposed solution; Sect. 5 analyzes and discusses the obtained results; and, finally, Sect. 6 presents the last considerations of the research.

2 Literature Review

2.1 Organizational Culture Theory

In order to analyze employee performance, engagement and satisfaction in the context of organizations, it is necessary to understand organizational culture and its influence on these factors. [20]. The most commonly used and accepted definition of organizational culture is the one proposed by Schein [45, p. 7]:

A pattern of basic assumptions, invented, discovered, or developed by a given group, as it learns to cope with its problems of external adaptation and internal integration, that has worked well enough to be considered valid and, therefore is to be taught to new members as the correct way to perceive, think, and feel in relation to those problems.

As part of the Organizational Culture Theory, Schein [45] also describes an organization's culture as a set of levels that represent its elements, as shown in Fig. 1.

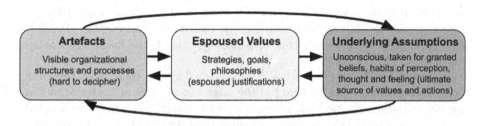

Fig. 1. The levels of organizational culture. Adapted from [45]

In the context of human performance, **Artifacts** represent what people effectively accomplish and which directly reflect on performance and goal achievement. This level is the most evident in the culture, although some organizational actions and structures can be difficult to understand and justify.

The **Espoused Values** are the strategies, objectives, norms and philosophies openly propagated by the organization, aiming, for example, the effectiveness of the performance management. The organization's actions have the most significant effect at this cultural level.

Finally, **Underlying Assumptions** are taken-for-granted beliefs based on thoughts, perceptions, and feelings. At this level, cultural elements become visible only through the analysis of behavioral patterns. These underlying assumptions exist in order to simplify complex issues of organizational reality, such as the reasons why one person is promoted over another [32].

It is evident that the elements of each level of organizational culture are capable of influencing all the others, however, underlying assumptions of an organization have a great impact on its artifacts, supplanting, in some situations, the influence of declared values [32,45].

Organizational culture can be seen as a preponderant factor in performance management but also as part of the results of this management, that is, by promoting the performance improvement of employees and their teams, organizational culture ends up being directly influenced by this improvement [22].

Regarding the performance of an organization, it is possible to build a culture that emphasizes essential points, such as meritocracy, transparency and recognition [33]. All these positive changes that take place in the organizational culture have the power to provide employees with the possibility to act proactively, identifying, mitigating and eliminating human errors and correcting the organization's vices and weaknesses [49].

A favorable cultural posture results in actions that can, if carried out accordingly, guide the institution towards an effective management of human performance. [49].

2.2   Human Performance Management

Interest in the effectiveness of Human Resource Management is not a recent phenomenon, relevant and frequent studies can be found from the 1970s s onwards [21]. Human Performance Management is considered one of the main pillars of Human Resource Management and, for this reason, the concern of researchers about human performance within organizations also began more than half a century ago. [3,6,12,23,38].

Aspects related to this branch of organizational management have, therefore, a rich literature that can be found in the most varied areas of research, such as psychology, administration, sociology, information systems and economics [35].

In addition to the Organizational Culture Theory, HPM is based on a wide range of other theories [26,47], which demonstrates the high complexity and deepness of the subject.

Table 1 presents some fundamental theories to understand and develop Human Performance Management.

Table 1. Fundamental theories of human performance management [26, 47]

Theory	Author(s)
Theory of Action and Job Performance	Richard E. Boyatzis
Agency Theory	M. C. Jensen and W. H. Meckling
Attribution Theory	Fritz Heider
Bureaucracy Theory	Max Weber
Field Theory	Kurt Lewin
Competency Theory	David McClelland
Contract Theory	Oliver Hart and Bengt Holmström
Theory of Individual Differences in Task and Contextual Performance	S. J. Motowidlo, W. C. Borman and M. J. Schmit
Two-Factor Theory	Frederick Herzberg
Equity Theory	J. Stacy Adams
Expectancy Theory	V. Vroom, L. Porter and E. Lawler
Goal-setting Theory	E. Locke and G. Latham
General Systems Theory	Ludwig von Bertalanffy
Organizational Justice Theory	Jerald Greenberg
Theory of Behavioral Engineering Model	Thomas F. Gilbert
Theory of Human Motivation	Abraham Maslow
Achievement Motivation Theory	David McClelland
Theory of the Social Self	George H. Mead
Job Characteristics Theory	R. Hackman, E. Lawler and G. Oldham
Bases of Social Power Theory	J. French and B. Raven
Reinforcement Theory	B. F. Skinner

Based on the numerous definitions of HPM that can be found in the literature, it can be inferred that Human Performance Management is a cyclical and continuous process that is intended to identify, plan, measure, control and develop performance at work, both individually and as a team, while aligning this performance with the organization's strategic objectives and the value delivery from executed activities [13, 25, 48].

HPM is, therefore, a complex process that involves a series of methodologies, techniques and approaches focused on overcoming the challenges and difficulties inherent to this type of management and returning positive results for organizations [4]. Figure 2 presents a holistic and pragmatic view of the Human Performance Management Framework as proposed by [48].

2.3 Humanism

Humanism is essentially a philosophical stance that assigns preeminent importance to human beings, their experiences, interests and rights. The hallmark of humanist philosophy is, therefore, the development of people's potential, considering Protagoras' relativism (490-420 BCE) where "man is the measure of all things" [50].

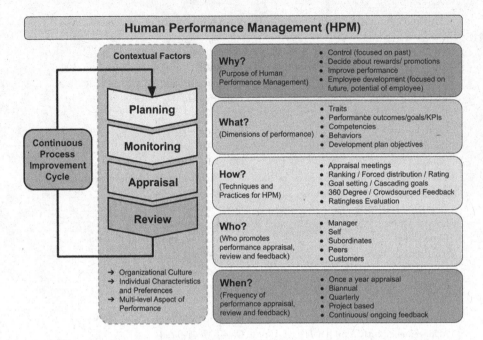

Fig. 2. Human performance management framework. Adapted from [48]

Among all the principles contemplated by humanism, some of them deserve to be highlighted: human value; individual dignity; the pursuit of civic culture; promotion of diversity and equality; and humanistic ethics [50].

· According to humanist ethics, the human being must "be considered as an end and never exclusively as a means or instrument for any purpose external to itself" [8]. Thus, moral rules are defined from the perspective of humanity, that is, *right* is everything that is good for human beings, values their life and develops their capacities, while *wrong* is everything that harms or takes away human dignity, represses individuality and dehumanizes people [8].

One of the main global aspirations of Humanism is found in the Universal Declaration of Human Rights, which establishes a commitment to promote universal respect for and observance of human rights and fundamental freedoms, demonstrating that human beings and their dignity must be above private power in any sphere [27].

Based on the fundamental idea of humanism, many other reflections have been developed, also covering the organizational context [56]. Thus, inside organizations, humanist management must place human dignity and rights as central concerns in all its subjects and methodologies. In this sense, economic transactions are considered, in essence, as relationships between people and, for this reason, organizations need to serve the objectives of humanity and not the opposite. In doing so, people are seen as active and central elements of the economic system and not passive and secondary objects of an economy guided by other goals [7].

In a concise manner, a humanistic management is concerned with human needs and oriented towards the complete and extensive development of human being virtues.

Thus, based on the concepts of this type of management, it is possible to describe a progressive model of 3 levels of entrepreneurial humanism [52,53], as shown in Fig. 3. In the same sense, humanistic management is composed of 5 dimensions [56]:

- Managerial responsibility;
- Employee motivation;
- Personal promotion;
- Interpersonal relationships;
- Organizational culture.

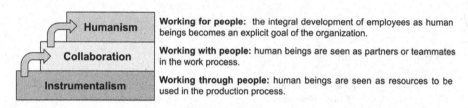

Fig. 3. Levels of entrepreneurial humanism. Based on [52].

Regarding the relationship between technology and humanism, it is important to note that this is not a recent issue [41], but the advancement of Artificial Intelligence and its application in real Information System problems has leveraged new initiatives seeking to discuss this relationship [24]. Such efforts are known as Digital Humanism, which has proclaimed and disclosed a manifesto with principles on current and future technological development, as well as, on the co-evolution of technology and humanity [15].

2.4 Social Support

The social support theory establishes that interpersonal relationships produce beneficial effects on people's physical and mental health, especially on issues related to stress [44]. Thus, according to a great number of researchers, social support affects, directly or indirectly, the well-being of those who receive support, eliminating or buffering negative impacts of daily events [10,51,54].

Social support is a source of study for several research areas, such as anthropology, medicine, psychology, sociology, and economics. Considering the fact that it has multiple facets, there is some difficulty in contextualizing, defining and measuring social support, since each area proposes a different approach regarding this construct [54].

Despite this, most of definitions found in the literature have convergent characteristics. In this sense, social support commonly refers to any positive interaction, helpful behaviour, or material assistance provided to a person in need of support by significant others, individuals or groups, such as family members, friends, co-workers, and neighbors [10,44,51,54]. Besides, for some authors, the concept of social support may also include the nature of the support network, the individual's perception of the support available or received, and the reciprocity of helping actions [44].

Although the idea about what is provided in terms of support may vary, many authors recognize that there are at least four common types or functions of social support: emotional support, informational support, tangible support, and belonging support [44,51,54]. It is important to note that each of these categories may include multiple subcategories. A more detailed view of this typology is provided in Table 2.

Table 2. Common types of social support [51,54]

Type of Support	Definition	Example
Emotional	Expressions of comfort, encouragement and confidence	A person who listen to your problems and encourages you.
Informational	Provision of advice, feedback and guidance	Someone who can give you trusted advice on a stressful situation.
Tangible	Provision of material goods, financial assistance, and services	A friend who could look after your home when you travel.
Belonging	Sense of social belonging and companionship, shared social activities	A family member with whom you could talk when you feel lonely.

Briefly, one can say that emotional support is related to offering empathy, love, care, concern and encouragement, among others. While informational support involves providing advice, guidance, suggestions, mentoring or any other useful information with potential to help in solving problems or in other situations. Tangible or instrumental support, on the other hand, refers to the provision of material needs, services or other practical assistance, for example financial, in a concrete and direct way. Finally, companionship or belonging support is the type of support that aims to expand the sense of social belonging and to promote engagement in shared social activities, creating social ties and support groups with similar interests or situations [44,54].

It is important to emphasize that, although they are presented individually here, in practice these social support functions are often interrelated, which makes it difficult to identify separately how they relate to health and well-being. In addition, establishing and developing social bonds does not guarantee health promotion, since, in some cases, these bonds may become significant sources of stress or encourage deviant or unhealthy behaviors [54].

In this sense and considering the work environment, professional relationships may be the main sources of stress and tension for a person, which makes the presence of social support inside organizations even more relevant. The sources and effects of social support may vary according to the types of work relationships that exist, moreover, the support provided is not necessarily work-related [10]. In addition, it is important that social support is incorporated into the organizational culture. Figure 4 represents the relation between social support and work environment.

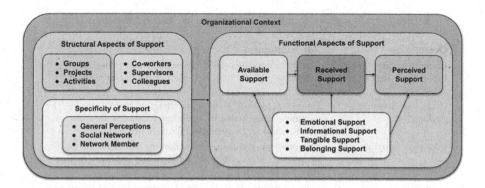

Fig. 4. Social support and work environment. Based on [54]

2.5 IT Professional Profile

There is a vast literature devoted to the study of professionals working in the area of Information Technology, there are many documents that analyze or propose aspects related to the profile of this type of profession. Authors from the 60s and 70s were already concerned with the topic and proposed ways of defining and evaluating the fundamental characteristics of these professionals [2,3,6,12, 23,38]. On the other hand, more recent studies point to an extremely complex and plural profile, capable of acting in different areas of the organization [31,36, 39,40].

For this reason, precisely defining the IT professional and his/her profile has become a controversial task, where the conclusion can even be that everyone in the organization is somehow part of the workforce that works in IT area [31]. Despite this, this study proposes and uses a simple and broad definition of IT professionals that summarizes the mission of these workers [30,37]:

Professionals who have attributions and perform activities, primarily, aimed at delivering information technology products and services with effectiveness and security, reducing risks and costs and increasing reliability, productivity and quality.

Based on the presented definition, this research and the model proposed considered that any professional related directly to the fields of Information Systems (IS) or Information Technology (IT), such as Software Developer, Cyber Security Analyst or Data Scientist, is an IT professional and has a differentiated profile.

Moreover, according to the U.S. Bureau of Labor Statistics (BLS) [18], computer and information technology workers "are professionals who create or support computer applications, systems, and networks". Considering this approach, BLS identified the main computer and information technology occupations, as presented on Table 3 [18].

Table 3. Main computer and information technology occupations [18]

Occupation	Job Summary
Computer and Information Research Scientists	Computer and information research scientists design innovative uses for new and existing computing technology.
Computer Network Architects	Computer network architects design and build data communication networks, including local area networks (LANs), wide area networks (WANs), and Intranets.
Computer Programmers	Computer programmers write, modify, and test code and scripts that allow computer software and applications to function properly.
Computer Support Specialists	Computer support specialists maintain computer networks and provide technical help to computer users.
Computer Systems Analysts	Computer systems analysts study an organization's current computer systems and design ways to improve efficiency.
Database Administrators and Architects	Database administrators and architects create or organize systems to store and secure data.
Information Security Analysts	Information security analysts plan and carry out security measures to protect an organization's computer networks and systems.
Network and Computer Systems Administrators	Network and computer systems administrators are responsible for the day-to-day operation of computer networks.
Software Developers, Quality Assurance Analysts, and Testers	Software developers design computer applications or programs. Software quality assurance analysts and testers identify problems with applications or programs and report defects.
Web Developers and Digital Designers	Web developers create and maintain websites. Digital designers develop, create, and test website or interface layout, functions, and navigation for usability.

Even with the diversity of characteristics and classifications pertinent to IT profile, it is possible to identify convergent aspects common to all professionals from this area [36]. IT specialists have unique identity, knowledge, skills, attitudes and interests, and their focus at work tends to be more centered on technical issues, to the detriment of interpersonal skills such as communication [1].

Considering this scenario, the IT profile can be defined as a set of special abilities (hard and soft skills) necessary for Information Technology professionals to perform well in activities related to their jobs. These skill can be classified into 3 broad categories [36, 57]:

- **Technical Skills:** knowledge and competences related to the use and application of technologies.
- **Humanistic Skills:** temperance, resilience, interpersonal relationships (e.g., teamwork, leadership, communication), promotion of well-being.
- **Business Skills:** business domain knowledge, project management, ethics, problem and conflict resolution.

When compared to professionals from other areas, IT personnel have a greater desire for opportunities, challenges and autonomy [57], in addition, they are motivated by achievements, recognition, constant learning and personal growth [1].

These are also common elements of the IT area [36]:

- Supply and demand for IT professionals continually changing;
- Requirement of a combined set of technical, humanistic and business skills;
- Professional environment in constant change, requiring adaptation and update of specific skills in short periods of time;
- Activities developed are essentially cognitive and difficult to monitor and evaluate.

In 2022, according to the Occupational Requirements Survey of BLS, most of IT workers are required to have particular skills and prior work experience. Furthermore, for these professionals, the specific preparation time, necessary for average performance in Information Technology area, may vary from 2 to 10 years [19].

The definitions and all other considerations just presented are what make Information Technology professionals singular inside organizations, demanding differentiated attention and approach from human resource management and, more specifically, from human performance management [1, 29, 36, 37, 57].

3 Research Methodology

In order to develop the solution proposed in this research, the *Design Science Research* paradigm was used [11, 55]. Based on this paradigm, the first 4 steps of the process model proposed by Peffers et al. [34], known as *Design Science Research Methodology* (DSRM), were carried out, as shown in Fig. 5.

Thus, this research, which has a qualitative approach and positivist epistemological position, was developed in 4 phases or stages:

1. Problem identification and motivation;
2. Definition of solution objectives;

3. Design and development;
4. Demonstration.

In the first stage, an extensive literature review was performed, which made it possible to identify the context and domain of the problem. Additionally, the motivation and reasons for seeking a solution were also determined.

Continuing in the second phase, with the problem identified, it was possible to establish the objectives of the proposed solution, the assumptions and requirements that the produced artifact should follow. At this point, the need to build a human performance management model specifically focused on information technology professionals was defined, encompassing the precepts and characteristics of humanism.

In the third stage, the design and construction of the proposed model allowed a better understanding of the problem domain and its solution.

Finally, in the last step, the applicability of the model was demonstrated through evaluation methods of static and architectural analysis [11], verifying the structure of the model and studying its suitability to the requirements and theoretical assumptions postulated.

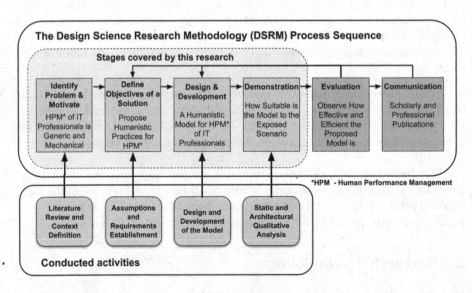

Fig. 5. Research implementation using the DSRM process model. Adapted from [34]

4   Research Findings

Based on the context and issues described previously, the present work proposes a humanistic model for performance management focused on developing the needs of IT employees as human beings, guided by the principles of ethics and appreciation of life.

The solution has the following fundamental assumptions and requirements:

- **Promotion of the human person:** all the steps on the process must preserve and improve IT employees' well-being and expectations;
- **Ethics:** all tasks related do performance evaluation need to be based on ethics principals defined by society and organizational culture;
- **Transparency:** actions and decisions of performance management must be communicated widely and transparently;
- **Justice, Equality and Inclusion:** the process must pursue and guarantee organizational justice, equality and inclusion;
- **Objectivity and Celerity:** HPM should avoid excessive bureaucracy, prioritizing simplicity, objectivity and celerity;
- **Active stakeholder participation:** all the steps must permit and promote the participation of organization community;
- **Formative Appraisal:** performance evaluation must prioritize a formative method (perceptions) over a summative one (grades and rates);
- **Respect for individuality and dignity:** all persons involved in the process must be treated with respect and dignity;
- **Personal and professional development:** HPM must ensure the personal and professional development of IT employees.

The details of the proposed model can be seen in Fig. 6, there are 4 distinct phases in the human performance management process (planning, performance appraisal, review, monitoring and improvement), where each step is specified according to humanistic foundations.

As can be seen from the model, **human being** must be the central concern of HPM, this indicates that management success depends, primarily, on how the issues related to humans are treated.

IT Profile is the next element that deserves consideration in the model, this represents all characteristics, skills, competences, knowledge and needs that compose and differentiate IT professionals from the others. The actions taken during the performance management process must respect and consider this profile.

The **planning** stage defines and presents the individual and collective purposes for evolution of human performance of organization's members. Planning must have a person-centered approach, be public and objective, in addition, it must address the personal and professional growth needs of each individual, contemplating the specificity of the IT profile. Its realization has collaborative characteristics, where decisions about what to produce, develop, improve or remedy are taken jointly and equitably.

Performance appraisal has a formative character and occurs continuously, being encouraged and carried out by all members of the organizational community. It should not use a summative method, the absence of values prevents comparisons and, at the same time, develops empathy and critical thinking in employees when interpreting feedback received or evaluating a colleague or themselves.

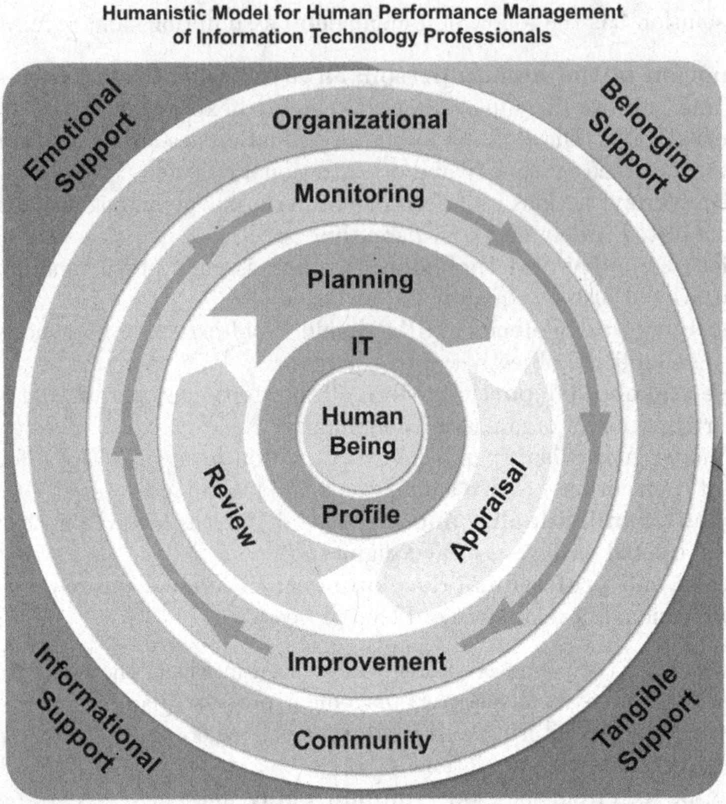

**Humanistic Model for Human Performance Management
of Information Technology Professionals**

Fig. 6. Humanistic model for human performance management of information technology professionals.

The **review** stage, which is also participatory, analyzes what has been carried out, allowing the necessary points to be adjusted and improving HPM proposals and mechanisms for the new cycle that will begin.

In the **monitoring and improvement phase (follow-up and support)**, the entire organizational community is invited to collaborate with the development of personal and professional goals, both individual and collective, which were defined in the planning stage. This step occurs throughout HPM process and can be executed in the form of mentoring, coaching, physical and mental health support, transfer and promotion of knowledge, among others possibilities. In addition, actions that seek to improve the management process itself are also promoted and encouraged.

The model also considers the positive and humanist influence of social support into human performance. There are several significant beneficial effects and positive behaviours resulting from social support on Human Performance Management process, especially related to cope with stressful situations, emotional and psychological well-being and reduction of job turnover. Table 4 resumes some of social support effects according to the phases of the HPM model proposed.

Table 4. Social support beneficial effects on the HPM model proposed

Emotional Support

Phase	*Planning*
Example	Discussing feelings or emotions about performance drivers and goals.
Beneficial Effects	- Active participation in planning; - Improvement of sense of justice, equality and inclusion.
Phase	*Performance Appraisal*
Example	Pointing out the strengths a person has.
Beneficial Effects	- Personal recognition and appreciation; - Self-esteem development.
Phase	*Review*
Example	Asking or giving personal advice about executed activities.
Beneficial Effects	- Process continuous improvement; - Perception of being cared for and supported by co-workers.
Phase	*Monitoring and Improvement*
Example	Listening and empathizing in stressful work situations.
Beneficial Effects	- Stresses and strains mitigation or buffering; - Encouragement and confidence improvement.

Informational Support

Phase	*Planning*
Example	Sharing information that can help to promote one's skills, abilities, and intrinsic value.
Beneficial Effects	- Preservation and improvement of expectations; - Reinforcement of ethical principles.
Phase	*Performance Appraisal*
Example	Providing informational help or professional advice in defining and coping with performance problems.
Beneficial Effects	- Formative Appraisal; - Promotion of personal and professional development.
Phase	*Review*
Example	Gathering and sharing information that can help co-workers know of potential HPM next steps that may work well.
Beneficial Effects	- Process transparency; - Respect and promotion of individuality.
Phase	*Monitoring and Improvement*
Example	Providing guidance, technical advice and mentoring.
Beneficial Effects	- Equality to deal with work issues or decision making based on information; - Assistance with moral and intellectual development.

(*continued*)

Table 4. (*continued*)

Tangible Support

Phase	*Planning*
Example	Taking on responsibilities or brainstorming solutions for performance drivers and goals.
Beneficial Effects	- Collaborative work development; - Practical and direct aid that enable the fulfillment of job-related obligations.
Phase	*Performance Appraisal*
Example	Assisting actively in definition and application of performance evaluation instruments.
Beneficial Effects	- Empathy and critical thinking development; - Reduction of comparison and competition.
Phase	*Review*
Example	Promoting and coordinating feedback meetings.
Beneficial Effects	- Job turnover prevention; - Simplicity and celerity fostering.
Phase	*Monitoring and Improvement*
Example	Teaching or showing the other person something about work.
Beneficial Effects	- Correct tools and techniques provision; - Direct help with personal and professional development.

Belonging Support

Phase	*Planning*
Example	Discussing guidance and evolution of human performance with all organizational community.
Beneficial Effects	- Active stakeholder participation; - Enhancement of organizational community and culture.
Phase	*Performance Appraisal*
Example	Having a team or co-workers with whom to count on in order to achieve performance goals.
Beneficial Effects	- Development of trust and engagement; - Encouragement of teamwork.
Phase	*Review*
Example	Crowdsourcing performance reviews.
Beneficial Effects	- Democracy promotion. - Inclusive environment at work.
Phase	*Monitoring and Improvement*
Example	Being allies in difficult interpersonal situations at work.
Beneficial Effects	- Formation of people clusters with similar interests or situations; - Promotion of social connectivity and companionship.

5   Discussion

As demonstrated in Fig. 2, Human Performance Management is a complex process that involves numerous variables, methodologies, people and applications. In addition, HPM is based on a vast amount of theories, in the most diverse areas of research, which makes the study on the subject very extensive and deep.

Considering the theories studied, the Organizational Culture theory proved to be the central point of analysis, through which it is possible to understand how the actions defined in the HPM are actually performed and the effects that this management has on employees.

Added to this, there are the unique characteristics of IT professionals and their work environment, which require, from Human Performance Management, a differentiated and individualized treatment for employees working in this area.

The particularities, problems and difficulties faced by Information Technology professionals have been subject of study for many years [40], considering the issues addressed by the researchers, the following items deserve to be highlighted:

- Ethics in IT and Conflicts at work;
- Job or career turnover;
- Gender imbalance/prejudice in IT;
- Treatment of minorities in IT;
- Evolution/Change of project and work models;
- Overload, stress, exhaustion and burnout;
- Work versus social life conflicts;
- Speed of technological evolution;
- Perception of professional stagnation or obsolescence.

It is important to understand that an effective HPM has the power to treat, mitigate or even solve the problems experienced in IT area. Additionally, it has demonstrated to be essential to study, develop and encourage a more humane, supportive and sustainable organizational management.

In this sense, the present research believes that human beings should have the following needs considered and managed by organizations [53]:

- Physical and mental health;
- Intellectual development;
- Emotional growth;
- Experiences in the fields of arts, culture and aesthetics;
- Social connectivity;
- Moral and spiritual development.

In order to ensure the true evolution of human performance, any HPM model must consider the humanistic aspects in its management premises. Therefore, it is essential to leave behind all models where workers are seen only as production resources, abolishing the view that monitoring and optimization should consider only productivity and efficiency [53].

Considering the proposed model, the analysis of the results relied on the evaluative precepts established by Design Science Research Methodology [11] and, from there, we sought to understand how adequate the solution is in relation to the human performance management framework, to the humanist and social support principles and to the characteristics and particularities of the IT professional profile.

Regarding the human performance management framework (Fig. 2), it is possible to verify that the proposed model is fully adherent to it. The solution presents a management process with well defined phases and elements, deals with organizations' contextual factors and allows the adoption of existing approaches and methodologies related to the field of HPM.

Considering the problems covered in this research in relation to humanist and social support principles, we believe that the following points are contemplated in the solution, as proposed by Farah [8, p. 150]:

- Respect for human beings and equal treatment;
- Improvement of Organizational Justice;
- Concern with personal (physical, mental, moral and spiritual) and professional development (skills, knowledge and technological evolution);
- Planning and evolution of human performance in an appropriate manner, linked to both, personal and organizational, expectations;
- Collaboration in IT talent retention.

Regarding the connections in the model between the IT specialist's requirements and their actual implementation in the organization, Table 5 demonstrates some possible application examples of the model, considering the IT occupations, work activities and context, as proposed by the U.S. Bureau of Labor Statistics and O*NET OnLine [18, 28].

Table 5. Application examples of the model, considering the IT occupations, work activities and context

Occupation	*Computer and Information Research Scientists*
Sample task	Analyze problems to develop solutions involving computer hardware and software.
Work context	High responsibility for outcomes and results
Proposed model application/connection	HPM must recognize and reward good results rather than blame and punish poor outcomes
Actual implementation example	Rewards and Recognition program specially designed for IT professionals
Occupation	*Computer Network Architects*
Sample task	Develop conceptual, logical, or physical network designs.
Work context	Being exact or accurate is important
Proposed model application/connection	HPM enhances the beneficial effects of social support
Actual implementation example	Advanced tools and techniques usage in the decision-making process, such as mentoring, continuous monitoring, business intelligence, and automation
Occupation	*Computer Programmers*
Sample task	Write, analyze, review, and rewrite computer programs
Work context	Daily time pressure
Proposed model application/connection	HPM promotes organizational justice and workload balance, respecting individuality and dignity
Actual implementation example	Use of Agile methodologies, like Scrum and Kanban, for project, task and time management.
Occupation	*Computer Support Specialists*
Sample task	Collaborate with others to resolve information technology issues.
Work context	Constant contact with others
Proposed model application/connection	HPM stimulates and encourages empathy and active listening.
Actual implementation example	Design Thinking approach to problem solving
Occupation	*Computer Systems Analysts*
Sample task	Supervise computer programmers or other systems analysts or serve as project leaders for particular systems projects.
Work context	Strong working relationships, necessity to coordinate or lead others
Proposed model application/connection	HPM should provide a supportive work environment for collaboration and positive leadership
Actual implementation example	Use of communication, collaboration and productivity apps, like Google Workspace or GitLab, to ensure that team members don't feel left out.

(*continued*)

Table 5. (continued)

Occupation	Database Administrators and Architects
Sample task	Administer, test, and implement computer databases
Work context	Consequences of errors are very serious
Proposed model application/connection	HPM must be aware that errors are a normal part of human existence
Actual implementation example	Design of fail-safe/fault-tolerant systems, involving, for example, hardware redundancy, containerized applications or data replication, in order to improve reliability and safety
Occupation	**Information Security Analysts**
Sample task	Implement security measures for computer or information systems.
Work context	Staying up to date on Information Security matters is important
Proposed model application/connection	HPM must address the personal and professional growth needs
Actual implementation example	Cybersecurity Certifications, like Security+ and CISSP
Occupation	**Network and Computer Systems Administrators**
Sample task	Maintain computer networks to enhance performance and user access
Work context	Execution of repetitive and controlled tasks
Proposed model application/connection	HPM should prioritize simplicity, objectivity and celerity
Actual implementation example	Processes and activities standardization through the adoption of the ITIL framework
Occupation	**Software Developers, Quality Assurance Analysts, and Testers**
Sample task	Analyze project data to determine specifications or requirements
Work context	Daily interactions, collaborations and discussions
Proposed model application/connection	HPM must permit active stakeholder participation
Actual implementation example	Use of DevOps/DevSecOps methodologies and practices
Occupation	**Web Developers and Digital Designers**
Sample task	Design websites or web applications.
Work context	Highly demanding and competitive job
Proposed model application/connection	HPM must ensure and promote personal and professional development based on the principles of ethics, equality and transparency
Actual implementation example	Continuous and accessible learning as an IT governance strategy

Furthermore, this study is also considered to be innovative because it proposes an unprecedented and supportive model capable of improving, from a humanist perspective, the human performance management of information technology professionals.

In order to corroborate with this statement, most of the authors analyzed by this research focused their studies on directly applicable methods or management practices for performance evaluation, and, only in few cases, the characteristics of IT professionals are encompassed, however, leaving aside the question of humanism. The authors who dealt with humanistic management, on the other hand, do not, specifically, address performance management or the profile of the IT professional.

6   Conclusions

For humanism, every person is worthy of development [50]. This research was conducted based on this humanistic axiom and it is hoped that this study can somehow contribute to a better and more sustainable world, aware of the importance of valuing life and human dignity.

The main implications of this work for researchers and practitioners reside on the possibility to adopt, implement and extend the concepts, guidance, processes, phases and good practices established by the model, moreover, they can use this study to transform the culture of an organization, incorporating humanism and social support into daily work routine.

The limitations of the model and its usage are primarily related to the issues concerning the initial adoption, since the study considered a generic process of HPM focused on Information Technology professionals, for more specific scenarios or situations on IT area, it will be necessary make adaptations and develop extensions in order to deliver the expected results. Its important to emphasize that the model is prepared to be adapted and evolved according to organizational culture, management and governance, mainly with regard to the IT area.

Others probable limitations to the use of the proposed model are:

- Complexity of performance measurement mechanisms;
- Low adherence or acceptance by the organizational community;
- Lack of clearer or more practical instructions;
- Mandatory aspects due to regulations or laws.

Another point, to be considered, is that the model is based on the ways of working and tools used by most organizations today, concepts such as robotic process automation and the evolution and expansion of Artificial Intelligence usage in the work environment can significantly transform, in the near future, the way performance management are carried out, directly impacting the model's applicability. These issues or limitations can lead to partial adoption or even non-adoption of the model.

As future work, the development of complementary researches is indicated, which, based on the proposed model, are able to produce new artifacts capable of leveraging the evolution of Human Performance Management of Information Technology professionals. Surveys, maturity models, good practices, processes, methodologies, and information systems are just a few examples of important artifacts that can be defined and explored.

References

1. Allen, M.W., Armstrong, D.J., Reid, M.F., Riemenschneider, C.K.: It employee retention: employee expectations and workplace environments. In: Proceedings of the Special Interest Group on Management Information System's 47th Annual Conference on Computer Personnel Research. SIGMIS CPR 2009, New York, NY, USA, pp. 95–100. Association for Computing Machinery (2009). https://doi.org/10.1145/1542130.1542148

2. Bartol, K.M., Martin, D.C.: Managing information systems personnel: a review of the literature and managerial implications. MIS Quart. **6**, 49–70 (1982). https://www.jstor.org/stable/248991

3. Berger, R.M., Wilson, R.C.: Correlates of programmer proficiency. In: Proceedings of the Fourth SIGCPR Conference on Computer Personnel Research. SIGCPR 1966, pp. 83–95, New York, NY, USA. Association for Computing Machinery (1966). https://doi.org/10.1145/1142620.1142629

4. De Oliveira Góes, A.S., De Oliveira, R.C.L.: A process for human resource performance evaluation using computational intelligence: an approach using a combination of rule-based classifiers and supervised learning algorithms. IEEE Access **8**, 39403–39419 (2020). https://doi.org/10.1109/ACCESS.2020.2975485

5. DelPo, A.: Performance Appraisal Handbook, The: Legal & Practical Rules for Managers. Performance Appraisal Handbook, NOLO (2007)

6. Dickmann, R.A.: A programmer appraisal instrument. In: Proceedings of the Second SIGCPR Conference on Computer Personnel Research. SIGCPR 1964, New York, NY, USA, pp. 45–64. Association for Computing Machinery (1964). https://doi.org/10.1145/1142635.1142640

7. Dierksmeier, C.: What is 'Humanistic' About Humanistic Management? Humanistic Manage. J. **1**(1), 9–32 (2016). https://doi.org/10.1007/s41463-016-0002-6

8. Farah, F.: A Ética da Avaliação de Desempenho. Master's thesis, EAESP/FGV, São Paulo (2000)

9. Fernández-Sanz, L.: Personal skills for computing professionals. Computer **42**(10), 110–111 (2009). https://doi.org/10.1109/MC.2009.329

10. Henderson, M., Argyle, M.: Social support by four categories of work colleagues: Relationships between activities, stress and satisfaction. J. Occupat. Behav. **6**(3), 229–239 (1985). https://www.jstor.org/stable/3000094

11. Hevner, A.R., March, S.T., Park, J., Ram, S.: Design science in information systems research. MIS Quart. **28**(1), 75–105 (2004). https://www.jstor.org/stable/25148625

12. Hoyle, J.C., Arvey, R.D.: Development of behaviorally based rating scales. In: Proceedings of the Tenth Annual SIGCPR Conference. SIGCPR 1972, New York, NY, USA, pp. 85–103, Association for Computing Machinery (1972). https://doi.org/10.1145/800156.805029

13. Huibao, C., Lei, L.: The study on appraisal of enterprise employee performance. In: 2009 First International Workshop on Database Technology and Applications, pp. 632–637. Institute of Electrical and Electronics Engineers (2009). https://doi.org/10.1109/DBTA.2009.45

14. Idell, K., Gefen, D., Ragowsky, A.: Managing it professional turnover. Commun. ACM **64**(9), 72–77 (2021). https://doi.org/10.1145/3434641

15. Initiative, T.D.H.: Vienna manifesto on digital humanism (2019). https://dighum.ec.tuwien.ac.at/dighum-manifesto/

16. Kanij, T., Grundy, J., Merkel, R.: Performance appraisal of software testers. Inf. Softw. Technol. **56**(5), 495–505 (2014)
17. Killingsworth, B.L., Hayden, M.B., Crawford, D., Schellenberger, R.: A model for motivating and measuring quality performance in information systems staff. Inf. Syst. Manage. **18**(2), 8–14 (2001). https://doi.org/10.1201/1078/43195.18.2. 20010301/31271.2
18. U.B. of Labor Statistics: Computer and information technology occupations : Occupational outlook handbook, September 2022. https://www.bls.gov/ooh/computer-and-information-technology/
19. U.B. of Labor Statistics: Occupational requirements survey - u.s. bureau of labor statistics (2022). https://www.bls.gov/ors/factsheet/pdf/computer-and-mathematical-occupations.pdf
20. Larsen, K., Eargle, D.: Organizational culture theory (2011). https://is.theorizeit. org/wiki/Organizational_culture_theory
21. Latham, G., Wexley, K.N., Wexley, K.: Increasing Productivity Through Performance Appraisal. Addison-Wesley series on managing human resources. Addison-Wesley (1981)
22. Martinez, E.A., Beaulieu, N., Gibbons, R., Pronovost, P., Wang, T.: Organizational culture and performance. Am. Econom. Rev. **105**(5), 331–35 (2015)
23. Mayer, D.B., Stalnaker, A.W.: Selection and evaluation of computer personnel- the research history of sig/cpr. In: Proceedings of the 1968 23rd ACM National Conference. ACM 1968, New York, NY, USA, pp. 657–670. Association for Computing Machinery (1968). https://doi.org/10.1145/800186.810630
24. Messner, D.: Redefining and renewing humanism in the digital age [opinion]. IEEE Technol. Soc. Mag. **39**(2), 35–40 (2020). https://doi.org/10.1109/MTS.2020. 2991498
25. Miller, E.: The performance appraisal. IEEE Potentials **16**(2), 20–21 (1997). https://doi.org/10.1109/MP.1997.582455
26. Miner, J.B.: Organizational behavior I. Essential theories of motivation and leadership. M.E. Sharpe, Inc (2005)
27. das Nações Unidas, O.: Declaração universal dos direitos humanos (1948), https:// www.ohchr.org/en/udhr/documents/udhr_translations/por.pdf
28. Network, O.I.: Occupational information network (o*net) online (2022). https:// www.onetonline.org/
29. Niederman, F., Crosetto, G.: Valuing the it workforce as intellectual capital. In: Proceedings of the 1999 ACM SIGCPR Conference on Computer Personnel Research. SIGCPR 1999, New York, NY, USA, pp. 174–181. Association for Computing Machinery (1999). https://doi.org/10.1145/299513.299659
30. Niederman, F., Ferratt, T.W., Trauth, E.M.: On the co-evolution of information technology and information systems personnel. SIGMIS Database **47**(1), 29–50 (2016). https://doi.org/10.1145/2894216.2894219
31. Niederman, F., Kaarst-Brown, M., Quesenberry, J., Weitzel, T.: The future of it work: computers and people. In: Proceedings of the 2019 on Computers and People Research Conference. SIGMIS-CPR 2019, New York, NY, USA, pp. 28–34. Association for Computing Machinery (2019). https://doi.org/10.1145/3322385. 3322403
32. Packer, C.: A framework for the organizational assumptions underlying safety culture. Technical report, International Atomic Energy Agency (IAEA) (2002). https://inis.iaea.org/search/search.aspx?orig_q=RN:34007162

33. Patnaik, M., Pattanaik, B.: Performance evaluation of employees in public sector banks. In: IEEE-International Conference On Advances In Engineering, Science And Management (ICAESM -2012), pp. 19–25. Institute of Electrical and Electronics Engineers (2012)

34. Peffers, K., Tuunanen, T., Rothenberger, M.A., Chatterjee, S.: A design science research methodology for information systems research. J. Manage. Inf. Syst. **24**(3), 45–77 (2007). https://doi.org/10.2753/MIS0742-1222240302

35. Perkins, S.J.: Processing developments in employee performance and reward. J. Organizat. Effect. People Perform. **5**(3), 289–300 (2018). https://doi.org/10.1108/JOEPP-07-2018-0049

36. Potter, L.E.: Preparing for projects: It student self-evaluation of technical and professional skills. In: Proceedings of the 2020 on Computers and People Research Conference. SIGMIS-CPR 2020, New York, NY, USA, pp. 63–69. Association for Computing Machinery (2020). https://doi.org/10.1145/3378539.3393868

37. Potter, L.E.C., von Hellens, L.A., Nielsen, S.H.: Childhood interest in it and the choice of it as a career: the experiences of a group of it professionals. In: Proceedings of the Special Interest Group on Management Information System's 47th Annual Conference on Computer Personnel Research. SIGMIS CPR 2009, pp. 33–40, New York, NY, USA, Association for Computing Machinery (2009). https://doi.org/10.1145/1542130.1542138

38. Powell, B.: Performance evaluation of programmers and analysts. In: Proceedings of the 3rd Annual ACM SIGUCCS Conference on User Services. SIGUCCS 1975, New York, NY, USA, pp. 19–21. Association for Computing Machinery (1975). https://doi.org/10.1145/800115.803716

39. Prommegger, B., Arshad, D., Krcmar, H.: Understanding boundaryless it professionals: an investigation of personal characteristics, career mobility, and career success. In: Proceedings of the 2021 on Computers and People Research Conference. SIGMIS-CPR 2021, New York, NY, USA, pp. 51–59. Association for Computing Machinery (2021). https://doi.org/10.1145/3458026.3462162

40. Prommegger, B., Wiesche, M., Krcmar, H.: What makes it professionals special? a literature review on context-specific theorizing in it workforce research. In: Proceedings of the 2020 on Computers and People Research Conference. SIGMIS-CPR 2020, New York, NY, USA, pp. 81–90, Association for Computing Machinery (2020). https://doi.org/10.1145/3378539.3393861

41. Rapp, F.: Humanism and technology: the two-cultures debate. Technol. Soc. **7**(4), 423–435 (1985)

42. Renaud, S., Morin, L., Saulquin, J.Y., Abraham, J.: What are the best HRM practices for retaining experts? a longitudinal study in the Canadian information technology sector. Int. J. Manpower **36**(3), 416–432 (2015). https://doi.org/10.1108/ijm-03-2014-0078

43. Riemenschneider, C., Allen, M., Reid, M.: Potencial antecedents to the voluntary turnover intentions of women working in information technology. In: Proceedings of 2002 Americas Conference on Information Systems (AMCIS), pp. 2018–2022. Association for Information Systems (2002). https://aisel.aisnet.org/amcis2002/277

44. Sarason, I.G., Sarason, B.R. (eds.): Social Support: Theory, Research and Applications. Springer, Netherlands (1985). https://doi.org/10.1007/978-94-009-5115-0

45. Schein, E.H.: Organizational culture. In: Working paper (Sloan School of Management). No. 2088–88 in Working paper (Sloan School of Management), Sloan School of Management, Massachusetts Institute of Technology (1988). https://hdl.handle.net/1721.1/2224

46. Sethunga, S., Perera, I.: Impact of performance rewards on employee turnover in Sri Lankan it industry. In: 2018 Moratuwa Engineering Research Conference (MERCon), pp. 114–119. Institute of Electrical and Electronics Engineers (2018). https://doi.org/10.1109/MERCon.2018.8421961

47. Shafagatova, A., Looy, A.V.: Developing a tool for process-oriented appraisals and rewards: design science research. J. Software: Evol. Process **33**(3) (2020). https://doi.org/10.1002/smr.2321

48. Shafagatova, A., Van Looy, A.: A conceptual framework for process-oriented employee appraisals and rewards. Knowl. Process Manag. **28**(1), 90–104 (2021)

49. Spang, R.J., Spang, N.D.: Human performance, error precursors and the tool kit. In: 2020 IEEE IAS Electrical Safety Workshop (ESW), pp. 1–8 (2020). https://doi.org/10.1109/ESW42757.2020.9188332

50. Steelwater, E.: Humanism. In: Chadwick, R. (ed.) Encyclopedia of Applied Ethics 2nd edn., pp. 674–682. Academic Press, San Diego (2012). https://doi.org/10.1016/B978-0-12-373932-2.00208-8, https://www.sciencedirect.com/science/article/pii/B9780123739322002088

51. Taylor, S.E.: Social Support: A Review. Oxford University Press (2011). https://doi.org/10.1093/oxfordhb/9780195342819.013.0009

52. Teehankee, B.: Humanistic entrepreneurship: an approach to virtue-based enterprise. Asia Pac. Soc. Sci. Rev. **8**(1), 89–110 (2008)

53. Teehankee, B.: Principles and practices of humanistic management (2021). https://doi.org/10.32907/RO-120-8689

54. Uchino, B.N.: Social Support and Physical Health. Current Perspectives in Psychology. Yale University Press, New Haven, CT, February 2004

55. Walter, M.: An approach to transforming requirements into evaluable UI design for contextual practice - a design science research perspective. In: Proceedings of the 2018 Federated Conference on Computer Science and Information Systems. IEEE, September 2018. https://doi.org/10.15439/2018f235

56. Wang, C.j., Xu, H.m., Jiang, M.h.: Research on the dimensions and influencing factors of enterprise humanism management - an empirical study based on the questionnaire of dongguan enterprises. In: 2020 16th International Conference on Computational Intelligence and Security (CIS), pp. 169–173. Institute of Electrical and Electronics Engineers (2020). https://doi.org/10.1109/CIS52066.2020.00044

57. Zylka, M.P.: Putting the consequences of it turnover on the map: a review and call for research. In: Proceedings of the 2016 ACM SIGMIS Conference on Computers and People Research. SIGMIS-CPR 2016, New York, NY, USA, pp. 87–95. Association for Computing Machinery (2016). https://doi.org/10.1145/2890602.2890618

Companies in Multilingual Wikipedia: Articles Quality and Important Sources of Information

Włodzimierz Lewoniewski(✉) [iD], Krzysztof Węcel[iD], and Witold Abramowicz[iD]

Department of Information Systems, Poznan University of Economics and Business, Al. Niepodleglosci 10, Poznan 61-875, Poland
{wlodzimierz.lewoniewski,krzysztof.wecel,witold.abramowicz}@ue.poznan.pl

Abstract. In this paper, we provide a method for the identification and assessment of reliable internet sources about companies. We first identified 516,586 Wikipedia articles related to companies in 310 language versions, and then extracted and analyzed references contained in them using three different models for article quality assessment. As a result, we compiled a ranking of reliable sources. We found that there are several universal sources shared by many languages, but usually each language has its own specific sources. Our ranking of sources can be useful for Wikipedia editors looking for source material for their articles. Companies themselves can leverage this ranking for public relations activities. Moreover, our method can be used to automatically maintain a list of reliable internet sources.

Keywords: Information quality · Credibility of information sources · Wikipedia · Wikidata · DBpedia

1 Introduction

Information presented in Wikipedia articles should be based on reliable sources [9]. The source can be understood as the work (book, paper, etc.), the author, or the publisher. Such sources must have a proper reputation and should present all majority and significant minority views on some piece of information. Following this rule ensures that the readers of the Wikipedia article can be assured that each specific statement provided is supported by a published and reliable source. Therefore, before adding any information to this online encyclopedia, Wikipedia editors (volunteer authors) should ensure that the facts presented in the article can be verified by other people who read Wikipedia [11].

Few developed language versions of Wikipedia contain a non-exhaustive list of sources whose reliability and use in Wikipedia are frequently discussed. Even English Wikipedia, the largest chapter, has such a general list with information on reliability for only approximately 400 websites [10]. Sometimes we can find such lists for specific topics (e.g., video games and movies).

It could take significant human effort to produce a more complete list of trusted Internet sources - there are more than a billion websites available on the

© The Author(s), under exclusive license to Springer Nature Switzerland AG 2023
E. Ziemba et al. (Eds.): FedCSIS-AIST 2022/ISM 2022, LNBIP 471, pp. 48–67, 2023.
https://doi.org/10.1007/978-3-031-29570-6_3

Internet [15,27] and many of them can be considered a source of information. Therefore, it can be a very challenging and time-consuming task for Wikipedia volunteers to assess the reliability of each source. Moreover, the reputation of each website can change with time; hence, such lists must be updated regularly. Each source may also have a different reliability score depending on the topic and language version of Wikipedia.

On one hand, we can state that such a list of reliable information sources would be helpful to editors. On the other hand, we have not identified such an approach in the literature. The lack of methods for maintaining a list of reliable sources is a significant research gap. This study presents a method for automating this process by analyzing existing and accepted content with sources from Wikipedia articles on companies in different languages. We use existing and new models to assess the reliability and popularity of websites. We found that, depending on the models, it is possible to find such important sources in selected Wikipedia languages. Additionally, the assessment of the same sources can vary, depending on the language of this encyclopedia.

The paper is structured as follows. Section 2 provides a literature review. In Sect. 3 we explain our research methodology, i.e. how articles related to companies were identified and what data was collected along with its characteristics. Section 4 extends the research methodology with regard to the extraction of references from previously identified articles. The research findings using three models for source assessment are presented in Sect. 5. A discussion of the results is carried out in Sect. 6. Conclusions and future work can be found in Sect. 7.

2   Related Work

Researching the quality of Wikipedia content is a fairly developed topic in scientific work. As one of the key factors influencing the quality of Wikipedia articles is the presence of references, some studies focused on researching information sources. Some works use the number of references to automatically assess the quality of the information on Wikipedia [3,34]. Such important measures are implemented in different approaches to automatic quality assessment of Wikipedia articles (for example, WikiRank [39]). References often contain external links (URL addresses) where cited information is placed. Such links can be assessed by indicating the degree to which they conform to their intended purpose [36]. Furthermore, these links can be used separately to assess the quality of Wikipedia articles [6,42].

Some of the studies focused on the metadata analysis of sources in Wikipedia references. One of the previous works used ISBN and DOI identifiers to unify references and find the similarity of sources between various Wikipedia language editions [21]. It is becoming more common practice to include scientific sources in references in Wikipedia articles [21,22,29,33]. At the same time, it should be noted that such references often link to open-access works [35] and recently published journal articles [16]. One of the studies devoted to scientific work related to COVID-19 cited in Wikipedia articles found that information comes from about 2% of the scientific works published at that time [5].

News websites are also one of the most popular sources of information in Wikipedia, and there is a method to automatically suggest new references to the selected piece of information [13]. Particularly popular are references about recent content or life events [30]. For example, for information related to the COVID-19 pandemic, Wikipedia editors tend to cite the latest scientific articles and insert more recent information into Wikipedia shortly after the publication of these works [5].

The previous publication [22], relevant to this article, proposed and implemented 10 models for the evaluation of sources in Wikipedia articles. The evaluation results are also implemented in the online tool "BestRef" [2]. Such approaches use features (or measures) that can be extracted from publicly available data (Wikimedia Downloads [38]) so that anyone can use those models for different purposes.

This work is a continuation of the previous study [23]. Compared to the previous article, this study significantly expanded the scope of the analyzed language versions (all language versions available during the period analyzed). We also used more recent data from Wikipedia and Wikidata in order to obtain the results - November 2022. In addition, we conducted an analysis of some aspects of the quality of Wikipedia articles on companies in different languages.

3   Wikipedia Articles Related to Companies

To find such articles, we used data from DBpedia and Wikidata. Data from these open databases are widely used in a number of domains, such as web search, life sciences, art market, digital libraries, and business networks [12,14,19,26].

DBpedia ontology has a hierarchical structure, and if some resource is aligned with other company-related classes, we can use connections between those classes to detect Wikipedia articles related to companies. For example, some organizations can be aligned to 'Bank', 'Publisher', 'BusCompany', or another company-related class of the DBpedia ontology, and after generalization, we can find that all of them belong just to the 'Company' class. Based on DBpedia dumps related to instance types [7] (the specific part of the dumps for each available language), we found that Wikipedia articles can be aligned directly to one of the 634 classes of the DBpedia ontology. After considering transitive DBpedia dumps, we have obtained resources in the 'Company' class. Next, we took similar data extracted by DBpedia from other Wikipedia languages and finally collected an extended list of articles related to companies.

In the next stage, we analyzed Wikidata items that were presented as a collection of different statements structured as Subject—Predicate—Object. Based on Wikidata statements, out of more than 100 million items, we determined more than 100 thousand items that were related to companies. Often they had a statement in the form `Property:P31 Q783794`, meaning 'instance of a company'. We also enriched our knowledge base with statements related to **business**

(Q4830453), `enterprise` (Q6881511), `public company` (Q891723), `technology company` (Q18388277), and other similar items. The resulting list of Wikidata items about companies can provide links to related Wikipedia articles in different languages.

Compared to DBpedia ontology classes, Wikidata has roughly 100 times more possible alignments for different items [23]. There are various possibilities to automate the process of identifying company-related items in Wikidata. One of them is to analyze Wikidata items related to companies selected using DBpedia extraction and find the most popular alignments in `instance of` statements. In total, we collected more than 3000 various classes, and the most popular are business, enterprise, public company, company, automobile manufacturer, airline, record label, publisher, bus company, video game developer, organization, commercial organization, and bank.

Before we could identify relevant articles about companies, we introduced several tweaks to our procedure. First, we kept only alignments that appeared at least 200 times to avoid insignificant errors that could be introduced by less experienced users editing Wikidata. Furthermore, we removed the alignment to `organization` (Q43229) which was too general. As a result, we have more Wikidata items with articles on the list of companies; overall, 296,180 Wikidata items were identified with at least one related Wikipedia article in considered language versions. Since each Wikidata item can have one or more links to Wikipedia articles in some language versions, we were able to identify 516,586 articles related to companies in 310 language versions of Wikipedia. A more detailed description of the approach that allowed the search of Wikipedia articles on companies was described in our previous study [23].

Table 1 shows statistics for some of the language versions of Wikipedia (with more than 1000 articles related to companies). Please note that the average and median values were rounded to whole numbers. More extended results are available in the supplementary materials on the Web [8].

It is important to note that the other 30 language versions have only one article about a company, the next 68 languages have 2–10 articles related to companies, and 110 language editions of Wikipedia have over 10 but less than 1000 articles that describe various companies. There are also 51 language versions of Wikipedia that do not have any distinguished articles about a company.

The largest number of articles on companies was found in English Wikipedia – 133,220, which is 2.03% of all articles in that language version. The second largest number of articles about companies has German Wikipedia - 51,700 (2.08% share). Japanese Wikipedia is third in terms of the number of articles (37,292), but it has the highest share of articles on companies among other Wikipedia languages - 2.76%.

Usually, the total number of edits correlates with the number of articles; therefore, we could expect that the largest number of edits will be in the English, German, and Japanese Wikipedia. However, if we analyze the number of unique authors who edited articles on companies, we can observe slightly different results. We considered only edits from registered authors (with an account

Table 1. Statistics on the identification of Wikipedia articles related to companies in different languages. Source: own calculations in November 2022.

Language	Articles number	share	Total Edits	Authors avg.	med.	Article Len. avg.	med.	Page Views avg.	med.
ar - Arabic	12,505	1.05%	1,371,350	8	4	9,882	4,704	5,188	577
arz - Egyptian Arabic	1,245	0.08%	50,018	3	3	2,123	1,406	318	41
az - Azerbaijani	1,357	0.72%	118,823	7	4	6,276	4,058	1,247	158
azb - South Azerbaijani	1,957	0.81%	101,985	4	4	3,047	2,812	38	20
be - Belarusian	1,216	0.54%	116,822	6	5	9,153	5,482	197	80
bg - Bulgarian	1,893	0.66%	263,727	11	8	9,680	5,855	3,033	546
bn - Bangla	2,391	1.85%	209,108	8	5	13,331	8,617	2,156	263
ca - Catalan	6,639	0.93%	778,498	8	5	7,128	4,004	410	84
cs - Czech	6,280	1.23%	826,522	13	9	8,385	4,980	2,689	596
da - Danish	4,183	1.46%	529,293	12	6	4,691	2,929	1,241	237
de - German	57,100	2.08%	11,280,527	32	20	8,597	5,313	5,951	1,011
el - Greek	2,200	1.03%	274,575	10	6	11,722	6,904	3,995	601
en - English	133,220	2.03%	38,459,600	46	24	10,636	6,540	21,652	2,890
eo - Esperanto	1,033	0.32%	105,768	6	5	4,934	2,832	92	34
es - Spanish	19,874	1.10%	3,876,285	19	8	10,393	6,286	12,410	1,363
et - Estonian	1,953	0.85%	225,326	8	6	4,686	2,383	599	143
fa - Persian	8,986	0.96%	847,192	9	3	5,945	3,514	4,485	288
fi - Finnish	9,567	1.77%	1,534,720	14	9	5,518	3,531	1,831	431
fr - French	36,652	1.49%	6,805,196	26	15	9,951	6,033	6,294	882
gl - Galician	1,607	0.84%	167,349	8	5	7,189	4,495	147	51
he - Hebrew	5,033	1.55%	776,861	23	13	10,064	6,692	3,420	702
hi - Hindi	1,266	0.82%	147,389	13	9	17,562	7,421	8,002	1,402
hr - Croatian	1,072	0.50%	136,106	10	6	6,771	4,045	3,093	590
hu - Hungarian	4,063	0.79%	607,256	16	8	10,034	6,090	3,139	479
hy - Armenian	2,078	0.71%	168,097	9	7	10,313	6,416	458	75
id - Indonesian	8,668	1.37%	1,017,284	8	4	8,086	4,424	4,344	412
it - Italian	17,486	0.98%	3,223,485	29	19	9,186	5,612	7,227	1,127
ja - Japanese	37,292	2.76%	7,862,134	26	13	13,342	6,931	12,526	2,659
ko - Korean	7,824	1.28%	1,357,212	14	7	7,458	4,410	5,225	637
lt - Lithuanian	1,461	0.71%	208,089	8	5	5,034	3,528	1,534	286
lv - Latvian	1,125	0.97%	132,502	8	5	6,938	5,053	979	207
ml - Malayalam	1,059	1.33%	107,189	7	5	10,722	6,898	589	126
ms - Malay	4,001	1.11%	308,476	5	3	7,293	4,268	801	120
nl - Dutch	9,939	0.47%	1,750,944	24	13	6,765	4,397	3,290	667
no - Norwegian	6,624	1.10%	1,021,525	18	12	4,383	2,619	1,029	220
pl - Polish	13,662	0.89%	2,181,898	16	9	7,211	4,213	5,063	769
pt - Portuguese	16,148	1.47%	2,591,292	14	7	7,470	4,406	6,260	687
ro - Romanian	5,017	1.15%	742,558	7	4	5,267	2,928	2,636	322
ru - Russian	22,012	1.18%	3,984,793	20	11	16,573	10,494	15,902	1,882
simple - Simple English	2,482	1.12%	271,982	13	7	4,118	2,712	757	139
sk - Slovak	1,251	0.52%	171,155	10	7	7,464	4,702	2,239	520
sr - Serbian	1,852	0.28%	233,473	10	7	12,641	7,582	2,432	508
sv - Swedish	10,597	0.41%	1,742,965	19	11	4,920	3,238	1,962	414
ta - Tamil	1,403	0.94%	146,982	6	4	12,879	6,964	1,297	236
th - Thai	2,114	1.40%	348,045	12	6	13,213	7,724	7,558	975
tr - Turkish	7,060	1.34%	783,320	13	6	6,338	3,692	6,723	648
uk - Ukrainian	9,928	0.83%	1,069,776	10	6	13,497	8,731	3,034	271
ur - Urdu	1,411	0.79%	113,174	3	3	3,869	2,096	168	32
uz - Uzbek	1,342	0.74%	44,999	5	4	13,978	7,579	646	34
vi - Vietnamese	4,061	0.32%	480,356	11	5	11,375	6,128	4,596	500
zh - Chinese	19,673	1.50%	3,329,049	18	9	9,222	5,067	8,289	1,409

on Wikipedia) and excluded bots (which also appear as separate accounts). It must be taken into account that one author may make many insignificant edits (e.g., adding a dot, removing spaces, etc.), while another author may include the entire section(s) in a single edit. In addition, the number of authors may also indicate the degree of objectivity of the content, because each of the authors may have their own opinion on the described organization and the way of presenting information about it. Taking into account the average number of unique authors per article, the top 5 Wikipedia languages include English (46 authors), German (32), Italian (29), French (26), and Japanese (25). This ranking looks similar in the case of median values. The lowest value of the average number of authors per article is in South Azerbaijani, Egyptian Arabic, and Urdu Wikipedia.

The length of the Wikipedia article can also be related to the quality of the content, e.g., completeness of the information about the described company. The length was measured as a volume in bytes of the wiki markup of the Wikipedia article. The largest average length values have the following Wikipedia languages: Hindi (17,562 bytes), Russian (16,573), Uzbek (13,978), Ukrainian (13,497), Japanese (13,342), Bangla (13,331), Thai (13,213), Tamil (12879), Serbian (12,641). When comparing median values, the longest articles belong to Russian (10,494 bytes), Ukrainian (8,730), and Bangla Wikipedia (8,617). Egyptian Arabic Wikipedia has the lowest average and median length of the articles: 2,123 bytes and 1,406 bytes per article, respectively.

The popularity of the articles can not only reflect the demand for information on Wikipedia in a specific language version but can also positively affect the quality of the content (especially on the timeliness of the information on current events). In this study, we considered only page views from real users (not automated or bots) from the last 12 months (November 2021 - October 2022). The largest number of page views per article (average and median) is available in English, Russian, Japanese, Spanish, Chinese, and Hindi Wikipedia.

4   Extraction of References

The following sections present results for the 51 language versions of Wikipedia with at least 1000 articles related to companies. To extract information on references, we prepared our own parser (implemented in Python) and applied it to Wikimedia dumps with articles in HTML format [38].

The presence of references in a Wikipedia article may indicate the degree of verifiability of information. More importantly, this information must come from reliable sources. External links (or URL addressees) in the references were used to indicate the main address of the source website. However, each web source can use a different structure of URL addresses. For example, some websites use subdomains for separate topics of information or news. Also, some organizational units (e.g., departments) of the same company may post their own information on separate subdomains of the main organization. To determine which level of domain indicates the source, we used the Public Suffix List, which is a cross-vendor initiative to provide an accurate list of domain name suffixes [31].

Some sources may have several different domains. For example, Google can be listed in sources as 'google.com', 'google.pl', 'google.de', etc. We, therefore, unified such sources to a single occurrence. Taking into account the fact that various useful services are placed under the 'google.com' (e.g., books) and separate blogs on 'wordpress.com' subdomains, we additionally provide subdomain distinction for these portals.

Table 2 presents the general extraction statistics. It has three groups of columns: 1) Total references – we count all references encountered in articles, without removing duplicates; 2) References tags share – share of references (in percent), described with respective tag; 3) Unique references – numbers after removing duplicated references, where duplicated were identified based on existing identifiers and similarity between references. The first and third groups comprise three columns: count, showing the absolute numbers; avg, the average number of references per article about a company; med, the median number of references per article about a company. The second group concerns the share of the following features of references: archived, books, and sci score (scientific references). 'Archived' means that the reference has a link to one of the archive services with the referenced web page. This often means that the original source may no longer be available or unavailable at the original URL address. In order to identify references related to 'books,' we analyzed if there is a link to the Google Books service. 'Sci' score counted based on references that contained the DOI identifier [20].

Taking into account the absolute numbers, the language with the highest number of references is English, both when unique and when all references are counted. The next with less than a quarter of references are German and Japanese, but German is using more unique references (second place). The number of references is a consequence of a large number of articles in these languages, therefore we also calculated the number of references per article. The highest number of average references per article, 21, is found in the Uzbek language, although it features only 27.8 thousand articles. The second place is taken by English with an average value of 18. The typical number is in the range of 5–7. However, the largest median is for English - 9. Taking into account the unique references, the situation is similar: English and Uzbek top the list. A "references tags share" promotes other languages. The highest share of archived references belongs to Polish (3.03%), Hindi (2.75%), and Malayalam (2.42%). The books are most often encountered in Indonesian (2.87%), Catalan (2.84%), and Serbian (2.70%). Scientific references are preferred in the following language versions: Arabic (1.75%), Serbian (1.38%), and Malayalam (1.37%).

5   The Information Sources in Wikipedia About Companies

This section presents the results of the evaluation of the most important sources of information about companies described in various Wikipedia languages and assessed using different models.

Table 2. Statistics on references extraction from Wikipedia articles related to companies in different languages. Source: own calculations in November 2022.

Language	Total references			References tags share			Unique references		
	count	avg	med	archived	books	sci	count	avg	med
ar - Arabic	123,743	10	4	1.28%	1.28%	1.75%	105,572	8	3
arz - Egyptian Arabic	5,732	5	3	1.31%	0.42%	0.85%	4,053	3	3
az - Azerbaijani	9,141	7	3	1.61%	1.43%	0.34%	7,542	6	3
azb - South Azerbaijani	7,665	4	3	0.51%	0.09%	0.04%	4,168	2	2
be - Belarusian	9,114	7	4	0.89%	0.21%	0.34%	7,513	6	3
bg - Bulgarian	13,523	7	3	0.92%	0.71%	0.30%	11,379	6	3
bn - Bangla	23,551	10	5	2.06%	1.30%	0.96%	19,750	8	5
ca - Catalan	61,134	9	5	0.56%	2.84%	0.80%	50,321	8	4
cs - Czech	67,032	11	5	0.57%	0.38%	0.42%	50,267	8	4
da - Danish	23,653	6	3	1.84%	0.63%	0.22%	20,386	5	3
de - German	602,498	11	6	0.52%	0.93%	0.25%	488,127	9	4
el - Greek	20,629	9	5	1.47%	1.62%	1.21%	18,184	8	4
en - English	2,344,978	18	9	1.62%	2.01%	0.82%	1,857,221	14	8
eo - Esperanto	4,954	5	2	1.11%	2.04%	0.52%	4,396	4	2
es - Spanish	242,210	12	6	1.34%	1.29%	0.46%	200,098	10	5
et - Estonian	12,994	7	3	0.74%	0.50%	0.06%	10,073	5	2
fa - Persian	46,403	5	2	1.15%	1.22%	0.56%	38,994	4	2
fi - Finnish	88,940	9	5	0.30%	0.23%	0.13%	60,889	6	4
fr - French	460,496	13	6	0.00%	1.41%	0.41%	366,338	10	5
gl - Galician	12,496	8	3	1.43%	1.26%	0.47%	9,989	6	3
he - Hebrew	48,761	10	5	0.51%	0.61%	0.23%	45,011	9	5
hi - Hindi	14,203	11	4	2.75%	0.78%	0.37%	12,044	10	4
hr - Croatian	7,183	7	3	0.72%	0.81%	0.35%	6,047	6	3
hu - Hungarian	41,389	10	5	0.73%	0.60%	0.33%	34,137	8	4
hy - Armenian	22,295	11	5	2.07%	1.43%	1.09%	18,759	9	5
id - Indonesian	102,297	12	5	1.49%	2.87%	0.51%	80,855	9	4
it - Italian	195,831	11	5	1.65%	1.19%	0.32%	155,619	9	4
ja - Japanese	620,815	17	6	0.37%	0.21%	0.27%	408,157	11	4
ko - Korean	54,797	7	3	0.83%	0.62%	0.62%	46,079	6	3
lt - Lithuanian	7,657	5	3	0.89%	0.57%	0.25%	6,935	5	3
lv - Latvian	7,579	7	4	0.75%	0.50%	0.21%	6,394	6	3
ml - Malayalam	9,683	9	5	2.42%	1.40%	1.37%	7,828	7	4
ms - Malay	41,866	10	5	0.90%	0.94%	0.22%	35,138	9	4
nl - Dutch	64,431	6	3	0.50%	0.48%	0.14%	52,548	5	3
no - Norwegian	37,836	6	3	0.65%	0.61%	0.23%	32,232	5	3
pl - Polish	131,539	10	4	3.03%	0.78%	0.17%	98,102	7	3
pt - Portuguese	169,459	10	5	0.80%	0.84%	0.45%	136,242	8	4
ro - Romanian	43,055	9	5	0.48%	0.64%	0.30%	29,221	6	3
ru - Russian	333,347	15	8	1.30%	0.80%	0.40%	259,880	12	6
simple - Simple English	14,560	6	3	1.74%	1.34%	0.89%	12,051	5	3
sk - Slovak	9,785	8	4	0.14%	0.72%	0.22%	7,725	6	3
sr - Serbian	20,129	11	5	1.84%	2.70%	1.38%	16,711	9	4
sv - Swedish	66,446	6	3	1.59%	0.39%	0.21%	55,124	5	3
ta - Tamil	10,742	8	4	1.70%	1.31%	0.66%	9,324	7	4
th - Thai	19,161	9	5	0.61%	1.27%	0.61%	15,940	8	4
tr - Turkish	47,141	7	3	1.24%	0.94%	0.41%	39,977	6	3
uk - Ukrainian	103,271	10	5	1.20%	0.62%	0.75%	85,099	9	4
ur - Urdu	4,769	3	1	0.67%	0.84%	0.27%	4,119	3	1
uz - Uzbek	27,828	21	8	1.43%	1.23%	0.49%	24,923	19	8
vi - Vietnamese	53,908	13	6	1.51%	1.29%	0.57%	44,584	11	5
zh - Chinese	220,141	11	5	1.43%	0.85%	0.18%	174,152	9	4

It is important to note that archive services (e.g., archive.org, archive.today) were excluded from the analysis, due to the frequent occurrence of such links alongside the original sources in the same reference. If the original source is no longer available, such archive services are very important because Wikipedia readers can verify information, but unavailable original web sources are not in the scope of this research. References to Wikipedia itself and Wikidata were also excluded. Many references contained links that are automatically inserted based on such identifiers as DOI (often links to doi.org) or ISBN (often links to books.google.com).

This work used the following modified and improved models from our previous articles on source assessment [22,23]:

1. **F-model** – how frequently (F) considered source appears in references.
2. **LRP-model** – how popular (P) Wikipedia articles are, in which the considered source appears.
3. **LRA-model** – how many authors (A) edited the articles, in which the considered source appears.

5.1   F-model

One of the most basic and commonly used approaches to assessing the importance of a web source is to count how frequently it was used in Wikipedia articles. This principle was used in relevant studies [16,21,28,32]. Therefore, the **F-model** assesses how many times a specific web domain occurred within the external links of the references. For example, if the same source is cited 50 times in 44 Wikipedia articles (each contains at least one reference with such web source), we count the (cumulative) frequency as 50. Equation 1 shows the calculation for the F-model.

$$F(s) = \sum_{i=1}^{n} X_s(i), \quad \text{where:}$$

s is the source (website or web domain),

n is the number of the considered Wikipedia articles,

$X_s(i)$ is the number of references that the source s uses

(e.g. domain in URL) in the article i.

$$(1)$$

The top web sources according to the F-model include websites such as nytimes.com (American daily newspaper: 76,072 references), worldcat.org (international union library catalog: 70,784), reuters.com (international news agency: 45,520), bloomberg.com (American multinational mass media corporation: 32,675), forbes.com (American business magazine: 29,552), bbc.co.uk (British public service broadcaster: 28,729), techcrunch.com (American technology news website: 25,962), wsj.com (American business-focused daily newspaper: 25,703).

Next, we created separate Web sources rankings for each language version. To provide cross-lingual analysis and due to the limited space in the next graph, we selected only websites that appeared at least seven times among the top 100 websites for each of the 51 selected language versions of Wikipedia (see Table 2). Websites that appear in the top 100 of each of the 51 languages are the following: nytimes.com, reuters.com, bloomberg.com, forbes.com. Figure 1 shows the positions in the ranking of the best web sources of information on companies in each of the 51 languages on Wikipedia according to the F-model.

5.2   LRP-Model

LRP-model uses page views (or visits) of Wikipedia articles within a certain period divided by the total number of references in each Wikipedia article considered. Some studies found a correlation between information quality and page views in Wikipedia articles [1,18]. Such a measure as page views can be considered a public interest in a specific topic [37,41]. The more people read a specific Wikipedia article, the more likely its content was checked by part of them (including the presence of reliable sources in references). So, the more readers see particular facts in Wikipedia, the bigger the probability that one of such readers will make an appropriate edit if such facts are incorrect (or if the source of information is inappropriate).

The visibility of a single reference is also important. If more references are present in the article, then a specific source for the particular reader (visitor) is less visible. At the same time, the more references Wikipedia articles have, the more visible a particular source is. Equation 2 shows the calculation using the *RLA*-model.

$$LRP(s) = \sum_{i=1}^{n} \frac{L(i)}{X(i)} \cdot X_s(i) \cdot P(i), \quad \text{where:}$$

s is the source (website or web domain),

n is the number of considered articles,

$X_s(i)$ is the number of references using the source s in the Wikipedia article i,

$X(i)$ is the total number of references in i,

$L(i)$ length of the Wikipedia article i,

$P(i)$ number of page views of the article i.

(2)

This model uses cumulative page views P from human users (excluding bots) in November 2021 - October 2022. Figure 2 shows the positions in the ranking of the best Web sources of information about companies in each of 51 language versions according to the LRP-model.

Comparing the results between LRP-model and F-model, we can find some important changes in the web sources rankings. These are some examples of such changes in the multilingual ranking (in all Wikipedia languages):

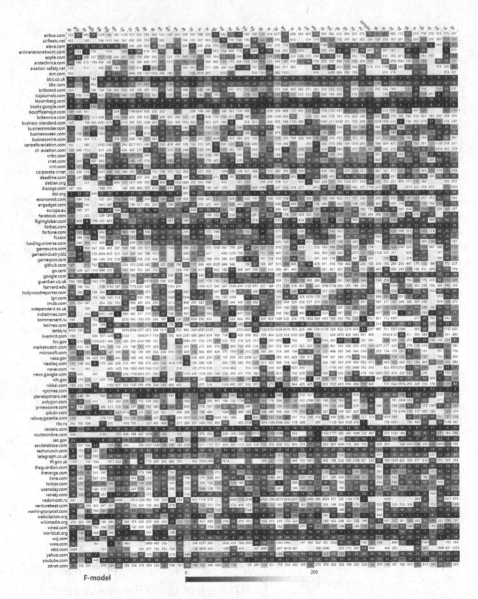

58   W. Lewoniewski et al.

Fig. 1. Positions in rankings of the best web sources of information about companies in each of 51 languages on Wikipedia according to F-model. Interactive and extended versions of this chart can be found on [8]

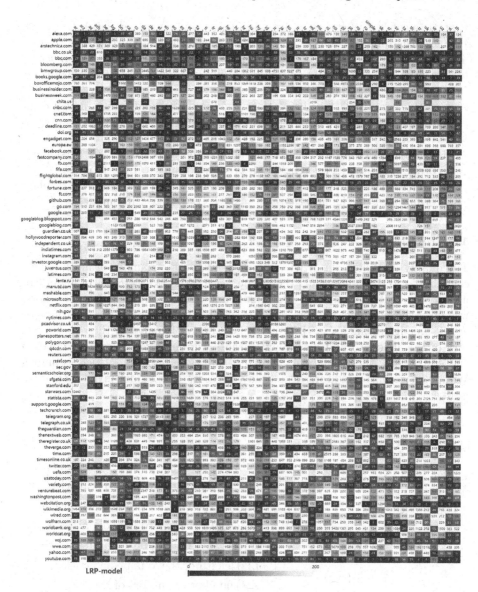

Fig. 2. Positions in rankings of the best web sources of information about companies in each of 51 language versions according to the LRP-model. Interactive and extended versions of this chart can be found on [8]

– statista.com (platform specialized in market and consumer data): the 287th place according to F-model and the 127th place according to LRP-model
– imdb.com (online database of information related to films, television series, and video games): the 86th place according to F-model and the 233rd place according to LRP-model
– mashable.com (digital media platform, news website, and entertainment company): the 155th place according to F-model and the 31st place according to LRP-model.
– discogs.com (website and database about audio recordings): the 101st place according to F-model and the 968th place according to LRP-model.
– fb.com (online social media and social networking service): the 1126th place according to F-model and the 76th place according to LRP-model.

5.3   LRA-Model

The quality of Wikipedia articles also depends on the number of authors who contributed to the content and their experience. Wikipedia articles of high quality are often edited jointly by a large number of different authors. This correlation was observed by many authors [4,17,24,25,40]. To assess the popularity of an article among editing users, there is the possibility of analyzing the revision history of the article to find how many authors were involved in content creation and editing. So, the AR-model characterizes how popular the article is among Wikipedia volunteer editors. Equation 3 presents this model in mathematical form.

$$LRA(s) = \sum_{i=1}^{n} \frac{L(i)}{X(i)} \cdot X_s(i) \cdot A(i), \quad \text{where:}$$

s is the source (website or web domain),
n is the number of considered articles,
$X_s(i)$ is the number of references using the source s in the Wikipedia article i,
$X(i)$ is the total number of references in i,
$L(i)$ length of the Wikipedia article i,
$A(i)$ number of authors of the article i.

(3)

Unlike our previous work, the LRA-model in this study uses the number of authors A who are registered on Wikipedia as users, excluding bots.

Figure 3 shows the positions in the ranking of the best Web sources of information about companies in each of the 51 language versions of Wikipedia according to the LRA-model.

Comparing results between LRA-model and F-model, we can also find some important changes in the web sources rankings. Below is a summary of the differences:

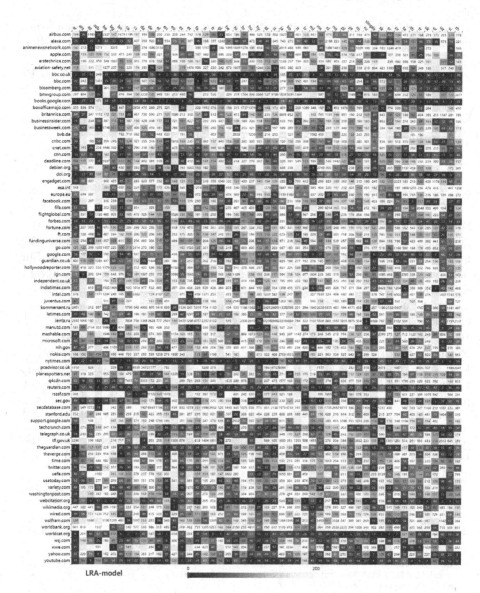

Fig. 3. Positions in rankings of the best web sources of information about companies in each of 51 Wikipedia language versions according to LRA-model. Interactive and extended versions of this chart can be found on [8]

- uefa.com (website of one of six continental bodies of governance in association football): the 736th place according to F-model and the 162nd place according to LRA-model
- nasdaq.com (American stock exchange): the 162nd place according to F-model and the 270th place according to LRA-model.
- loc.gov (research library of the United States Congress): the 52nd place according to F-model and the 105th place according to LRA-model.
- harvard.edu (research university in Cambridge, Massachusetts): the 103rd place according to F-model and the 70th place according to LRA-model.

6   Discussion of the Results

Some important websites for separate language versions are not presented in the heat maps Figs. 1, 2, and 2, due to poor support among at least six additional language versions. It means that some of the Web sources can be widely used in only one or two language versions of Wikipedia. For example, newspapers.com is the fourth most important source of information on companies in the English Wikipedia according to the F-model, but only one additional language version of Wikipedia (among the 51 languages considered) has this source in the top 100. Depending on the model, we can observe some differences between lists of sources that were selected for the heat maps (only websites that appeared at least seven times among the top 100 websites for each of 51 languages). However, there are many important sources for separate Wikipedia languages that are not presented in such heat maps.

The following is the list of sources that did not meet the threshold required to be placed in presented heat maps but are placed in the top 10 important sources according to one of the three models in some Wikipedia languages (the highest position among models in the local ranking is given in brackets):

- **ar (Arabic)**: grid.ac (7)
- **arz (Egyptian Arabic)**: grid.ac (2), charitynavigator.org (3), csfd.cz (3), wikisource.org (3), justice.cz (4), purl.org (4), youm7.com (4), staralliance.com (5), miningreece.com (6), ralphlauren.com (7), creativecommons.org (7), nashvillezoo.org (8), cbc.ca (8)
- **az (Azerbaijani)**: e-qanun.az (1), lent.az (2), president.az (3), deyerler.org (5), virtualaz.org (6), apa.az (6), shanghairanking.com (7), azertag.az (7), mediaforum.az (8), mta.info (10), qafqaz-info.az (10)
- **azb (South Azerbaijani)**: domaintools.com (8), the-afc.com (10)
- **be (Belarusian)**: zviazda.by (1), marketing.by (1), svaboda.org (2), tut.by (3), belta.by (3), minsk.by (4), gortransport.kharkov.ua (5), sigla.ru (6), nbrb.by (7), yandex.ru (7), rt.com (9), nn.by (9), metropoliten.by (10)
- **bg (Bulgarian)**: dnevnik.bg (1), mersenne.org (1), capital.bg (4), technologyreview.com (6), brra.bg (7), btv.bg (8), bas.bg (10)
- **bn (Bangla)**: thedailystar.net (1), bdnews24.com (4), indianrailways.gov.in (7), prothomalo.com (8), irfca.org (10)
- **ca (Catalan)**: elpais.com (3), gencat.cat (4), lavanguardia.com (5), enciclopedia.cat (6), ara.cat (7), vilaweb.cat (8), bcn.cat (10)
- **cs (Czech)**: justice.cz (1), idnes.cz (1), lupa.cz (3), denik.cz (4), ihned.cz (5), zdopravy.cz (6), ceskatelevize.cz (6), lidovky.cz (7), e15.cz (8), aktualne.cz (9), novinky.cz (10)
- **da (Danish)**: dr.dk (1), business.dk (2), dsb.dk (2), brondby.com (2), politiken.dk (3), finans.dk (4), starwarsplaces.com (5), berlingske.dk (6), borsen.dk (7), tv2.dk (8), computerworld.dk (9)
- **de (German)**: spiegel.de (1), zdb-katalog.de (1), mementoweb.org (2), heise.de (3), handelsblatt.com (4), tagesspiegel.de (4), faz.net (6), welt.de (7), sueddeutsche.de (7), bundesbank.de (10), zeit.de (10)
- **el (Greek)**: et.gr (1), similarweb.com (1), kathimerini.gr (2), utm.edu (6), e-tetradio.gr (6), typologies.gr (7)

- **en (English)**: newspapers.com (4)
- **eo (Esperanto)**: yandex.ru (1), wikiwix.com (2), liberafolio.org (3), vc.ru (4), staralliance.com (5), creativecommons.org (5), aidh.org (6), rezo.net (7), metromadrid.es (8), zelpage.cz (10)
- **es (Spanish)**: elpais.com (1), issn.org (2), elmundo.es (6), lanacion.com.ar (8)
- **et (Estonian)**: postimees.ee (1), delfi.ee (2), err.ee (3), aripaev.ee (4), muinas.ee (4), riigiteataja.ee (4), nasdaqbaltic.com (5), digar.ee (5), efis.ee (8), swedbank.ee (8), staralliance.com (10)
- **fa (Persian)**: tehran.ir (4), radiofarda.com (5), hamshahrionline.ir (6), isna.ir (7), mehrnews.com (9)
- **fi (Finnish)**: yle.fi (1), hs.fi (1), kauppalehti.fi (3), hel.fi (3), is.fi (4), talouselama.fi (6), iltalehti.fi (7), stat.fi (8), habbo.fi (8), finder.fi (9), espoo.fi (9), tekniikkatalous.fi (10), taloussanomat.fi (10)
- **fr (French)**: lesechos.fr (1), lemonde.fr (1), lefigaro.fr (2), wikiwix.com (5), bnf.fr (7), googleusercontent.com (7), ozap.com (7), societe.com (8), liberation.fr (8)
- **gl (Galician)**: elpais.com (1), lavozdegalicia.es (1), skyrocket.de (1), jstor.org (4), rinoceronte.gal (9), formulatv.com (9), numista.com (10), laopinioncoruna.es (10)
- **he (Hebrew)**: globes.co.il (1), nli.org.il (2), themarker.com (2), haaretz.co.il (4), ynet.co.il (4), calcalist.co.il (5), tase.co.il (7), walla.co.il (7), mako.co.il (8), makorrishon.co.il (10)
- **hi (Hindi)**: pib.nic.in (3), rbi.org.in (5), annualreports.com (6), ndtv.com (9)
- **hr (Croatian)**: hrt.hr (1), mojarijeka.hr (2), vecernji.hr (3), dnevnik.hr (3), jutarnji.hr (6), casopis-gradjevinar.hr (6), enciklopedija.hr (7), htmlgoodies.com (9), rtl.hr (9), poslovni.hr (10), tportal.hr (10)
- **hu (Hungarian)**: index.hu (1), origo.hu (2), hvg.hu (2), iho.hu (3), kaze.fr (4), telex.hu (4), villamosok.hu (6), 24.hu (6), sg.hu (7), mavcsoport.hu (7), crt-tv.com (8), blog.hu (9), media1.hu (10)
- **hy (Armenian)**: matenadaran.am (1), 1tv.am (3), cba.am (4), amazon.fr (5), asj-oa.am (6), csufresno.edu (7), unesco.org (9), stretfordend.co.uk (10)
- **id (Indonesian)**: detik.com (2), kompas.com (3), tempo.co (4), liputan6.com (7), tribunnews.com (8), thejakartapost.com (8), transjakarta.co.id (10)
- **it (Italian)**: repubblica.it (1), corriere.it (2), ilsole24ore.com (2), rai.it (4), ansa.it (6), lastampa.it (7), beniculturali.it (7), cm-lisboa.pt (8), primaonline.it (10)
- **ja (Japanese)**: catr.jp (1), ndl.go.jp (2), sponichi.co.jp (3), edinet-fsa.go.jp (4), impress.co.jp (4), asahi.com (5), itmedia.co.jp (5), nikkansports.com (7), jreast.co.jp (8), prtimes.jp (9), eirparts.net (10)
- **ko (Korean)**: kbs.co.kr (2), gg.go.kr (2), chosun.com (3), donga.com (4), yonhapnews.co.kr (5), ytn.co.kr (6), mt.co.kr (6), joins.com (7), hani.co.kr (8), hankyung.com (9), mois.go.kr (9), mk.co.kr (10)
- **lt (Lithuanian)**: vz.lt (1), delfi.lt (2), 15min.lt (3), vle.lt (4), litrail.lt (4), lrt.lt (5), lrytas.lt (6), lrs.lt (9)
- **lv (Latvian)**: db.lv (1), delfi.lv (2), tvnet.lv (3), lursoft.lv (4), lsm.lv (4), diena.lv (6), airbaltic.com (6), lattelecom.lv (8), inbox.lv (9), ldz.lv (9), ltv.lv (10), porsche.com (10)
- **ml (Malayalam)**: mathrubhumi.com (1), manoramaonline.com (2), madhyamam.com (4), thehindu.com (5), kerala.gov.in (5), nhrc.nic.in (7), jal.co.jp (8), eci.nic.in (8), ncert.nic.in (9), kseb.in (10)
- **ms (Malay)**: thestar.com.my (1), utusan.com.my (2), malaysiaairlines.com (2), mstar.com.my (4), airasia.com (5), bernama.com (6), rtm.gov.my (6), themalaysianinsider.com (7), astroawani.com (8), bharian.com.my (9)
- **nl (Dutch)**: nrc.nl (1), volkskrant.nl (1), nos.nl (2), nu.nl (2), fd.nl (3), kb.nl (5), ad.nl (5), telegraaf.nl (6), standaard.be (8), trouw.nl (8), tijd.be (10)
- **no (Norwegian)**: nb.no (1), nrk.no (2), brreg.no (3), regjeringen.no (3), aftenposten.no (4), e24.no (5), dn.no (6), stretfordend.co.uk (6), snl.no (8), proff.no (9), dagbladet.no (9), hafen-hamburg.de (10)
- **pl (Polish)**: wirtualnemedia.pl (1), wyborcza.pl (2), plk-sa.pl (3), rynek-kolejowy.pl (4), wp.pl (4), sejm.gov.pl (6), satkurier.pl (7), mma.pl (7), transinfo.pl (8), transport-publiczny.pl (8), onet.pl (9), pwn.pl (10), tvp.pl (10)
- **pt (Portuguese)**: uol.com.br (1), globo.com (2), cm-lisboa.pt (3), abril.com.br (3), estadao.com.br (4), mziq.com (5), terra.com.br (5), sapo.pt (8), tecmundo.com.br (9)
- **ro (Romanian)**: wall-street.ro (1), zf.ro (1), money.ro (3), adevarul.ro (4), arma.org.ro (4), afi.com (5), arabcrunch.com (5), capital.ro (6), mediafax.ro (6), evz.ro (7), paginademedia.ro (7), hotnews.ro (8), acasatv.ro (9), metrorex.ro (10)
- **ru (Russian)**: ria.ru (6), vk.com (6), tass.ru (7), forbes.ru (9), vkontakte.ru (10), gazeta.ru (10)
- **simple (Simple English)**: mathvault.ca (6), baskinrobbins.com (7)
- **sk (Slovak)**: sme.sk (2), socialblade.com (2), dennikn.sk (3), finstat.sk (4), imhd.sk (4), orsr.sk (5), pravda.sk (6), aktuality.sk (6), etrend.sk (7), hnonline.sk (8), techbyte.sk (8), zoznam.sk (9), visibility.sk (10)
- **sr (Serbian)**: b92.net (2), rts.rs (3), novosti.rs (5), exyuaviation.com (7), nb.rs (8), nbs.rs (9), blic.rs (9)

- **sv (Swedish)**: allabolag.se (1), svt.se (1), kb.se (2), dn.se (2), svd.se (3), sverigesradio.se (4), resume.se (6), historiskt.nu (8), expressen.se (8), trafikverket.se (8), di.se (9), aftonbladet.se (9), runeberg.org (10)
- **ta (Tamil)**: indianrailways.gov.in (1), tn.gov.in (1), thehindu.com (2), rbi.org.in (5), theekkathir.org (7), thehindubusinessline.com (8), dinamani.com (9)
- **th (Thai)**: soc.go.th (1), mcot.net (1), listedcompany.com (2), gotomanager.com (2), set.or.th (3), mgronline.com (4), thairath.co.th (6), prachachat.net (7), settrade.com (8), dbd.go.th (10), positioningmag.com (10)
- **tr (Turkish)**: hurriyet.com.tr (1), milliyet.com.tr (2), haberturk.com (3), ntv.com.tr (6)
- **uk (Ukrainian)**: rada.gov.ua (2), rbc.ua (3), uprom.info (3), epravda.com.ua (4), pravda.com.ua (5), detector.media (7), ukrinform.ua (8), anisearch.de (9), president.gov.ua (10)
- **ur (Urdu)**: ourairports.com (1), booleanstrings.com (2), zerohedge.com (3), dawn.com (4), nlpd.gov.pk (4), tribune.com.pk (7), radio.gov.pk (7), pakrail.com (8), piac.com.pk (10)
- **uz (Uzbek)**: kun.uz (2), ziyouz.com (3), uztelecom.uz (7)
- **vi (Vietnamese)**: vtv.vn (1), tuoitre.vn (2), vnexpress.net (4), hoinhabaovietnam.vn (8)
- **zh (Chinese)**: nii.ac.jp (1), sina.com.cn (1), qq.com (3), udn.com (4), ltn.com.tw (4), on.cc (5), xinhuanet.com (6), hk01.com (7), hkexnews.hk (8), sohu.com (9), people.com.cn (10), appledaily.com (10)

The results also showed that many references contained links that are automatically inserted based on such identifiers as DOI and ISBN numbers, which often link to doi.org and books.google.com, respectively. Such web services provide works written by different authors and shared by various organizations (including publishing houses). In that case, a more detailed analysis can be performed in future work.

In this paper, we present a cross-lingual comparison only for 51 selected language versions of Wikipedia. Extended and interactive results for all 310 language versions of Wikipedia can be found in the supplementary material [8].

7 Conclusion and Future Work

This study focused on the analysis of the quality of Wikipedia articles on companies and their sources of information in different languages. Using the semantic representation of information in DBpedia and user-generated knowledge in Wikidata, this study provides the method for identifying Wikipedia articles that describe separate companies. After determining the titles of Wikipedia articles and extracting references from their content, we traced the URLs of these references and determined the main site addresses. As a result, we identified the websites of the sources considered. Each identified web source of information was assessed using an improved version of the three models from our previous research.

The approach presented in this work can help not only Wikipedia volunteer editors in selecting websites that can provide valuable information on companies, but also help other Internet users better understand how to find valuable sources of information for a specific topic on the Web using open data from Wikipedia.

The models we used in the research have some limitations. Some of them use page views and the number of authors of Wikipedia articles. These measures can be imprecise or not always available. For example, some of the page views can be accidental: the Internet user, shortly after visiting the Wikipedia article, can realize that information is not relevant and search for another page in the encyclopedia or move on to another website. Another example is "short page views", where the reader spends a relatively short time studying only a few sentences and their sources from the beginning of the article. In this case, the reader will not see all the content and references to sources in the Wikipedia article. Unfortunately, Wikipedia does not provide data on the duration of each user's visit to the website. Regarding data on Wikipedia authors, it allows for analysis of the reputation of the particular user, who provides some changes to the Wikipedia article. It is even possible to analyze each contribution of any author. Therefore, some of the models presented can be improved in future work by providing more complex measurements of some features.

We plan to extend this research in the future by providing additional features on the identification of companies on Wikipedia. So far, we have been concerned with various aspects of the quality of Wikipedia articles on companies, including objectiveness, completeness, timeliness, and verifiability. In addition, we will group organizations by sectors (industries) to find the differences in the reliability of information sources. Future work will also focus on the extension of reliability models and the use of different methods in topic classification. One of the directions is to develop ways of weighing the importance of a reference based on its position within a Wikipedia article.

Acknowledgement. This research is supported by the project "OpenFact – artificial intelligence tools for verification of the veracity of information sources and fake news detection" (INFOSTRATEG-I/0035/2021-00), granted within the INFOSTRATEG I program of the National Center for Research and Development, under the topic: Verifying information sources and detecting fake news.

References

1. Apollonio, D.E., Broyde, K., Azzam, A., De Guia, M., Heilman, J., Brock, T.: Pharmacy students can improve access to quality medicines information by editing Wikipedia articles. BMC Med. Educ. **18**(1), 1–8 (2018). https://doi.org/10.1186/s12909-018-1375-z

2. BestRef: Popularity and Reliability Assessment of Wikipedia Sources. https://bestref.net (2022)

3. Blumenstock, J.E.: Size matters: word count as a measure of quality on Wikipedia. In: Proceedings of the 17th International Conference on World Wide Web, pp. 1095–1096. ACM (2008). https://doi.org/10.1145/1367497.1367673

4. Callahan, E.S., Herring, S.C.: Cultural bias in Wikipedia content on famous persons. J. Am. Soc. Inform. Sci. Technol. **62**(10), 1899–1915 (2011). https://doi.org/10.1002/asi.21577

5. Colavizza, G.: COVID-19 research in Wikipedia. Quant. Sci. Stud. **1**(4), 1349–1380 (2020). https://doi.org/10.1162/qss_a_00080

6. Conti, R., Marzini, E., Spognardi, A., Matteucci, I., Mori, P., Petrocchi, M.: Maturity assessment of Wikipedia medical articles. In: 2014 IEEE 27th International Symposium on Computer-Based Medical Systems (CBMS), pp. 281–286. IEEE (2014). https://doi.org/10.1109/CBMS.2014.69

7. Databus: DBpedia Ontology instance types. https://databus.dbpedia.org/dbpedia/mappings/instance-types/ (2022)

8. data.lewoniewski.info: Supplementary materials for this research (2022). https://data.lewoniewski.info/company/
9. English Wikipedia: Wikipedia: Reliable sources (2022). https://en.wikipedia.org/wiki/Wikipedia:Reliable_sources
10. English Wikipedia: Wikipedia: Reliable sources/Perennial sources (2022). https://en.wikipedia.org/wiki/Wikipedia:Reliable_sources/Perennial_sources
11. English Wikipedia: Wikipedia:Verifiability (2022). https://en.wikipedia.org/wiki/Wikipedia:Verifiability
12. Färber, M., Ell, B., Menne, C., Rettinger, A.: A comparative survey of dbpedia, freebase, opencyc, wikidata, and yago. Semantic Web J. **1**(1), 1–5 (2015)
13. Fetahu, B., Markert, K., Nejdl, W., Anand, A.: Finding news citations for Wikipedia. In: Proceedings of the 25th ACM International on Conference on Information and Knowledge Management, pp. 337–346 (2016)
14. Filipiak, D., Filipowska, A.: Improving the quality of art market data using linked open data and machine learning. In: Abramowicz, W., Alt, R., Franczyk, B. (eds.) BIS 2016. LNBIP, vol. 263, pp. 418–428. Springer, Cham (2017). https://doi.org/10.1007/978-3-319-52464-1_39
15. Internet Live Stats: Total number of Websites (2022). https://www.internetlivestats.com/total-number-of-websites/
16. Jemielniak, D., Masukume, G., Wilamowski, M.: The most influential medical journals according to Wikipedia: quantitative analysis. J. Med. Internet Res. **21**(1), e11429 (2019). https://doi.org/10.2196/11429
17. Kane, G.C.: A multimethod study of information quality in wiki collaboration. ACM Trans. Manage. Inf. Syst. (TMIS) **2**(1), 4 (2011). https://doi.org/10.1145/1929916.1929920
18. Lerner, J., Lomi, A.: Knowledge categorization affects popularity and quality of Wikipedia articles. PLoS ONE **13**(1), e0190674 (2018). https://doi.org/10.1371/journal.pone.0190674
19. Lewańska, E.: Towards automatic business networks identification. In: Abramowicz, W., Alt, R., Franczyk, B. (eds.) BIS 2016. LNBIP, vol. 263, pp. 389–398. Springer, Cham (2017). https://doi.org/10.1007/978-3-319-52464-1_36
20. Lewoniewski, W.: Identification of important web sources of information on Wikipedia across various topics and languages. Procedia Comput. Sci. **207**, 3290–3299 (2022)
21. Lewoniewski, W., Węcel, K., Abramowicz, W.: Analysis of references across Wikipedia languages. In: Damaševičius, R., Mikašytė, V. (eds.) ICIST 2017. CCIS, vol. 756, pp. 561–573. Springer, Cham (2017). https://doi.org/10.1007/978-3-319-67642-5_47
22. Lewoniewski, W., Węcel, K., Abramowicz, W.: Modeling Popularity and Reliability of Sources in Multilingual Wikipedia. Information **11**(5), 263 (2020). https://doi.org/10.3390/info11050263
23. Lewoniewski, W., Węcel, K., Abramowicz, W.: Identifying reliable sources of information about companies in multilingual Wikipedia. In: 2022 17th Conference on Computer Science and Intelligence Systems (FedCSIS), pp. 705–714. IEEE (2022). https://doi.org/10.15439/2022F259
24. Lih, A.: Wikipedia as Participatory Journalism: Reliable Sources? Metrics for evaluating collaborative media as a news resource. In: 5th International Symposium on Online Journalism, p. 31 (2004)
25. Liu, J., Ram, S.: Using big data and network analysis to understand Wikipedia article quality. Data Knowl. Eng. (2018). https://doi.org/10.1016/j.datak.2018.02.004

26. Metilli, D., Bartalesi, V., Meghini, C.: A Wikidata-based tool for building and visualising narratives. Int. J. Digit. Libr. **20**(4), 417–432 (2019). https://doi.org/10.1007/s00799-019-00266-3

27. Netcraft: August 2021 Web Server Survey (2021). https://news.netcraft.com/archives/2021/08/25/august-2021-web-server-survey.html

28. Nielsen, F.Å.: Scientific citations in Wikipedia. arXiv preprint arXiv:0705.2106 (2007). https://doi.org/10.48550/arXiv.0705.2106

29. Nielsen, F.Å., Mietchen, D., Willighagen, E.: Scholia, scientometrics and wikidata. In: Blomqvist, E., Hose, K., Paulheim, H., Ławrynowicz, A., Ciravegna, F., Hartig, O. (eds.) ESWC 2017. LNCS, vol. 10577, pp. 237–259. Springer, Cham (2017). https://doi.org/10.1007/978-3-319-70407-4_36

30. Piccardi, T., Redi, M., Colavizza, G., West, R.: Quantifying engagement with citations on Wikipedia. In: Proceedings of The Web Conference 2020, pp. 2365–2376 (2020). https://doi.org/10.1145/3366423.3380300

31. Public Suffix List: List (2022). https://publicsuffix.org/learn/

32. Redi, M.: Characterizing Wikipedia Citation Usage. Analyzing Reading Sessions (2019). https://meta.wikimedia.org/wiki/Research:Characterizing_Wikipedia_Citation_Usage/Analyzing_Reading_Sessions. Accessed 01 Sept 2021

33. Singh, H., West, R., Colavizza, G.: Wikipedia citations: a comprehensive data set of citations with identifiers extracted from English Wikipedia. Quant. Sci. Stud. **2**(1), 1–19 (2021). https://doi.org/10.1162/qss_a_00105

34. Stvilia, B., Twidale, M.B., Smith, L.C., Gasser, L.: Assessing information quality of a community-based encyclopedia. In: Proceedings of the ICIQ, pp. 442–454 (2005)

35. Teplitskiy, M., Lu, G., Duede, E.: Amplifying the impact of open access: Wikipedia and the diffusion of science. J. Am. Soc. Inf. Sci. **68**(9), 2116–2127 (2017). https://doi.org/10.1002/asi.23687

36. Tzekou, P., Stamou, S., Kirtsis, N., Zotos, N.: Quality assessment of Wikipedia external links. In: WEBIST, pp. 248–254 (2011)

37. Weiner, S.S., Horbacewicz, J., Rasberry, L., Bensinger-Brody, Y.: Improving the quality of consumer health information on Wikipedia: case series. J. Med. Internet Res. **21**(3), e12450 (2019). https://doi.org/10.2196/12450

38. Wikimedia Downloads: Main page (2021). https://dumps.wikimedia.org

39. WikiRank: Quality and Popularity Assessment of Wikipedia Articles (2022). https://wikirank.net/

40. Wilkinson, D.M., Huberman, B.a.: Cooperation and quality in wikipedia. Proceedings of the 2007 international symposium on Wikis WikiSym 2007, pp. 157–164 (2007). https://doi.org/10.1145/1296951.1296968

41. Wulczyn, E., West, R., Zia, L., Leskovec, J.: Growing Wikipedia across languages via recommendation. In: Proceedings of the 25th International Conference on World Wide Web, pp. 975–985 (2016). https://doi.org/10.1145/2872427.2883077

42. Yaari, E., Baruchson-Arbib, S., Bar-Ilan, J.: Information quality assessment of community generated content: a user study of Wikipedia. J. Inf. Sci. **37**(5), 487–498 (2011). https://doi.org/10.1177/0165551511416065

Approaches to Improving Society

Analysis for Women's' Menstrual Health Disorders Using Artificial Intelligence

Łukasz Sosnowski[1]([✉]) [iD], Soma Dutta[2] [iD], and Iwona Szymusik[3] [iD]

[1] Systems Research Institute, Polish Academy of Sciences, Newelska 6, 01-447 Warsaw, Poland
sosnowsl@ibspan.waw.pl

[2] University of Warmia and Mazury in Olsztyn, Słoneczna 54, 10-710 Olsztyn, Poland
soma.dutta@matman.uwm.edu.pl

[3] Department of Obstetrics and Gynecology, Medical University of Warsaw, Żwirki i Wigury 61, 02-091 Warsaw, Poland

Abstract. This paper presents some developments related to a project aiming to develop an AI-based model which can determine the possible ovulation dates as well as possibility of some health risks based on the input of a woman for a finite number of menstrual cycles. In some earlier papers, the AI schemes for some health risks, such as PMS, LPD, are already discussed. In this paper, additionally the schemes for hypothyroidism and polycystic ovary syndrome (PCOS) are presented. The model is based on a ontology of medical concepts, mathematical formulations of which are designed based on the data obtained from different users over a finite number of menstrual cycles and usual relationships among different parameters determining such concepts. The mathematical formulations of the concerned medical concepts are developed by using some notions of fuzzy linguistic labels and comparators.

Keywords: Menstrual disorders · Menstrual cycles anomaly recognition AI algorithms · Fuzzy linguistic summaries · Fuzzy comparators

1 Introduction

1.1 Research Problem

According to the statistics every fifth couple, trying to conceive (TTC), has a problem to achieve pregnancy in the first 12 months of efforts, and this tendency is increasing [1]. Gradually the age at which women, nowadays, are trying for the first child, is shifting towards 35. This consequently increases a risk in pregnancy, including the birth of a child with defects. So, an AI based drive has become significant for the natural endeavour of family planning [17].

Under the project OvuFriend 1.0[1] [5, 18–20], the attempt has been to establish a platform for helping women in determining the possibility of conceiving as

---

[1] www.ovufriend.pl.

E. Ziemba et al. (Eds.): FedCSIS-AIST 2022/ISM 2022, LNBIP 471, pp. 71–90, 2023.
https://doi.org/10.1007/978-3-031-29570-6_4

well as in understanding the hidden health risks based on their data input. The platform is developed as a mobile app where an user can put the data related to her physical and mental states during a number of specific menstrual cycles, and get an analysis of the possibility of conceiving or not conceiving. The project OvuFriend 1.0 [19] brought the company a big commercial success [20].

The R&D project OvuFriend 2.0 is aimed at extending the previous platform by adding the ability of assessing the risk of certain health disorders of a woman. In particular, the project focuses on the analysis of whether a particular user has the possibility of Premenstrual Syndrome (PMS[2]), Luteal Phase Defect (LPD[3]), benign growths like polyps, fibroids[4] in the uterus, Polycystic Ovary Syndrome (PCOS[5]) or hypothyroidism[6]. In [21], the specific algorithms for determining the risks of PMS, LPD, polyps and fibroids are discussed. In addition to that, in this paper we extend the study for PCOS and hypothyroidism.

Application of AI on healthcare industry is not now new. However, the way of developing AI does not have change much from the time of its initiation. IBM's dream project Watson was supposed to revolutionize everything from diagnosing patients and recommending treatment options to finding candidates for clinical trials. However, it failed as it was not trained with real patient data, but instead with hypothetical cases provided by a small group of doctors. The model's success with test data cannot directly reflect the scenario in reality. This clarify, that one way to improve the performance of an AI system[7] is to incorporate ways to engage users and improve the performance based on their continuous feedback. The proposed schemes for determining different health risks of women, expecting for conceiving child, are designed in a way that the above mentioned loopholes of AI based technologies are addressed to some extent.

1.2 Related Works

After the years of developments made in AI, from different aspects of human needs, the scientific community and the researchers are slowly getting convinced to the necessity of building AI systems which respect the perception and inter-action process of the system with the users and/or the physical reality for whose support the system is supposed to be designed. As a result, the terms like 'human-centered AI', 'human-in-the-loop of machine learning' [22] are often popping up in the literature of AI. AI in the medical industry is not different in this context.

---

[2] https://www.womenshealth.gov/menstrual-cycle/premenstrual-syndrome.

[3] https://www.webmd.com/infertility-and-reproduction/guide/luteal-phase-defect.

[4] https://progyny.com/education/female-infertility/understanding-uterine-fibroids-polyps/.

[5] In this condition the ovaries produce an abnormal amount of androgens, that are usually present in women in small amounts [9].

[6] Hypothyroidism means the thyroid gland does not produce enough thyroid hormones, which can lead to changes in the menstrual cycle. (https://helloclue.com/articles/cycle-a-z/hypothyroidism-and-the-menstrual-cycle).

[7] https://qz.com/2129025/where-did-ibm-go-wrong-with-watson-health.

In [6], different arguments are placed in favour of a paradigmatic changes in the healthcare industry where in contrary to the traditional way of medical support an evidence based, personalized medical support [10,11] is deemed of. The key issue is to create the protocols for medical care by combining the knowledge from the medical literature, experience of the professionals, and input parameters, e.g., habits, life style, preferences of the individual patients. That is, such an endeavour needs to standardize protocols with respect to the consensus of a group, and be sensitive by considering treatments out of the guidelines in the context of the patients who have different responses to that standard.

The content of the chapter is organized as follows. Section 2 presents the general research methodology that is followed in OvuFriend 2.0. Section 3 is divided into several subsections presenting the particular research findings related to the proposed schemes for determining risks for PMS, LPD, indicating anatomical changes related to polyp, fibroids, and risks related to PCOS and hypothyroidism. Section 4 presents the reference sets for conducting experiments and the results obtained from there. The paper ends with a concluding section.

2 Research Methodology Behind AI Based Schemes

The general methodology of the AI based app of OvuFriend 2.0, determining the possible days of ovulation as well as the possibility of the above mentioned health risks, incorporates the following features. Each AI based scheme consists of three hierarchical levels, namely *Detector level*, *Cycle level*, and *User level*.

(i) At the *detector's level* the user, on a daily basis, can put information related to her mental and physical health for one complete cycle. Then the data is grouped into time series for a given type of data (e.g. basal body temperature, cervical mucus, more than 80 subjective symptoms, moods, etc.), which together form a multidimensional time series indexed with the number of the day of the menstrual cycle. Based on the input of an user the values for a pre-fixed set (created by a team of medical experts) of attributes are determined and they are tagged against the information details of the patient. Thus this level corresponds to preprocessing of the data by aggregating the perception of the user and the knowledge of a team of experts.

(ii) After completion of a full cycle, based on the values computed for the attributes, certain compound concepts such as *ovulation happened, days of ovulation, follicular phase interval, luteal phase interval, PMS score* etc. are determined. These are the *cycle-level concepts* and are defined by some relevant formulas representing relationships among different attributes as described by a team of medical experts based on their knowledge from the literature and personal experiences. The attributes involved in the formulas are determined at the detector level, and the formulas are fed to the algorithms in order to determine the cycle level concepts. Thus, the mathematical formulations of the interrelationships among different attribute values are discovered by aggregating a team of medical experts' opinions.

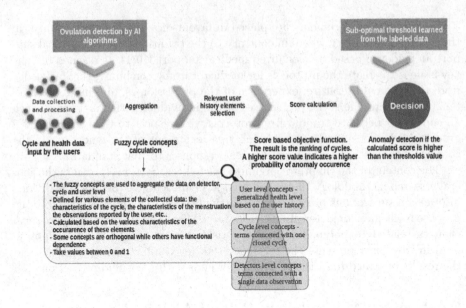

Fig. 1. General scheme for OvuFriend 2.0

(iii) In the *user's level*, the system aggregates the data related to the detector level as well as the cycle level concepts of a particular user for a finitely many cycles. The examples of the user level concepts are: *cycle length fluctuations, long cycles, short luteal phases, irregular periods in length, intermenstrual bleedings, frequent possible no ovulation,* and many others, to finally designate final concepts such as *risk of PMS, risk of LPD, risk of infertility, risk of PCOS* etc. Here, the system calculates the probabilistic ratio of the above mentioned cycle level concepts over the total number of cycles considered for a particular user. The system is also fed with a threshold value for each such user level concepts. Moreover, these threshold values are learned and adapted based on the opinions of the medical experts and the histories of already recorded and analysed cases. If the respective ratio for a particular user level concept is greater than the prefixed threshold for that concept the system notifies the user about the possibility of such health risk. Thus, it is clear that the threshold chosen for a particular health risk is set based on the experts' knowledge as well as existing evidences of such cases.

Figure 1 represents the above discussed scheme. The process of determining ovulation was described in [19].

It is visible that the model incorporates a three-layered hierarchical learning and reasoning mechanism based on the knowledge and experiences of a team of medical experts, perceptions of the users, and already recorded evidences to the system. Furthermore, the hierarchy of approximating fuzzy concepts is developed by using the quantifiers of fuzzy linguistic summaries in the process of inferring and making local decisions [14,15]. Thus, the model of OvuFriend 2.0 complies to a great extent to the need of personalized and evidence based medicine. Moreover, the model also incorporates perception of the current health situation of a woman based on the individual spatio-temporal windows of the physical world and actual physical interactions in the form of measuring attributes in the given space and time windows. Thus, to some sense the model also endorses some features of Interactive Granular Computing (IGrC) [4,12].

3   Research Findings: AI Algorithms Analyzing Health Risks

In this section we would present AI algorithms and schemes for determining whether a user has the risks of certain health diseases. Specifically, we focus on the health diseases such as PMS, LPD, Fibroids, Polyps, PCOS and hypothyroidism. All these schemes are discussed below in separate subsections.

The general prerequisite for all the algorithms determining risks of different disorders, that are described in this paper, is similar; they differ in details. It starts with collecting data related to the physical and mental health of a woman before, during, and after a complete menstrual cycle. After the completion of a cycle, the data is gathered for analyzing the risk of different disorders. Initially, the data is processed to investigate whether the ovulation has occurred and whether it is possible to determine the day of its occurrence. All concepts pertaining to the detector level are analysed and determined at this phase of data processing.

3.1   Scheme to Determine Risk of PMS

At the beginning, it is checked if the ovulation has occurred, and in case of positive answer an attempt is made to indicate two intervals of equal length falling into the follicular phase and the luteal phase of the cycle respectively.

The length of the intervals depends on the length of menstruation, the day of ovulation, and the length of the total cycle. A complete cycle means number of days between starting of the menstruation in one period to the starting of the same in the next period. The beginning point of the first interval is chosen as the k-th day after the end of the menstruation of the current cycle, where the value for k is prefixed in the algorithm. If the length of the cycle is x and the number of days of the current cycle's menstruation is m, then each interval has to be of length $\frac{x-(k+m)}{2}$. Thus, the beginning point and the end point of the first interval are respectively $m + k$ and $\frac{x+(k+m)}{2}$. Consequently, the second interval is $[\frac{x+(k+m)}{2}, x]$, where x is the last day of the cycle.

After successful determination of the intervals, the coefficients of occurrence of the physical symptoms and mood symptoms characteristics of PMS are computed. For the set of mood symptoms, the readers are referred to Fig. 6. Based on the consensus of gathered knowledge and experiences of a team of medical experts about variations of different moods, feelings and physical impacts observed in women during the menstrual cycles, this set of symptoms and formulas for calculating the coefficients are defined. All such symptoms related to

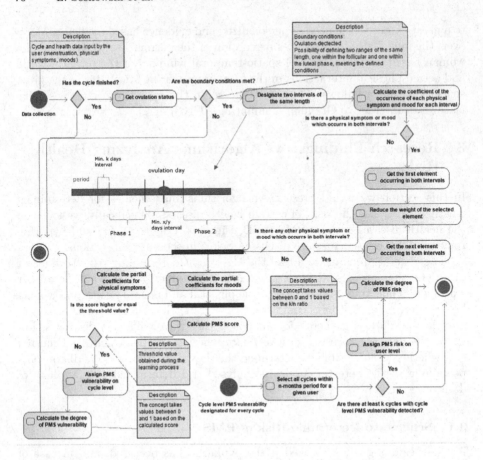

Fig. 2. Complete scheme for calculating PMS risk vulnerability (2 diagrams)

the physical or mental health are counted. Then it is checked whether they occur in both the phases or only in the second phase. If there is at least one physical symptom or mood symptom occurring in both the phases, the algorithm reduces the weights in the respective formula calculating the mood feel coefficient or physical feel coefficient. In case of PMS, usually the physical or mood symptoms are observed during the second phase. Due to this, when some symptoms are observed in both the phases, the possibility for PMS is decreased by reducing the weights. Finally, by aggregating the number of physical symptoms and the mood symptoms in a particular phase, according to the following formulas, the coefficients for the physical symptoms and the mood symptoms are calculated. Figure 2 shows the algorithmic flowchart behind the described process for determining the cycle level concept *PMS score*, denoted as PMS_{score}.

Let us denote the two phases as P_1 and P_2 respectively. $P_i MoodFeelCoeff$ and $P_i PhysFeelCoeff$ denote respectively the coefficients for mood symptoms and physical symptoms in phase P_i.

$$P_i MoodFeelCoeff = \frac{(SumOfOccurrenceP_iMood)}{K_1 \times PhaseLength} \times \alpha + (1 - \alpha) \quad (1)$$

where $i = 1, 2$ and $\alpha \in (0, 1)$,

$$P_2 PhysFeelCoeff = \frac{(SumOfOccurrenceP_2Phys)}{K_2 \times PhaseLength} \times \beta + (1 - \beta) \quad (2)$$

where $\beta \in (0, 1)$.

The symbols $SumOfOccurrenceP_iMood$ and $SumOfOccurrenceP_iPhys$ respectively indicate the number of mood and the number of physical symptoms occurred in a particular phase P_i. The symbols K_1 and K_2 represent respectively the total number of all moods and physical symptoms listed in the system. The factors α and β are parameters to control the significance of the given components in the final calculation. These formulas are designed by a team of scientific experts based on the general description given by the medical experts regarding the effect on physical and mental health of women during a cycle as well as keeping into account the observed patterns of cases available in the record. Based on the above coefficients the *PMS score* is calculated by the following formula.

$$PMS_{score} = \frac{P_2 MoodFeelCoeff}{P_1 MoodFeelCoeff} + \frac{P_2 PhysFeelCoeff}{w_1} \quad (3)$$

where w_1 is the weight chosen by a team of medical experts.

At the beginning, the algorithm also sets a threshold for PMS score by considering already available records of patients. This threshold may vary over time based on the changes in the patients' record. So, in some sense the underlying algorithm keeps a possibility of learning the threshold for PMS score based on the current evidences. Based on this threshold whether a user has the PMS susceptibility or not is determined just by checking if the obtained score is greater or equal to the prefixed threshold. If during the current cycle the algorithm determines PMS susceptibility for a user the algorithm passes to the next level where the degree of PMS risk is calculated for a particular user based on the observations of finitely many cycles. If over the selected period of n months there are at least k cycles with PMS susceptibility, then the degree PMS risk, assigned to the user, is $\frac{k}{n}$. The flowchart, presented in Fig. 2, shows a complete overview of the algorithm specifying PMS susceptibility and PMS risk for a particular user.

3.2   Scheme to Determine Risk for LPD

As mentioned before, the general prerequisite for running the algorithm to determine the risk of Luteal Phase Defect (LPD) [7] is common to all the considered disorders. After analyzing the data first it is determined whether ovulation has occurred, and then based on that the boundary conditions are determined. These conditions are verified using fuzzy quantifiers of linguistic summaries operating on multivariate time series (e.g., the quantifier *exists*) [13]. The specific scheme

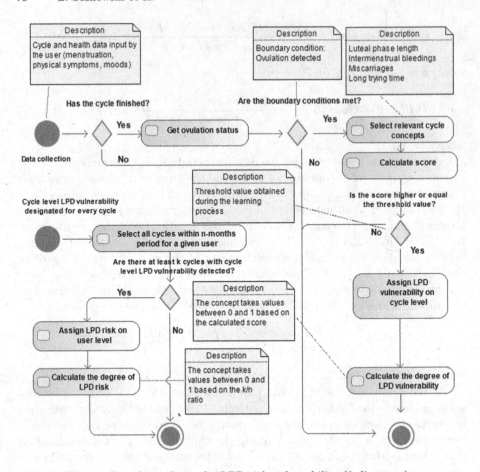

Fig. 3. Complete scheme for LPD risk vulnerability (2 diagrams)

of LPD differs from that of PMS in the formula calculating the susceptibility of LPD and consequently the degree of risk for LPD.

Similar like, PMS score, here the AI algorithm is fed with a formula for calculating LPD score, given by the following equation.

$$LPD_{score} = w_1 * LutParameters + w_2 * DecFer \tag{4}$$

The parameters $LutParameters, DecFer \in [0,1]$ and respectively denote the values for *Luteal Phase Parameters* and *Decreased Fertility*. The *Luteal Phase Parameters* are obtained based on the luteal phase length and various other factors related to the nature of bleeding during the luteal phase. The *Decreased Fertility* pertains to the observation of the period of time in which the attempts for conceiving a child are made, the number of miscarriages etc. These are estimated with the help of pregnancy tests and the length of the cycle compared to the typical lengths of the cycle and luteal phase for a given user. The respective values for *LutParameters, DecFer* are calculated based on the input data of a particular user, and the weights w_1, w_2 are chosen by the team of experts based on the significance of $LutParameters$ and $DecFer$.

After determining the possibility of LPD in the cycle level, the algorithm passes to the next level and calculates the degree of risk for LPD; if in the selected period of ɳ months there are at least k cycles with LPD susceptibility, then the LPD risk is simply $\frac{k}{n}$. Overview of the scheme is presented in Fig. 3.

3.3 Scheme for Indicating Anatomical Changes: Polyps and Fibroids

The algorithm for determining anatomical anomalies starts with the data of a complete cycle of a user. It focuses on the data related to inter-menstrual bleeding or spots. After initial investigation of whether the ovulation has occurred and determination of the possible ovulation date, all the detector level concepts, needed for the required analysis, are determined. Then cycle level concepts are analyzed in the same fashion as mentioned in the previous cases.

The cycle level concepts, selected at this stage, are associated to the symptoms characterizing the particular diseases like polyp or fibroids. Based on these cycle level concepts, a score is calculated using the following formula.

$$Score = w_1 * DisMens + w_2 * DecFer + w_3 * PhysSymp \qquad (5)$$

From the input data of a user $DisMens$, the value for the parameters corresponding to disordered menstruation, $DecFer$, the value for decreased fertility, and $PhysSymp$, the values corresponding to physical symptoms related to such diseases, are calculated. The weights w_1, w_2, w_3 are chosen by the team of experts. All these values are scaled in the interval $[0, 1]$ based on the information related to inter-menstrual bleeding, long-lasting menstruation, intensity of menstruation, miscarriage, long trying time for conceiving, pelvis pain, polyuria etc.

As before, if in a cycle the score is greater than or equal to the cut-off value, set through some learning process, the anatomical susceptibility is assigned at that particular cycle level. The grade is calculated by considering that in how many cycles, out of n cycles, the algorithm notifies the susceptibility of anatomical changes for a particular user, and it is simply $\frac{k}{n}$ if in k such cycles susceptibility of anatomical changes is detected. The readers are referred to Fig. 4 for the full scheme of determining the possibility of polyp, fibroids etc.

3.4 Scheme to Determine the Risk of PCOS

In order to start the analysis for the risk of PCOS, at first the system needs the data of an individual user for a few months. Different cycle level concepts such as *increasing level of anxiety, depressive mood, lower self-esteem, family history of PCOS, family history of diabetes, high BMI, long cycle, extended trying time for conceiving* etc. are determined based on the detector level parameters such as stress, gloomy mood, appetite, depression, hypersensitivity, insomnia, fatigue, problem in concentration, BMI, length of cycle etc. Some of the above mentioned cycle level concepts are marked with binary values and some with

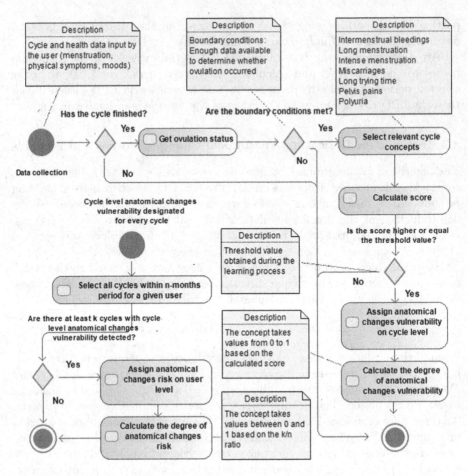

Fig. 4. Complete scheme for determining risk vulnerability of polyps and fibroids (2 diagrams)

fuzzy values, specifically on a scale of $0 \leq 0.33 \leq 0.66 \leq 1$; these values are marked over a span of time. After completion of a cycle, all cycle level concepts are determined and they describe information characterizing the entire cycle based on a multidimensional time series.

Some groups of symptoms allow for both a qualitative indication such as whether any of the symptoms belonging to the group occurred at least once on a given day, as well as quantitative indication such as how many symptoms from the group occurred on a day. The frequency of occurrence of a symptom usually is analyzed based on the selected time period. For example, the occurrence of fatigue 4 times in a 45-day cycle may indicate the greater value for anxiety than occurrence of the same symptom 4 times in half of the cycle. Based on need there are different forms available for deeper analysis of some of the above mentioned detector or cycle level concepts. For example, if a user meets the

PCOS boundary conditions, she is asked to provide some specific parameters in the follicular phase of the cycle for consecutive 3 days. If the user rates them three times negatively, the label for *low self esteem* is activated. This causes the user to complete a more detailed low self-esteem survey.

The analysis for PCOS starts with, as usual, by determining the possibility of ovulation and respective intervals as mentioned in above sections. To enable PCOS susceptibility analysis, the cycle must be completed, with a duration of at least 10 days; the same data for previous two cycles must also be available meeting the same conditions. One cycle is not enough to reliably assess the presence of PCOS, as it is a disease whose symptoms persist for a long time. Exploring three consecutive cycles increases also the likelihood that the observations made by the user are not accidental. Then for each of these series of cycles, possible ovulation or anovulation is determined. Here, to be remembered that if any of the cycle in a series lacks in necessary data, that series of cycles is not considered for further analysis.

The coefficient value for $cycle_n Score$ for the nth cycle is calculated on the basis of the issued cycle labels from the sequence according to the following formula.

$$cycle_n Score = X_{1n} * w_1 + X_{2n} * w_2 + X_{3n} * w_3 + X_{4n} * w_4 + X_{5n} * w_5$$
$$+ X_{6n} * w_6 + X_{7n} * w_7 \quad (6)$$

where X_{in} is calculated based on the number points obtained for the i-th group of concepts that have appeared in the n-th cycle. For example $X_{5n} = \frac{increased\_anxiety + depressive\_mood}{2}$ where the two operands in the numerator represent the number of points obtained for those two parameters from the 5-th group of concepts in the n-th cycle. The weights w_i, $1 \leq i \leq n$ are selected based on the significance of a group of symptoms over other. Then the sum of the points of each cycle from the sequence is added and normalized according to the formula below.

$$normScore = \frac{\sum_{i=1}^{3} cycle_i Score}{3 * \sum_{j=1}^{7} w_j} \quad (7)$$

Based on the values for *nomScore*, different possible sequences of cycles, recorded over a time period, are ranked in descending order. While selecting the desired cycle, it should be remembered that the sequences of three cycles can be overlapping; that is one of the cycles can be the first in one sequence and middle in another sequence. However, the sequence with the highest number for *normScore* is selected for the analysis of PCOS.

The scheme of the algorithm prototype is shown in Fig. 5. In order to determine the PCOS susceptibility for a particular sequence of cycles, one sequence of cycles, which is completed in last six months, is selected from the history of a user. If among these cycles at least two are detected with a vulnerability of PCOS, the respective user is assigned to a PCOS risk. Then, at the user level the degree of risk is calculated based on the ratio of the number of PCOS-susceptible cycles to the number of months over which the observation is made.

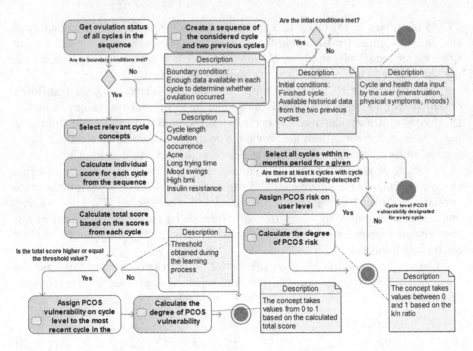

Fig. 5. Complete scheme for determining risk vulnerability of PCOS (2 diagrams)

3.5 Scheme for Hypothyroidism

The scheme for determining the possibility of hypothyroidism is quite similar to the scheme for PCOS. Here in order to start the analysis, data corresponding to a particular user for three consecutive cycles is needed. Initially, data for each of the three cycles are processed to test whether ovulation has occurred and whether it is possible to determine the date of its onset. At the same time, the detector level concepts and the cycle level concepts are determined. Usually ovulation can be determined based on mucus, basal body temperature (bbt), cervix, physical symptoms, ovulation tests, ovulation monitor etc. collected from a particular cycle. Sometimes, there are situations where the obtained data is not enough to quantify ovulation. If, in each cycle of the sequence, enough data has been marked for the algorithm to determine the occurrence of ovulation or anovulation, the algorithm can proceed to the next stage. Those cycle level concepts, for which the symptoms characteristic are related to this disease, are selected; these include symptoms like feeling cold, feeling sleepy, concentration problems, decreased appetite, constipation, swelling, decreased libido, mood swings, memory problems, etc. On their basis, for each cycle, a score, denoted as Sc_n, is determined from the sequence in accordance with the formula presented below.

$$Sc_n = w_1 * PhySym_n + w_2 * Len_n + w_3 * Ov_n$$
$$+ w_4 * DecFer_n + w_5 * PsySym_n \tag{8}$$

As before the weights $w_1, \ldots, w_5$ are selected by the experts, and the values for the other parameters are obtained based on the user's data. The symbol $PhySym_n$ stands for the value corresponding to the physical symptoms during the n-th cycle, Len_n denotes the length of the n-th cycle, Ov_n denotes the number of ovulations occurred in the n-th cycle, $DecFer_n$ corresponds to the value for the decreased fertility in the n-th cycle, and $PsySym_n$ represents the value corresponding to the psychological symptoms in the n-th cycle.

Based on the scores accumulated from three consecutive cycles the score for the risk of hypothyroidism is calculated for the whole sequence; specifically,

$$Score_{Hypth} = Sc_1 + Sc_2 + Sc_3 \tag{9}$$

where 1 denotes the number of the first cycle of three consecutive cycles.

Finally, if the score is greater than or equal to the cut-off value, which is set by the learning process based on the available records, the most recent cycle in the sequence is assigned a hypothyroidism susceptibility at the cyclic level and the score is then calculated just by adding the score obtained in three consecutive cycles. The score obtained for each such single cycle from a chain of three consecutive cycles is used to assess the risk of developing hypothyroidism at the level of the user. First, all completed cycles, that have occurred during the last n months, are selected. Then all possible sequence combinations of three consecutive cycles are created from them, and the sum of the points is calculated for each sequence. If the sum of the points for any of the sequences is greater than or equal to the pre-fixed cut-off value, a risk of hypothyroidism is assigned to the user, and a grade is calculated in the range of $[0, 1]$.

Further, the data and analysis, obtained from the sequences, are also get assessed by medical experts and based on such history of sequences the cut-off point is learned.

4   Reference Set and Experiments: Discussion on Research Findings

To estimate how effectively the algorithms can detect anomalies, first a reference set needs to be created. In our case, this set consists of cycles of different user described by the experts. For each cycle the experts tag the information related to chance of an anomaly occurrence by a value in the range $[0, 1]$ and add comments explaining the reason behind the assessment. Each of the references is also attached with a cycle visualization containing the basic data which are needed to determine the ovulation, as well as the information of already predicted ovulation (product of the OvuFriend 1.0 project). In addition, the visualization contains a series of low level data (e.g., group of symptoms) broken down by observation days. As a whole it can be considered as a multidimensional time series indexed with the days of the ovulatory cycle. To have an idea of visualization labelling the readers are referred to the form for *PMS* presented in Fig. 6 [16], and the same for luteal phase deficiency (LPD) can be found in Fig. 7. The form for

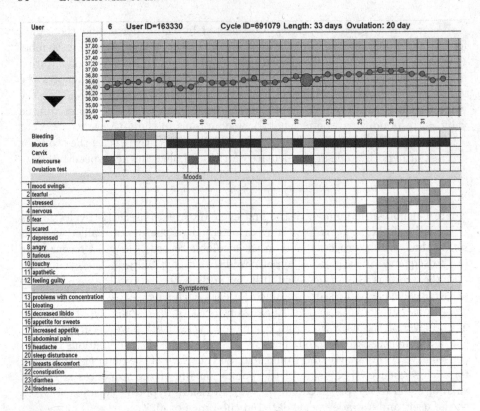

Fig. 6. PMS labelling form prepared for medical experts to evaluate susceptibility of selected cycles. Form is based on such attributes as: bleeding, mucus, bbt, cervix, mood swings, tearful, stressed, nervous, depressed, angry, furious, tiredness, bloating, problem with the concentration, appetite for sweets, sleep disturbance, breasts pains, constipation, etc.

tagging the other disorders are similar to the one for *LPD*. In case of polyps and fibroids the forms are extended with a few additional attributes (cf. Figure 7). The reference set consists of 1500 menstrual cycles (300 for each disorder). In the category of "Anatomical or hormonal abnormalities with inter-menstrual spots" each cycle is marked with both the presence of NFL and anatomical changes. It is observed that the number of items in the set has grown steadily as successive sets of cycles are submitted for tagging. Subsequent sets of cycles are drawn on the basis of the given criteria, selected in such a way that it helps to obtain a similar size in the positive class (minimum expert's score 0.5) and the negative class (score below 0.5). The size of each class, broken down by a group and the types of anomaly, is presented in Table 1. In each of the five groups of anomalies, the sample is well-balanced, where the share of the positive class ranges from 48% to 55% of the sample.

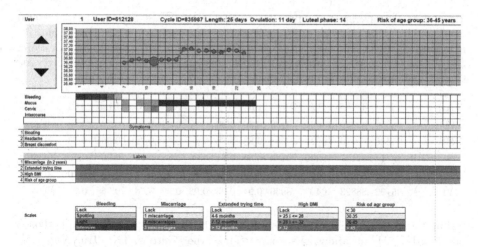

Fig. 7. Luteal phase deficiency and polyps tagging form prepared for medical experts to evaluate susceptibility of selected cycles. Form is based on such attributes as: bleeding, mucus, bbt, cervix, age group, increased BMI, extended trying time, miscarriages in history, etc.

Table 1. The sample size by class and type of anomaly. PC - positive class, NC - negative class

Anomaly	#	PC	% PC	NC	% NC
PMS	300	164	55%	136	45%
LPD	300	147	49%	153	51%
Polyps and Fibroids	300	160	53%	140	47%
PCOS	300	144	48%	156	52%
Hypothyroidism	300	157	52%	143	48%

Next comes the turn for evaluating the effectiveness of the prototypical algorithms. In this regard, four experiments have been conducted for each of the five disorders. In general, the following methodology is adopted for all the experiments.

Each of the experiments involves a different number of repetitions such as 1000, 500, 100, and 10, respectively for ReSample evaluation [8]. From the whole set of references, two disjoint subsets are selected; the training set contains 33% of the reference set, and testing is performed on the remaining 67%. The values of the cut-off thresholds of rankings for all described disorders are learned in each iteration of the training set that consists of 100 cycles (33% of 300 tagged cycles). Evolutionary algorithms with a fitting function based on a combination of the accuracy measure and the F1Score measure were used to train the thresholds. The test procedure that returned the values for contingency table are processed

Table 2. Results averaged over 1000 iterations of the ReSample routine (sample 200000 per disorder). Abbreviations: # - sample, TP - True Positives, TN - True Negatives, FP - False Positives, FN - False Negatives, PR - Precision, RE - Recall, F1 - F1 score, mn- min, mx- max, AC - accuracy, POL-FIBR - Polyps and fibroids, PCOS - Polycystic Ovary Syndrome, HYP - hypothyroidism

Type	TP	TN	FP	FN	PR	RE	F1	AC	$F1_{mn}$	$F1_{mx}$	AC_{mn}	AC_{mx}
LPD	88650	87920	13991	9439	0.86	0.90	0.88	0.88	0.78	0.93	0.80	0.92
PMS	96685	70710	19921	12684	0.83	0.88	0.86	0.84	0.72	0.90	0.73	0.89
POL-FIBR	86714	82157	10990	20139	0.89	0.81	0.85	0.84	0.73	0.90	0.76	0.90
PCOS	79436	88516	15446	16602	0.84	0.83	0.83	0.84	0.62	0.89	0.70	0.89
HYP	95792	88823	6449	8936	0.94	0.93	0.93	0.92	0.76	0.96	0.78	0.96

Table 3. Results averaged over 500 iterations of the ReSample routine (sample 100000 per disorder). Abbreviations: # - sample, TP - True Positives, TN - True Negatives, FP - False Positives, FN - False Negatives, PR - Precision, RE - Recall, F1 - F1 score, mn- min, mx- max, AC - accuracy, POL-FIBR - Polyps and fibroids, PCOS - Polycystic Ovary Syndrome, HYP - hypothyroidism

Type	TP	TN	FP	FN	PR	RE	F1	AC	$F1_{mn}$	$F1_{mx}$	AC_{mn}	AC_{mx}
LPD	44317	44071	7035	4577	0.86	0.90	0.88	0.88	0.79	0.92	0.80	0.92
PMS	48043	35454	9965	6538	0.83	0.88	0.85	0.84	0.75	0.90	0.75	0.89
POL-FIBR	43523	41078	5618	9781	0.89	0.82	0.85	0.85	0.75	0.91	0.77	0.90
PCOS	39775	44157	7898	8170	0.83	0.83	0.83	0.84	0.72	0.89	0.77	0.89
HYP	47773	44566	3173	4488	0.94	0.91	0.93	0.92	0.78	0.97	0.80	0.97

on 200 cycles. Single iteration results are stored in the contingency table. Finally, all TP (True Positive), TN (True Negative), FP (False Positive) and FN (False Negative) are summed and then measures of effectiveness are calculated. The obtained results for 1000 repetitions are presented in the Table 2.

The label TP is assigned when the cycle is tagged with at least 0.5 by the medical experts and the algorithm has classified the cycle in the positive set of a given disease; whereas, the case for FP is determined when the experts have given mark below 0.5 but the algorithm has classified the case into positive class. The case for TN is obtained when the experts have assigned less than 0.5 and the algorithm has calculated score under the learned threshold. Finally the cases for FN is indicated when the algorithm has calculated the score value under the learned threshold but from the experts it receives a mark greater or equal 0.5. The outcome of 500 repetitions of such process is presented in the Table 3.

The obtained results for 100 and 10 repetitions are presented in the Table 4 and Table 5 respectively.

In the project, the team of medical experts consists of three highly qualified medical scientists, and the decisions regarding tagging cycles have been made based on discussion within the team. As the values, selected after tagging,

Table 4. Results averaged over 100 iterations of the ReSample routine (sample 20000 per disorder). Abbreviations: # - sample, TP - True Positives, TN - True Negatives, FP - False Positives, FN - False Negatives, PR - Precision, RE - Recall, F1 - F1 score, AC - accuracy, POL-FIBR - Polyps and fibroids, PCOS - Polycystic Ovary Syndrome, HYP - hypothyroidism

Type	TP	TN	FP	FN	PR	RE	F1	AC	$F1_{min}$	$F1_{max}$	AC_{min}	AC_{max}
LPD	8808	8833	1394	965	0.86	0.90	0.88	0.88	0.78	0.92	0.80	0.92
PMS	9687	7025	2049	1239	0.83	0.89	0.86	0.84	0.76	0.91	0.76	0.90
POL-FIBR	8672	8245	1122	1961	0.89	0.82	0.85	0.85	0.75	0.90	0.78	0.89
PCOS	7854	8901	1505	1740	0.84	0.83	0.83	0.84	0.76	0.88	0.79	0.88
HYP	9550	8945	632	873	0.94	0.92	0.93	0.93	0.88	0.96	0.87	0.96

Table 5. Results averaged over 10 iterations of the ReSample routine (sample 2000 per disorder). Abbreviations: TP - True Positives, TN - True Negatives, FP - False Positives, FN - False Negatives, PR - Precision, RE - Recall, F1 - F1 score, AC - accuracy, POL-FIBR - Polyps and fibroids, PCOS - Polycystic Ovary Syndrome, HYP - hypothyroidism

Type	TP	TN	FP	FN	PR	RE	F1	AC	$F1_{min}$	$F1_{max}$	AC_{min}	AC_{max}
LPD	902	873	120	105	0.88	0.90	0.89	0.89	0.85	0.92	0.86	0.92
PMS	950	709	209	132	0.82	0.88	0.85	0.83	0.83	0.87	0.82	0.85
POL-FIBR	868	824	115	193	0.88	0.82	0.85	0.85	0.79	0.88	0.81	0.88
PCOS	789	906	119	186	0.87	0.81	0.84	0.85	0.81	0.87	0.83	0.86
HYP	936	902	51	111	0.95	0.90	0.92	0.92	0.85	0.95	0.86	0.95

are already agreed with the consensus of the whole team they do not require additional processing in order to be used for evaluation.

The presented results of the experiments pertain to the first stage of the project, in which the parameters of the algorithms are learned from the tagging of medical experts. The labels are made on the data constituting the subjective observations of the system users, the measurements of the physical parameters (e.g.,, BBT, cervical mucus, cervix position, etc.) and the subjective labels of the team of experts.

In future, we plan to run the experiments based on the data obtained from real test results, that are used by the doctors to make the diagnosis. Thus, the algorithm can be tested against the real hardcore medical data.

5   Conclusion

Dependence on AI and machine learning techniques is prevalent in every sphere of life. Reflection of the same is also visible in healthcare support. Contrary to the classical style of medical support, the technologies for treating a patient is getting inclined to a distributed process which does not depend on the subjective knowledge and experience about a particular field of medicine of an individual medical expert. In other words, it demands a standardization in the protocols of treating a particular disease, followed by different practitioners.

The architecture of OvuFriend 2.0 is developed in such a way that the system has an interface of user in order to gather input data as well as an interface of a team of medical experts to have a possibility of shared knowledge. Based on the consensus of these medical experts a protocols for standardizing lowest level concepts, known as detector level concepts, as well as methodologies for calculating their values, are created. Based on the data of a complete cycle the values for detector level concepts are selected and then cycle level concepts are analyzed and evaluated. Combining the values obtained for the cycle level concepts for a finitely many cycles the degrees of risk for respective cycle level concepts are computed.

So, it can be noticed that through the user interface the decision support system designed by OvuFriend attempts to be sensitive to the user's perceptions. On the other hand, the interface for a team of medical experts keeps the possibility open for discussion and standardization of the protocol of medical support, and at the same time the process of treatment becomes distributive. Moreover, the underlying AI algorithm incorporates a learning mechanism which based on records of the already available patients changes certain thresholds for analyzing health risks. Thus, we can notice that the model, developed by OvuFriend, appears to be close to the needs of personalized and evidence based medical support.

However, there are some aspects where the model needs to be more dynamic and interactive. A few of such limitations are listed below.

(i) Though the model incorporates two interfaces respectively for the user and for the team of experts, there is not much possibility of keeping these two interfaces interactive all through the process of decision making. Hence, the decisions are made based on one time accumulation of data, and thus there is no room for improving accidentally obtained faulty or noisy data.

(ii) Presently, the formulas determining the values for the cycle level concepts and the user level concepts are fixed.

In regard to the above mentioned limitations, different future research directions open up. The aspect, mentioned in (i), can be improved by introducing a language of dialogue [2,3]. So we plan to add such an environment for dialogue between the interfaces, which may allow the model to update and revise the underlying treatment protocol based on a particular user's input. In the present model, certain weights for a particular health disease does not depend on the input of a particular user. The inclusion of a possibility of dialogue among different interfaces may help the model to dynamically learn the optimized care for a particular user. Secondly, in reference to (ii), instead basing on a fixed rule for determining certain concept, we plan to include a possibility of using machine learning techniques which can help to learn a set of possible rules or formulas for diagnosing certain health risks. These techniques may take as input the already existing evidences, and based on that modify the existing formulas from different aspects of approximations. This may generate a more flexible and evidence driven process of diagnosis.

Though the existing algorithms shows a very good quality of the results, the real test will be their modernization and incorporation of data from medical examinations into operation. It will be a milestone which, if achieved, will guarantee another success for applications and system users.

Acknowledgement. The research presented in this paper is co-financed by the EU Smart Growth Operational Program 2014-2020 under the project "Developing innovative solutions in the domain of detection of frequent intimate and hormonal health disorders in women of procreative age based on artificial intelligence and machine learning - OvuFriend 2.0", POIR.01.01.01-00-0826/20.

References

1. Bablok, L., Dziadecki, W., Szymusik, I., et al.: Patterns of infertility in Poland - multicenter study. Neuro Endocrinol Lett. **32**(6), 799–804 (2011)
2. Dutta, S., Wasilewski, P.: Dialogue in Hierarchical Concept Learning using Prototypes and Counterexamples. Fundamenta Informaticae **162**, 17–36 (2018). https://doi.org/10.3233/FI-2018-1711
3. Dutta, S., Skowron, A.: Concepts Approximation Through Dialogue with User. In: Mihálydeák, T., et al. (eds.) IJCRS 2019. LNCS (LNAI), vol. 11499, pp. 295–311. Springer, Cham (2019). https://doi.org/10.1007/978-3-030-22815-6_23
4. Dutta, S., Skowron, A.: Toward a computing model dealing with complex phenomena: interactive granular computing. In: Nguyen, N.T., Iliadis, L., Maglogiannis, I., Trawiński, B. (eds.) ICCCI 2021. LNCS (LNAI), vol. 12876, pp. 199–214. Springer, Cham (2021). https://doi.org/10.1007/978-3-030-88081-1_15
5. Fedorowicz, J., et al.: Multivariate Ovulation Window Detection at OvuFriend. In: Mihálydeák, T., et al. (eds.) IJCRS 2019. LNCS (LNAI), vol. 11499, pp. 395–408. Springer, Cham (2019). https://doi.org/10.1007/978-3-030-22815-6_31
6. Fernandez-Llatas, C., Munoz-Gama, J., Martin, N., Johnson, O., Sepulveda, M., Helm, E.: Process mining in healthcare. In: Fernandez-Llatas, C. (ed.) Interactive Process Mining in Healthcare. HI, pp. 41–52. Springer, Cham (2021). https://doi.org/10.1007/978-3-030-53993-1_4
7. Ginsburg, K.A.: Luteal phase defect: etiology, diagnosis, and management. Endocrinol. Metabolism Clin. North Am. **21**(1), 85–104 (1992). Reproductive Endocrinology. https://doi.org/10.1016/S0889-8529(18)30233-0
8. Good, P.: Resampling methods: a practical guide to data analysis. Birkhäuser Boston (2005)
9. Goodman, N.F., Cobin, R.H., Futterweit, W., Glueck, J.S., Legro, R.S., Carmina, E.: American Association of Clinical Endocrinologists, American College of Endocrinology, and Androgen Excess and PCOS Society Disease State Clinical Review: Guide to the Best Practices in the Evaluation and Treatment of Polycystic Ovary Syndrome - Part 1. Endocr. Pract. **21**(11), 1291–1300 (2015). https://doi.org/10.4158/EP15748.DSC
10. Hamburg, M.A., Collins, F.S.: The Path to Personalized Medicine. New England J. Med. **363**(4), 301–304 (2010). https://doi.org/10.1056/NEJMp1006304
11. Haynes, B., Haines, A.: Barriers and bridges to evidence based clinical practice. BMJ **317**(7153), 273–276 (1998). https://doi.org/10.1136/bmj.317.7153.273

12. Jankowski, A., Skowron, A., Swiniarski, R.W.: Interactive complex granules. Fundam. Informaticae **133**(2–3), 181–196 (2014). https://doi.org/10.3233/FI-2014-1070

13. Kacprzyk, J., Owsinski, J.W., Szmidt, E., Zadrozny, S.: Fuzzy linguistic summaries for human centric analyses of sustainable development goals (sdg) related to technological innovations. In: Verdegay, J.L., Brito, J., Cruz, C. (eds.) Computational Intelligence Methodologies Applied to Sustainable Development Goals, Studies in Computational Intelligence, vol. 1036, pp. 19–35. Springer, Cham (2022). https://doi.org/10.1007/978-3-030-97344-5_2

14. Kacprzyk, J., Yager, R.R., Merigó, J.M.: Towards human-centric aggregation via ordered weighted aggregation operators and linguistic data summaries: a new perspective on zadeh's inspirations. IEEE Comput. Intell. Mag. **14**(1), 16–30 (2019). https://doi.org/10.1109/MCI.2018.2881641

15. Kacprzyk, J., Zadrozny, S.: Fuzzy logic-based linguistic summaries of time series: a powerful tool for discovering knowledge on time varying processes and systems under imprecision. Wiley Interdiscip. Rev. Data Min. Knowl. Discov. **6**(1), 37–46 (2016). https://doi.org/10.1002/widm.1175

16. Kalhor, M., Yuseflo, S., Kaveii, B., Mohammadi, F., Javadi, H.: Effect of yarrow (Achillea Millefolium L.) extract on premenstrual syndrome in female students living in dormitory of Qazvin university of medical sciences. J. Medicinal Plants **18**(72), 52–63 (2019). https://doi.org/10.29252/jmp.4.72.S12.52

17. Smoley, B., Robinson, C.: Natural family planning. Am. Fam. Physician **86**(10), 924–928 (2012)

18. Sosnowski, Ł., Penza, T.: Generating fuzzy linguistic summaries for menstrual cycles. Annal. Comput. Sci. Inf. Syst. **21**, 119–128 (2020). https://doi.org/10.15439/2020F202

19. Sosnowski, Ł, Szymusik, I., Penza, T.: Network of fuzzy comparators for ovulation window prediction. In: Lesot, M.-J., et al. (eds.) IPMU 2020. CCIS, vol. 1239, pp. 800–813. Springer, Cham (2020). https://doi.org/10.1007/978-3-030-50153-2_59

20. Sosnowski, Ł., Wróblewski, J.: Toward automatic assessment of a risk of women's health disorders based on ontology decision models and menstrual cycle analysis. In: Chen, Y., et al. (eds.) 2021 IEEE International Conference on Big Data (Big Data), Orlando, FL, USA, 15–18 December 2021, pp. 5544–5552. IEEE (2021). https://doi.org/10.1109/BigData52589.2021.9671481

21. Sosnowski, Ł., Zulawinska, J., Dutta, S., Szymusik, I., Zygula, A., Bambul-Mazurek, E.: Artificial intelligence in personalized healthcare analysis for womens' menstrual health disorders. In: Ganzha, M., Maciaszek, L.A., Paprzycki, M., Slezak, D. (eds.) Proceedings of the 17th Conference on Computer Science and Intelligence Systems, FedCSIS 2022, Sofia, Bulgaria, 4–7 September 2022. Annal. Comput. Sci. Inf. Syst. **30**, 751–760 (2022). https://doi.org/10.15439/2022F59

22. Wu, X., Xiao, L., Sun, Y., Zhang, J., Ma, T., He, L.: A survey of human-in-the-loop for machine learning. Future Gener. Comput. Syst. **135**, 364–381 (2022). https://doi.org/10.1016/j.future.2022.05.014

Symptoms of Dementia in Elderly Persons Using Waveform Features of Pupil Light Reflex

Minoru Nakayama[1]([⊠])[iD], Wioletta Nowak[2][iD], and Anna Zarowska[2][iD]

[1] Tokyo Institute of Technology, Tokyo, Meguro, Japan
`nakayama@ict.e.titech.ac.jp`
[2] Wrocław University of Science and Technology, 50–370 Wrocław, Poland
`{wioletta.nowak,anna.sobaszek-zarowska}@pwr.edu.pl`

Abstract. A procedure for detecting cognitive impairment in senior citizens is examined using pupil light reflex (PLR) to chromatic light pulses and a portable measuring system. PLRs of both eyes were measured using blue and red light pulses aimed at either of the two eyes. The symptoms of cognitive function impairment were evaluated using a conventional dementia test during clinical surveillance. The extracted features of observed PLR waveforms for each eye remained at a comparable level for every group of participants. Three factor scores were calculated from the features, and a classification procedure for determining the level of dementia in a subject was created using regression analysis. As a result, the contribution of factor scores for blue light pulses on both eyes according to a participant's age was confirmed.

Keywords: Pupil · Pupil Light Reflex · Alzheimer's disease · Feature extraction · Logistic regression

1 Introduction

Symptoms of cognitive function impairment are used to diagnose Alzheimer's Disease (AD) and mild cognitive impairment (MCI). A major diagnostic procedure is the Mini-Mental State Examination (MMSE), which is based on a set of face-to-face clinical tests. These require participants to have sufficient communication skills, however. Therefore, a quicker and easier objective procedure should be developed using appropriate bio-makers. Pupillary responses are often observed to monitor mental activity as well as the pupil light reflex (PLR), which represents the dynamic characteristics of pupil behaviour [4,25].

The study of conventional PLR activity suggests that as this activity represents the visual information processing of retinal stimuli and the ability to activate neural signal transfers [5,12], it should be evaluated as an alternative means of diagnosing cognitive function impairment [3,26]. Also, PLR responses based on Melanopsin ganglion cells [15,21,40] can be applied to the study of Aged Macular Disease (AMD) and AD [8,15,21], and the possibility of their use

E. Ziemba et al. (Eds.): FedCSIS-AIST 2022/ISM 2022, LNBIP 471, pp. 91–107, 2023.
https://doi.org/10.1007/978-3-031-29570-6_5

in diagnosing these diseases has been studied [29,31,32,34]. A simple procedure to detect AMD and AD patients is required for medical and clinical staff who treat elderly people [33]. In a sense, a diagnostic procedure using ocular-motors may be an easy method, as it does not require verbal communication.

The authors have been conducting feasibility studies about how to conduct PLR observations at clinical institutions using a portable measuring system. During the current survey, additional elderly people were invited to participate, and their responses were analysed in order to examine the possibility of diagnostic prediction. Estimation performance and validity were evaluated. In this paper, the following points are addressed.

1. Features of PLRs for blue and red light pulses of the left and right eyes are compared, and the differences are extracted.
2. The ability of classifying participants as AD/MCI or normal control (NC) using MMSE scores and PLR features.
3. The contribution of the participant's age is also examined.
4. Procedures for predicting the performance of participants with AD or MCI are developed and evaluated.

The reminder of the paper is structured as follows. Section 2 reviews previous and related work. Section 3 introduces methodologies of experimental observation, such as feature characteristics of PLRs. Experimental results and regression analysis are detailed in Sect. 4. The Discussion and Conclusion of the results are summarised in the following sections.

2   Related Work

2.1   Diagnostic for Alzheimer's Disease (AD)

The study of Alzheimer's disease in clinical and pathological approaches has a long history [6,10]. Early diagnosis and appropriate treatment of the disease are required [35,36]. The diagnostic and testing procedures currently in use have been studied and their accuracy has often been discussed [2,7]. Though various clinical aspects of AD patients or patients with dementia, such as mild cognitive impairment (MCI) have been studied, the typical features which present AD symptoms have not yet been examined. Major diagnostic tools are almost always based on clinical and pathological measurement such as brain imaging and certain biomarkers [23,27] while clinical surveillance is frequently preferred using medical consultations.

Even so, clinical doctors have to diagnose using observations such as the MMSE (Mini-Mental State Examination) question inventory [11] or other procedures. As MMSE is used by observers to mark conditions during subject observation, the validity of the results depends on the activity of the targeted participant. Some improved consultation procedures are also being developed to enhance accuracy [38].

However, the diagnostic procedure is based on clinical observations using verbal communication. If the participants have sensor impairments, it may not be possible to conduct these types of tests. In another procedural approach to diagnosis, participant's behavioural responses, acoustic features of their spoken voice [17,24,41], gait features [1], and oculo-motors [31,32] have been analysed technically. Some new measurements using vision functions are also being studied to introduce new diagnostic approaches [8,26,39].

In particular, eye pupil reaction such as the pupil light reflex (PLR) is often referred to as one of the bio-markers for detecting AD patients since melanopsin related ganglion cells (ipRGC) have been discovered [14,21]. The detailed mechanism of the PLR and diagnostic procedures for detecting cognitive impairment based on ipRGCs and ipRGC-based PLRs have been studied [8,40]. Regarding the possibility of diagnosing AD patients, most conventional observations were conducted using a flash light and employing white light [13] of longer wavelengths, such as 585nm [5], 820nm [13], or other wavelengths [8,14]. The observation procedures and the characteristics extracted from PLRs have been discussed regularly. Some characteristics of PLR waveforms are extracted and compared with light wavelengths of colours such as blue or red [9,42] as suggested in previous works [18,20,21]. Though some PLR-based diagnostic prediction procedure using features of the waveforms are proposed [31,32], key features of PLRs and the appropriate procedures have not yet been extracted. As the previous studies have produced various successful assessments, feature extraction approaches to ipRGC based PLRs will be discussed in this work, with the most appropriate observation procedure for a PLR based diagnostic prediction procedures also being considered.

2.2 PLR Mechanism

Most of these procedures are based on the performance of signal transfer from retinal ganglion cells to the pretectal area via the optic chiasm, while the Edinger-Westphal (E-W) Nucleus also plays a major role in PLR [22,28,42]. Some impairment of the transfer path and the E-W Nucleus, such as neuronal loss, may influence AD patients [8,37]. Overall performance of the synaptic signal transfer may not be evaluated individually.

In the case of a proposed diagnostic procedure for Aged-Related Macular Disease (AMD) which also influences synaptic signal transfer, asynchronous PLR appearances between the eyes was focused on and evaluated quantitatively using waveform features [29]. It may be possible to consider using this type of experimental protocol to assess procedures for detecting symptoms in AD patients. These two diseases influence the extent of retinal damage or the contribution of photoreceptors and because they serve as pathways for signal transfer [22], they can be used as a means of simplifying AMD diagnosis [29]. In regards to the diagnostic issues, observation of these conditions should be focused on using the responses of each eye, even when the reactions of both eyes are measured synchronously. In most studies, the difference between the eyes is not considered since both pupils and eyes are thought of as changing synchronously, such as during consensual light response [42]. Also, similar processing can even be employed during diagnostic procedures which use PLR responses. This aspect should be considered using binocular synchronous observation in the analysis. For example, the following experiment may be introduced so that the PLR responses of both eyes are evaluated separately when either eye is irradiated by short or long wavelength light pulses. Therefore, the performance of the retinal signal transfer pathway of either eye and the reflex response signal transfer pathways of both eyes could be evaluated when a light pulse is presented to either eye. The following experiment introduces binocular pupillary observations in response to light pulses on either eye as a means of inducing chromatic stimulus.

2.3 Participant Factor

Most AD patients and persons presenting symptoms of dementia, including MCI, are elderly and almost all are receiving medication to treat health problems. In addition to individual differences including cognitive performance [16], pupil size generally decreases with age due to senile miosis. Cataract of the lens may also influence sensitivity to PLRs. In order to create a detection procedure for AD patients, a comparison of patients and normal control (NC) subjects is required initially. Even NC persons may exert some influence over their PLR responses.

Fundamentally, recruiting AD and MCI patient volunteers may not be easy once the experimental procedure is ethically approved [32]. Even a clinical doctor may only ask a limited number of candidates to participate. Therefore, most experiments have to be conducted by employing a small number of patients. If the number of participants grows, the condition of each individual with dementia and their health issues should be considered carefully during the evaluation of the results of experiments. Also, measured pupillary data should be carefully processed since participants may not be able to control blink and eyelid lift during observation. At minimum, the age and cognitive ability test scores of participants are required, but the deviations caused by individual differences need to be considered.

In order to invite elderly people to participate in an observation experiment which contained a balance between patients and NC group participants, family members of patients were encouraged to join so that a sufficient number of observations of additional elderly people could be made.

3 Method

Pupil light reflex was observed in senior citizens who may be AD patients, pseudo-positive participants, or have no cognitive impairment i.e., normal.

3.1 Experimental Procedure

Participants were introduced to a temporary dark space, where the 5 following experimental sessions were conducted for 10 s each.

Fig. 1. Equipment to observe pupillary changes

1. Condition1: Control session without light pulses
2. Condition2: Blue light pulse to the right eye
3. Condition3: Blue light pulse to the left eye
4. Condition4: Red light pulse to the right eye
5. Condition5: Red light pulse to the left eye

The experiment is designed to study the influence of light pulses on synaptic connections between both eyes in response to light pulses to either eye. Light pulses transfer from retinal ganglion cells on the irradiated eye to sphincters of both eyes via the Edinger-Westphal Nucleus, as mentioned above. The processes of miosis and restoration were observed in all 4 sessions. A short relaxation break was inserted between each session.

The size of pupil responses were measured in pixels 60 Hz using equipment with blue and red light sources, as shown in Fig. 1 (URATANI, HITOMIRU). The light sources were blue (469nm, $14.3cd/m^2$, 6.5lx) and red (625nm, $12.3cd/m^2$, 10.5lx). The size of both pupils during all conditions was measured. Blink artefacts were removed manually after measurement.

The experiment was conducted by a clinical physician at a medical institution, and the procedure was approved by an ethics committee of Osaka Kawasaki Rehabilitation University.

3.2 Participants

Valid data was obtained from 101 participants, of which 66 were female and 35 were male. Their mean age was 78.5 and the SD (standard deviation) was 8.9 years. Participants at a medical institute were selected, and an MMSE test was conducted. The results were classified into three groups according to MMSE scores. These were AD (Alzheimer's disease, with MMSE<=23), MCI (Mild cognitive impairment, with MMSE<=27) and others, whose conditions was NC (Normal Control). The distribution was as follows:

- AD: 31 (F:21, M:10), Mean age: 83.0, SD: 6.3 years.
- MCI: 9 (F:5, M:4), Mean age: 82.1, SD: 6.3 years.
- NC: 61 (F:40, M:21), Mean age: 75.6, SD: 9.2 years.

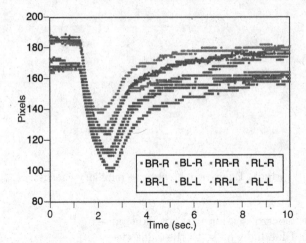

Fig. 2. Examples of PLR of both eyes for four conditions (NC participant, 76yo, M), categories:[light colour][irradiated eye]-[observed eye]

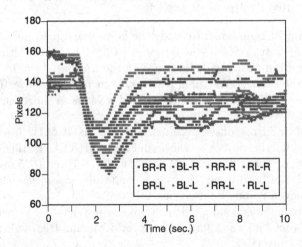

Fig. 3. Examples of PLR of both eyes for four conditions (AD participant, 87yo, F), categories:[light colour][irradiated eye]-[observed eye]

As the age of participants may influence their condition, four age levels were created: less than 66 years old (0), 66–75 years old (1), 76–85 years old (2), above 85 years old (3). Though participants were elderly and might have some health problems, these points were not considered during the following analysis.

Table 1. Features of PLR

Variables	Definitions
RA	Relative Amplitude of miosis
t_min	Time at minimum size
diff_min	Minimum differential of size
t_diff_min	Time at minimum differential
diff_max	Maximum differential of size
t_diff_max	Time at maximum differential
diff2_min	Minimum acceleration
t_diff2_min	Time at minimum acceleration
diff2_max	Maximum acceleration
t_diff2_max	Time at maximum acceleration

4   Results

4.1   PLR Waveforms

An example of PLR waveforms for a NC participant is shown in Fig. 2. The horizontal axis represents time, and the vertical axis represents pupil size in pixels for the experimental conditions 2–5. There are some differences in pupil size between the left and right eyes at the initial point. The legend "BR-R" means that Right pupil response when Blue light irradiates the Right eye, and also "RL-R" means that Right pupil response when Red light irradiates the Left eye. Also, levels of contraction are different between conditions, as in the previous work which presented PLR responses to blue or red light pulses [21]. Another example of an AD patient is shown in Fig. 3. Some typical features are observed, such as deviation during the restoration process after constriction. Several features of waveforms were extracted in order to compare groups of participants in relation to the previous study [31], as shown in Table 1.

The first hypothesis is that there is a feature difference between the left and right eyes when light pulses are directed at either eye. The hypothesis was examined using a t-test of features of both eyes, such as between the irradiated eye and the non-irradiated eye. The features were extracted from standardised waveforms in order to reduce the potential differences.

In the results of the test, there are no significant differences in any of the features. There were a few exceptions, but the results did not coincide with the results of either colour of light pulse.

4.2   Regression Analysis Based on Factor Scores

Since every feature includes measurement errors and individual differences, the latent factors are extracted using factor analysis according to the method used in the previous study [31].

The results of factor analysis are shown as a factor loading matrix in Table 2. In this paper, three factors are employed, and the overall contribution ratio of

Table 2. Factor loading matrix for PLR features

Variables	Factor1	Factor2	Factor3
diff_min	**0.87**	−.13	0.09
diff2_min	**0.76**	0.06	0.16
diff2_max	**−.83**	−.17	0.22
diff_max	−.36	0.08	0.15
RA	−.24	**0.78**	−.09
t_min	0.22	**0.73**	0.14
t_diff2_min	−.13	−.00	**0.49**
t_diff_min	−.05	−.03	0.36
t_diff_max	−.11	0.23	0.36
t_diff2_max	0.06	0.07	0.30

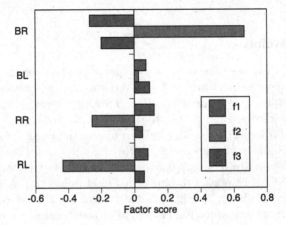

Fig. 4. Comparison of factor scores between stimuli (f1~f3: factor scores for factors 1–3)

the factors is 45.5%. Factor 1 represents the differential rate and acceleration of pupillary change, Factor 2 represents the features of contraction such as relative amplitude and its time, and Factor 3 represents the times for the differential rates and acceleration, as mentioned in Factor 1.

Three factor scores are calculated using the factor loading matrix. When the scores of both eyes are compared, there are also no significant differences.

The factor scores for experimental conditions are summarised and compared in Fig. 4. Changes in Factor-2 scores suggest a continuous decrease according to the experimental conditions. Also, there are significant differences in the three factor scores for blue and red stimuli. Within each colour stimulus condition, there are significant differences in the three factor scores for blue light pulses, and significant differences in Factor-2 scores for red light pulses ($t(402) = 2.13, p <$ 0.05). The differences between sessions using the same colour condition should

Table 3. Prediction models using factor scores of PLRs

Model	Variables	AUC
1	9 factor scores	0.77
2	9 factor scores + age group	0.84
3	9 factor scores + age	0.84
4	Selected variables: 5 factor scores + age group	0.84

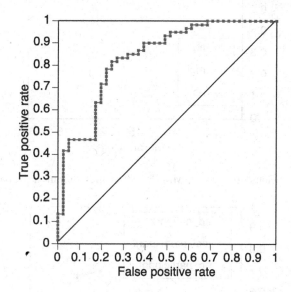

Fig. 5. ROC for Model 2 (AUC = 0.84)

be considered, and in particular the differences for blue light should be evaluated separately.

In addition, the factor of age level on factor scores is examined using two-way ANOVA of participant groups and age levels. Though the factor for the participant groups is not significant, the factor for age level is significant for Factor-1 scores ($F(3, 801) = 19.9, p < 0.01$), and the interaction between the two factors (age and participant group) is also significant ($F(2, 801) = 9.4, p < 0.01$). Therefore, the factor of age may affect the differential and the acceleration of pupillary change, as presented in Factor-1 scores.

The influence of a subject's level of dementia on PLR features was not confirmed in the above analysis. The factors of stimulus light wavelength and the age of the patient were significant and are the major components of the deviation. In order to examine the effectiveness of the extracted features for a prediction of cognitive function impairment, an estimation procedure using a logistic analysis which had been introduced in a previous study [31] was conducted. Here, both MCI and AD patients are merged as the "AD+MCI" group since the number of MCI participants is limited. The probability of cognitive impairment is calculated

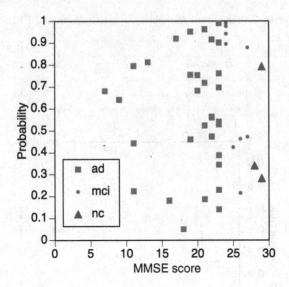

Fig. 6. Relationship between MMSE scores and computed probabilities

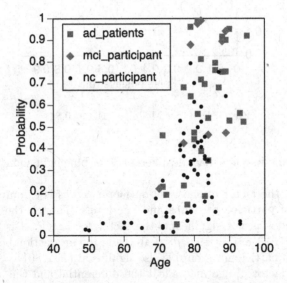

Fig. 7. Change in probability according to participant's age

using factor scores for each participant. As there are no significant differences between eyes, averaged features of responses of both eyes are employed. In considering the differences between session stimuli, two sets of features for blue light conditions and averaged features for red light conditions are introduced, for a total of 9 variables altogether.

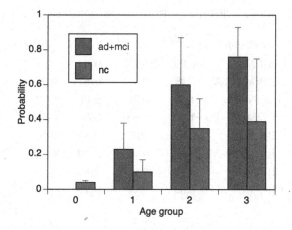

Fig. 8. Comparison of mean probabilities between AD+MCI and NC groups

Table 3 shows a summary of several prediction models and AUC (Area under the Curve) as an index of accuracy of binary classification for a ROC (Receiver Operating Characteristic Curve). Since the threshold for classification may depend on the diagnostic policy, such as reducing the False positive rate, accuracy is evaluated using AUC. An example of ROC for Model 2 is illustrated in Fig. 5. Model 1 consists of 9 factor scores, Models 2 and 3 include age level or age. Model 4 employs significant contributing variables using a step-wise selection technique. Participant's age information aids classification performance.

Probabilities for the classification of cognitive impairment based on Model-2 are calculated, and the relationships between MMSE scores and the probabilities are summarised in Fig. 6. The horizontal axis represents MMSE scores, and the vertical axis represents probability. Participants who were tested using MMSE are plotted in the figure according to their participant group, AD, MCI or NC. Confirmation of the contribution of a participant's age is shown in Fig. 7, where the horizontal axis represents age. In this figure, cognitive impairment can be observed in subjects over 70 years old, and the probability increases markedly from around 70 onward. When the threshold for AD+MCI is set to 0.5, 80% of participants are classified correctly. The AUC is 0.84 as shown in Table 3.

Mean probabilities for the groups of AD+MCI and NC by age level are summarised in Fig. 8, in order to evaluate the contribution of age level. Overall, mean probabilities increase with age level. In particular, the probability of AD+MCI increases over age 75, while mean probability of NC remains under 0.5. Model-4 in Table 3 was generated using a variable selection procedure. All 5 selected variables are factor scores for blue light pulses during two test sessions, and factor scores for red light pulses were not used. The AUC fitting index is comparable with the values of the other functions. This suggests the possibility that prediction can be made using responses to blue light pulses. A more detailed examination of this topic will be summarised in the following discussion section.

Table 4. Correlation coefficients for PLR waveforms between left and right eyes

Condition	1.0-2.5s	2.5-3.5s	3.5-10s	0.0-10s
BR:NC	0.99	0.98	**0.84**	0.97
BR:MCI+AD	0.99	0.97	**0.87**	0.97
BL:NC	1.00	0.99	**0.90**	0.98
BL:MCI+AD	1.00	0.99	**0.85**	0.97
RR:NC	0.99	0.97	**0.82**	0.96
RR:MCI+AD	0.99	0.96	**0.73**	0.97
RL:NC	0.99	0.96	**0.83**	0.96
RL:MCI+AD	0.99	0.96	**0.78**	0.96

5   Discussion

In the first hypothesis, cognitive impairment may be affected by the influence of the oculomotor nerve, which connects retinal ganglion cells to the pretectal area on the synaptic path. However, no significant differences in the extracted features were observed during several chromatic light pulses, though there were some differences between the experimental sessions, as shown in Fig. 2. One of the possible reasons is the dependence on the accuracy of measurement, because feature extraction is based on point estimation. In particular, the small pupils of senior citizens may influence the measurement of temporal change of pupil size. Another problem may be that the extracted features focused on the constriction phase of PLRs without allowing for the restoration phase which follows. The difference in PLR between the left and right eyes should be measured carefully in considering the above points. During the main analysis, the AD+MCI group was set as the specific target for prediction. As a diagnostic application, the level of cognitive impairment needs to be able to be estimated using features of PLRs if it is to be effective. If it is possible, AD and MCI should be classified using weighted levels.

The factor scores for blue but not red light pulses were selected once more for use in a regression model, following a step-wise procedure. The dominance of blue light pulses for prediction was confirmed in a previous study [31,32]. The possible reason for this may be based on the first hypothesis, which could not be confirmed according to the above evaluation, however. Therefore, a more detailed analysis needs to be conducted.

During the above waveform analyses, most features of both eyes were extracted from the constriction phase between 1.0 and 2.5 s. As the initial hypothesis states, the differences between eyes, such as a direct-irradiated eye and a non-irradiated eye, was examined using a statistical mean differential test. In the results, there was no significant difference and the hypothesis was rejected. However, some differences in waveform shapes are observed in Fig. 3, which illustrates the responses of an AD patient. Here, a more detailed analysis is tried using a simple mutual correlation analysis of two PLR waveforms for the left and right eyes. If the two eyes react synchronously, the correlation coefficient approaches 1. In considering the reaction phases such as constriction and the two stages of restoration, correlation coefficients are calculated and summarised across three phases for each stimulus condition in Table 4.

The overall correlation coefficients are presented in the right hand column, and nearly all approach the value of 1 (0.96–0.98). During the initial phases (1.0–2.5 s and 2.5–3.5 s), the coefficients approach 1 since the dynamical reaction occurred simultaneously during constriction and early restoration phases. The coefficients decrease to less than 0.9 during late restoration phase (3.5–10 s), however. These coefficients suggest asynchronous responses between the two eyes. In particular, coefficients for MCI-AD participants are less than 0.8 when red light pulses are used. This suggests that differences in response of some patients may have occurred as part of the conventional light response mechanism. Though pupil responses during the second stage of restoration are studied as a post-illumination pupil response (PIPR) [19,42], the synchronicity between the two eyes is not discussed sufficiently. As the phase difference appeared after the constriction phase, the reaction mechanism should be discussed carefully once more if the internal information processing for single eye irradiation with short and long wavelength light influenced responses. In regards to the hypothesis in this work, the details of this phenomenon could be resolved by referring to previous studies. Also, waveform features for the late restoration phase should be considered in the diagnostic procedure.

In addition to the above issues, there are some obvious limitations to this study. The first point is the accuracy of classification of patients. During the examination, the diagnostic category is only based on MMSE scores measured during consultations with a medical doctor. The degree of disease progress should be evaluated objectively. Also, the NC group may include some people who are patients. In this study, other metrics of cognitive functional ability have been observed, such as VSRAD (Voxel-based Specific Regional analysis system for Alzheimer's Disease), HDS-R (Hasegawa's Dementia Scale-Revised) and MoCA-J (a Japanese version of the Montreal Cognitive Assessment test). The development of an alternative diagnostic procedure which considers the level of cognitive function together with these metrics will be a subject of our further study. Even the design of the experimental conditions may have been insufficient. PLR responses were only observed for 10 s under certain conditions following a low intensity 1 s light pulse. Usually, observations should be conducted using at least two levels of light intensity. The second restoration phase after light pulse needs to be recorded for over 30 s in order to properly examine pupillary dynamics.

A revised experimental design which considers these limitations should be discussed. This will also be a subject of our further studies.

6   Conclusion

A procedure for detecting the level of cognitive impairment of senior citizens is examined using pupil light reflex (PLR) for chromatic light pulses and portable measuring equipment. Features of PLRs are compared between blue and red light pulses.

1. PLRs between left and right eyes are compared when light pulses are directed at either eye. In addition, the latent factor scores of PLR features are also extracted. There are no significant differences in features and factor scores between the left and right eyes, however.
2. Factor scores and participant's ages were analysed in order to classify individuals into groups such as AD+MCI and NC. Participant's age information contributed to classification of the groups. During the regression analysis using a variable selection procedure, factor scores for blue light pulses were extracted. PLRs for blue light pulses are key to accurate prediction.

As stated above, a more accurate prediction procedure and improvement of the method of analysis of the response mechanisms will be subjects of our further study.

Acknowledgements. This research was partially supported by the Japan Science and Technology Agency (JST), Adaptable and Seamless Technology transfer program through target driven R&D (A-STEP) [JPMJTM20CQ, 2020–2022].

The authors would like to thank Prof. Masatoshi Takeda and Prof. Takenori Komatsu of Osaka Kawasaki Rehabilitation University, Toshinobu Takeda, MD at the Jinmeikai Clinic, Yasuhiro Ohta and Takato Uratani of the Uratani Lab Company Ltd. for their kind contributions,

This paper is an extended version of the conference paper which has been presented at the 17th Conference on Computer Science and Intelligence Systems [30]. The authors also would like to thank the reviewers for their comments.

References

1. Aoki, K., et al.: Early detection of lower MMSE scores in elderly based on dual-task gait. IEEE Access **7**, 40085–40094 (2019). https://doi.org/10.1109/ACCESS.2019.2906908
2. Arevalo-Rodriguez, I., Segura, O., Solà, I., Bonfill, X., Sanchez, E., Alonso-Coello, P.: Diagonostic tools for Alzheimer's disease dementia and other dementias: an overview of diagnostic test accuracy (DTA) systematic reviews. BMC Neurol. **14**(183), 1–8 (2014). https://doi.org/10.1186/s12883-014-0183-2
3. Asanad, S., et al.: The retinal choroid as an oculavascular biomarker for Alzheimer's dementia: A histopathological study in severe disease. Alzheimer's & Dementia: Diagnosis, Assessment & Diesease Monitoring **11**, 775–783 (2019). https://doi.org/10.1016/j.dadm.2019.08.005
4. Beatty, J.: Task-evoked pupillary response, processing load, and the structure of processing resources. Psychol. Bull. **91**(2), 276–292 (1982). https://doi.org/10.1037/0033-2909.91.2.276
5. Bittner, D.M., Wieseler, I., Wilhelm, H., Riepe, M.W., Müller, N.G.: Repetitive pupil light reflex: Potential marker in Alzheimer's disease? J. Alzheimers Dis. **42**, 1469–1477 (2014). https://doi.org/10.3233/JAD-140969

6. Breijyeh, Z., Karaman, R.: Comprehensive review on Alzheimer's disease: causes and treatment. Molecules **25**(5789), 1–28 (2020). https://doi.org/10.3390/molecules25245789

7. Chávez-Fumagalli, M.A., et al.: Diagnosis of Alzheimer's disease in developed and developing countries: systematic review and meta-analysis of diagnostic test accuracy. J. Alzheimer's Disease Reports **5**, 15–30 (2021). https://doi.org/10.3233/ADR-200263

8. Chougule, P.S., Najjar, R.P., Finkelstein, M.T., Kandiah, N., Milea, D.: Light-induced pupillary responses in Alzheimer's disease. Front. Neurol. **10**(360), 1–12 (2019). https://doi.org/10.3389/fneur.2019.00360

9. Feigl, B., Zele, A.J.: Melanopsin-expressing intrinsically photosensitive retinal ganglion cells in retinal disease. Ophthalmol. Visual Sci. **91**D(8), August 2014. https://doi.org/10.1097/OPX.0000000000000284

10. Ferrari, C., Sorbi, S.: The comlexity of Alzheimer's disease: an evolving puzzle. Physiol. Rev. **101**, 1047–1081 (2021). https://doi.org/10.1152/physrev.00015.2020

11. Folstein, M.F., Folstein, S.E., McHugh, P.R.: MINI-MENTAL STATE - a practical method for grading the cognitive state of patients for the clinician. J. Psychiatr. Res. **12**, 189–198 (1975). https://doi.org/10.1016/0022-3956(75)90026-6

12. Fotiou, D.F., Setergiou, V., Tsiptsios, D., Lithari, C., Nakou, M., Karlovasitou, A.: Cholinergic deficiency in Alzheimer's and Parkinson's disease: evaluation with pupillometry. Int. J. Psychophysiol. **73**, 143–149 (2009). https://doi.org/10.1016/j.ijpsycho.2009.01.011

13. Fotiou, D., Kaltsatou, A., Tsiptsios, D., Nakou, M.: Evaluation of the cholinergic hypothesis in Alzheimer's disease with neuropsychological methods. Aging Clin. Exp. Res. **27**(5), 727–733 (2015). https://doi.org/10.1007/s40520-015-0321-8

14. Frost, S., Kanagasingam, Y., Sohrabi, H., Bourgeat, P., Villemagne, V., Rowe, C.C., Macaulay, L.S., Szoeke, C., Ellis, K.A., Ames, D., Masters, C.L., Rainey-Smith, S., Martins, R.N., Group, A.R.: Pupil response biomarkers for early detection and monitoring of Alzheimer's disease. Curr. Alzheimer Res. **10**(9), 931–939 (2013). https://doi.org/10.2174/15672050113106660163

15. Gamlin, P.D., McDougal, D.H., Pokorny, J.: Human and macaque pupil responses driven by melanopisn-containing retinal ganglion cells. Vision. Res. **47**, 946–954 (2007). https://doi.org/10.1016/j.visres.2006.12.015

16. Haj, M.E., Chapelet, G., Moustafa, A.A., Boutoleau-Bretonnière, C.: Pupil size as an indicator of cognitive activity in mild Alzheimer's disease. EXCLI J. **21**, 307–316 (2022). https://doi.org/10.17179/excli2021-4568

17. Jarrold, W., et al.: Aided diagnosis of dimentia type through computer-based analysis of spontaneous speech. In: Proceedings of Workshop on Computational Linguistics and Clinical Psychology: From Linguistic Signal to Clinical Reality, pp. 27–37. Association for Computational Linguistics (2014). https://doi.org/10.3115/v1/W14-3204

18. Kankipati, L., Girkin, C.A., Gamlin, P.D.: The post-illumination pupil response is reduced in Glaucoma patients. Visual Neurophysiol. **52**(5), 2287–2292 (2011). https://doi.org/10.1167/iovs.10-6023

19. Kankipati, L., Girkin, C.A., Gamlin, P.D.: Post-illumination pupil response in subjects without ocular disease. Invest. Ophthalmol. Visual Sci. **51**(5), 2764–2769 (2010). https://doi.org/10.1167/iovs.10-6023

20. Kardon, R.H., Anderson, S.C., Damarjian, T.G., Grace, E.M., Stone, E., Kawasaki, A.: Chromatic pupillometry in patients with retinitis pigmentosa. Ophthalmology **118**(2), 376–381 (2011). https://doi.org/10.1016/j.ophtha.2010.06.033

21. Kawasaki, A., Kardon, R.H.: Intrinsically photosensitive retinal ganglion cells. J. Neuroophthalmol. **27**, 195–204 (2007)
22. Kelbsch, C., et al.: Standards in pupillography. Front. Neurol. **10**(129), 1–26 (2019). https://doi.org/10.3389/fneur.2019.00129
23. Khoury, R., Ghossoub, E.: Diagnostic biomarkers of Alzheimer's disease: a state-of-the-art review. Biomarkers Neuropsychiatry **1**, 1–6 (2019). https://doi.org/10.1016/j.bionps.2019.100005
24. Klumpp, P., Fritsch, J., Noeth, E.: ANN-based Alzheimer's disease classification from bag of words. In: Proceedings of Speech Communication; 13th ITG-Symposium, pp. 1–4. IEEE (2018). https://ieeexplore.ieee.org/document/8578051
25. Kuhlmann, J., Böttcher, M. (eds.): Pupillography: Principles. Methods and Applications. W. Zuckschwerdt Verlag, Munchen (1999)
26. Lim, J.K.H., et al.: The eye as a biomarker for Alzheimer's disease. Front. Neurol. **10**(536), 1–14 (2016). https://doi.org/10.3389/fnins.2016.00536
27. Marcucci, V., Kleiman, J.: Biomarkers and their implications in Alzheimer's disease: a literature review. Expl. Res. Hypothesis Med. **6**(4), 164–176 (2021). https://doi.org/10.14218/ERHM.2021.00016
28. McDougal, D.H., Gamlin, P.D.: Autonomic control of the eye. Compr. Physiol. **5**(1), 439–473 (2015). https://doi.org/10.1002/cphy.c140014
29. Nakayama, M., Nowak, W., Ishikawa, H., Asakawa, K., Ichibe, Y.: Discovering irregular pupil light responses to chromatic stimuli using waveform shapes of pupillograms. EURASIP J. Bioinf. Syst. Biol. **2014**(1), 1–14 (2014). https://doi.org/10.1186/s13637-014-0018-x
30. Nakayama, M., Nowak, W., Zarowska, A.: Detecting symptoms of dementia in elderly persons using features of pupil light reflex. In: Proceedings of the Federated Conference on Computer Science and Information Systems (FedCSIS), pp. 745–749 (2022). https://doi.org/10.15439/2022F17
31. Nowak, W., Nakayama, M., Kręcicki, T., Hachoł, A.: Detection procedures for patients of Alzheimer's disease using waveform features of pupil light reflex in response to chromatic stimuli. EAI Endorsed Trans. Pervasive Health Technol. **6**, 1–11 (2020). https://doi.org/10.4108/eai.17-12-2020.167656, e6
32. Nowak, W., Nakayama, M., Kręcicki, T., Trypka, E., Andrzejak, A., Hachoł, A.: Analysis for extracted features of pupil light reflex to chromatic stimuli in Alzheimer's patients. EAI Endorsed Trans. Pervasive Health Technol. **5**, 1–10 (2019). https://doi.org/10.4108/eai.13-7-2018.161750, e4
33. Nowak, W., Nakayama, M., Trypka, E., Zarowska, A.: Classification of Alzheimer's disease patients using metric of oculo-motors. In: Proceedings of the Federated Conference on Computer Science and Information Systems (FedCSIS), pp. 403–407 (2021). https://doi.org/10.15439/2021F32
34. Oh, A.J., et al.: Pupillary evaluation of melanopsin retinal ganglion cell function and sleep-wake activity in pre-symptomatic Alzheimer's disease. PLoS ONE **14**(12), 1–17 (2019). https://doi.org/10.1371/journal.pone.0226197
35. Porsteinsson, A., Isaacson, R., Knox, S., Sabbagh, M., Rubino, I.: Diagnosis of early Alzheimer's disease: clinical practice in 2021. J. Prevent. Alzheimer's Disease **8**, 371–386 (2021). https://doi.org/10.14283/jpad.2021.23
36. van der Schaar, J., et al.: Considerations regarding a diagnosis of Alzheimer's disease before dementia: a systematic review. Alzheimer's Res. Therapy **14**(31), 1–12 (2022). https://doi.org/10.1186/s13195-022-00971-3
37. Scinto, L., Frosch, M., Wu, C., Daffner, K., Gedi, N., Geula, C.: Selective cell loss in Edinger-Westphal in asymptomatic elders and Alzheimer's patients. Neurobiol. Aging **22**(5), 729–736 (2001). https://doi.org/10.1016/s0197-4580(01)00235-4

38. Tombaugh, T., McDowell, I., Kristjansson, B., Hubley, A.: Mini-mental state examination (MMSE) and the modified MMSE (3MS): a psychometric comparison and normative data. Psychol. Assess. **8**(1), 48–59 (1996). https://doi.org/10.1037/1040-3590.8.1.48
39. Turner, R.S., Stubbs, T., Davies, D.A., Albensi, B.C.: Potential new approaches for diagnosis of Alzheimer's disease and related dementia. Front. Neurol. **11**(496), 1–10 (2020). https://doi.org/10.3389/fneur.2020.00496
40. Zele, A.J., Adhikari, P., Cao, D., Feigl, B.: Melanopsin and cone photoreceptor inputs to the afferent pupil light response. Front. Neurol. **10**(529), 1–9 (2019). https://doi.org/10.3389/fneur.2019.00529
41. Zhou, L., Fraser, K.C., Rudzicz, F.: Speech recognition in Alzheimer's disease and in its assessment. In: Proceedings of INTERSPEECH 2016. pp. 1948–1952. ISCA (2016). https://doi.org/10.21437/Interspeech. 2016–1228
42. Zivcevska, M., Blakeman, A., Lei, S., Goltz, H.C., Wong, A.M.F.: Binocular summation in postillumination pupil response driven by melanopsin-containing retinal ganglion cells. Vis. Neurosci. **59**, 4968–4977 (2018). https://doi.org/10.1167/iovs.18-24639

Assessment of Optimisation Results for Shared Cars

Janis Bicevskis[1]($\boxtimes$) (iD), Viesturs Spulis[2] (iD), Zane Bicevska[1] (iD), and Ivo Oditis[1] (iD)

[1] Department of Computing, University of Latvia, Raina Boulevard 19, Riga 1586, Latvia
{Janis.Bicevskis,Zane.Bicevska,Ivo.Oditis}@lu.lv
[2] DIVI Grupa Ltd., Avotu Street 40a-33, Riga 1009, Latvia
Viesturs.Spulis@di.lv

Abstract. This study is devoted to the assessment of potential additional income obtainable by dynamically relocating shared e-vehicles. The model describes one-way trips and dynamic relocations of e-vehicles between sectors by service personnel according to a dynamically compiled list of service trips. A MIP (Mixed-Integer Programming) type algorithm is used to optimize the transfer of dynamically selected e-vehicles. The developed solution has been implemented and validated for its practical application in Riga, Latvia. The study resulted in two types of assessments: (1) simulating e-vehicle relocations for different numbers of cars and service personnel resulted in an estimate of revenue growth between 9% and 18% compared with service income without an e-vehicle transfer, (2) relocation of shared cars according to a system-generated dynamically compiled optimized list of trips allowed the company to raise potential revenue by 29% to 52%, compared with relocations based on service personnel intuition and experience. The results demonstrate the efficiency of optimization algorithms for dynamic planning of shared e-vehicles' relocations.

Keywords: Shared cars · Optimization of relocations · Mixed-Integer Programming

1 Introduction

The UN has developed the programme Agenda 2030, which aims to address many of the pressing problems of human life, including the goal of moving to green economy. Karl Burkart [9] defined a green economy as based on six main sectors: Sustainable transport, Renewable energy, Green buildings, Water management, Waste management and Land management. This work will analyse the possibility of developing public transport by introducing widely shared e-vehicles, which could replace the individual transport systems currently in use.

According to [7] vehicle sharing systems benefit both users and the society in general. The two main benefits for individual users include reduced personal transport costs and improved mobility. Researches have shown that car sharing reduces the average number of kilometers travelled by a vehicle and is likely to reduce traffic congestions [11] and CO_2 emissions [25]. Ensuring mobility at affordable prices for economically vulnerable

E. Ziemba et al. (Eds.): FedCSIS-AIST 2022/ISM 2022, LNBIP 471, pp. 108–126, 2023.
https://doi.org/10.1007/978-3-031-29570-6_6

groups is another societal benefit of such public transport systems. The process without reservation enables the customer to receive information on the available e-vehicle on the city map. The customer can go to an e-vehicle location knowing that at this time another customer can take the same e-vehicle for his trip. If it happens, the client can repeatedly choose another e-vehicle and repeat the process. In cases where many e-vehicle are available, the client risks a little while not using the reservation process.

Compared to traditional vehicle rental systems the development and operation of e-vehicle (automotive) sharing systems face additional technological and practical challenges. The relatively limited autonomy of the currently available electric cars requires the recharging of vehicles multiple times in the case of longer trips. This can only be carried out at specific charging stations. Furthermore, e-vehicle charging time is significantly longer than the refueling of motor vehicles powered by internal combustion engines. Accrued statistics show that an e-vehicle used within the city area must be charged on average every three days. Because of high costs, the number of charging stations is sparse, and the total charging time can be quite long.

Vehicle rental approaches tend to be classified in two large groups [15]:

1. traditional rental - when customers receive and transfer vehicles after use at specially arranged points of leasing firms and rental will take one or more days;
2. vehicle sharing - when vehicles can be taken for use anywhere, even for a short time slot, and may be left anywhere at the end of the trip.

Vehicle sharing has quickly gained popularity. The growth rate of the service has particularly increased during the COVID-19 pandemic, as it allows urban populations to avoid the need to travel to their destination via public transport.

The main challenge facing e-vehicle sharing rental systems is to achieve the optimal (the most profitable) deployment of vehicles in a city. This requires relocating e-vehicles quickly to the most profitable sectors of the city which in turn causes additional costs. For example, the studies of [27] show that technical relocation of vehicles takes approximately 14% of the total distance carried out by the e-vehicles. Optimization algorithms are used to address this problem, which gives users or system holders recommendations on the need to relocate vehicles to achieve a "more cost-effective" deployment and, hence, higher returns.

The research is an extension of the previous studies published in [3–5, 22]. This paper focuses less on the design and optimisation of shared cars systems but focuses on assessing the effectiveness of optimized dynamic relocation of e-vehicles implemented within the framework. The study processed two types of assessments:

1. Simulating e-vehicle relocations for different numbers of cars and service personnel resulted in an estimate of revenue growth between 9% and 18% compared with service revenues without an e-vehicle transfer, and the relocation plans were generated rapidly (within 15 min).
2. Relocation of shared e-vehicles using a system-generated a dynamically compiled optimized list of service trips allowed the company to raise revenue from 29% to 59%, compared with relocations based on the experience of service staff.

The assessments obtained lead to the conclusion that the use of dynamic e-vehicle relocation is appropriate in shared cars systems.

The paper is structured as follows: a theoretical background on vehicle sharing models (Sect. 2), an original vehicle sharing model proposed by the authors (Sect. 3), a short discussion on the research findings (Sect. 4), and conclusions (Sect. 5).

2 Theoretical Background

This chapter deals with the results of other e-vehicle sharing studies that are necessary for discussing the ideas and solutions proposed.

2.1 Review of Sharing Models

The development of mobile communication infrastructure has opened the possibility to create electric vehicle (e-vehicle) sharing systems. In theoretical studies, they are considered at three levels:

- The strategic level determines the number of e-vehicle available for sharing and the maximum number of e-vehicle to be placed in each urban sector.
- At the tactical level, historical vehicle sharing data is used to assess the profitability of an e-vehicle depending on the season, the day of the week, the usage time and the city sector in which the e-vehicle is placed.
- At the operational level, the total daily income is estimated as a sum of the average expected income over a specific period of time from all e-vehicles placed in a specific sector.

2.1.1 Strategic Level

The strategic level corresponds to long-term decisions, with a horizon longer than a year. The most significant issues discussed in the literature are related to data, business models and system design. Two types of data are crucial for design and operation of a system:

- data describing demand, such as trip history, demographic information, mobility and travel-related variables, personal attitudes, and perceptions of e-vehicles,
- data describing system, such as configuration, city terrain characteristics and elevation, parking locations, and weather conditions.

Data about demand is recorded during system's operations in the past, e.g. trip history, or it is collected using preferences' surveys [1, 16] where respondents make decisions in hypothetical situations. Additionally, data about demand can be extracted from mobile phone trajectory of the users [21].

Using the data about demand, different models prediction models can be built. Such models estimate if users will prefer the offered serviceinstead of other transportation systems [1, 16]. In addition, the users may have a choice among different types of shared vehicles, such as between conventional and electric bikes, or among different systems configurations. The methodologies for building such models include logit models [1, 16], risky-choice behaviour models, or simulation [15].

The demand data, together with location characteristics and weather data, may also be used to model and forecast the average usage of a system for a certain period, such as hourly or daily. Here, the forecast may be at the station level [18], or at the zone level, which is usually used for free-floating e-vehicle systems. The forecast is created by using binomial models [18], microsimulation [1], or queuing theory [12].

At the strategic level, the authors approach the problem both from the operator's and user's points of view. In other words, the objective is to maximize the profitability of the system or the user's satisfaction. However, it is more common that the user satisfaction is incorporated in the performance measures which are modeled as constraints. The solution methodologies include optimization models, simulation tools, and various exact and heuristic algorithms.

2.1.2 Tactical Level

The bridge between the strategic and operational levels is defined by the tactical level. This section covers works from the literature coping with the mid-term decisions. There are three major aspects discussed in the literature: (1) demand modeling and pricing, (2) fleet sizing, and (3) system evaluation.

Demand modeling includes number of daily trips forecasting, the reaction of the users when pricing incentives are proposed, and what happens when a new type of mode is introduced into an already existing system.

The influencing factors on the number of daily trips can be determined using linear regression, user equilibrium models [19], or random intercept multilevel models [24]. The results of Li show that the fleet size, distribution and rental-parking price significantly influence the usage of free-floating systems. Furthermore, [24] observe that weather conditions, daylight, and employment are among the influencing factors.

Logit models can then be used to forecast the number of daily trip demand [18]. Moreover, the developed models can be compared using the number of daily trips' forecast as a performance measure. This way, the operator understands the demand structure in mid-term, and decides on the pricing strategy and the type of campaigns.

On the supply side, the most investigated challenge is the fleet sizing, as mentioned in [19]. For this purpose, the works either optimize the fleet size [7, 14, 17] or analyze the effect of it on the system [26]. One of the interesting aspect is combination of problems from different decision levels, such as network design [14, 26] and vehicle rebalancing [14, 17].

At the tactical level, a strong emphasis is put on the analysis of the system's usage, and the number of daily trips. Decisions made at the strategic level must also be reconsidered when more precise knowledge of the demand is available. Finally, it appears that several tactical decisions are supported by policy evaluation methods.

2.1.3 Operational Level

The last element of the framework consists of the operational level decisions. These decisions are concerned with the short-term time horizon. Therefore, the works that address daily/hourly operations and decisions are reviewed. Four main aspects are discussed in the literature with respect to this level: (1) demand forecasting, (2) dynamic pricing, (3) truck and staff routing for rebalancing and maintenance, and (4) system evaluation.

The demand forecasting models are designed to come up with the hourly demand per station/zone or the expected number of vehicles at stations/zones [2]. The main concern appears to be the correlation structures. This model is created for each sub-city district which makes it appropriate for usage in station-based systems. Instead of rebalancing operations, the balance of the system can be maintained by vehicle assignment and relays which denotes sequentially taking two vehicles to complete longer trips. Zhang works on such a strategy and uses a space-time-battery network flow model. This model is an extension of the conventional space-time network flow model where each node represents a specific pair of location and time. In the model, battery information is also included in nodes. The demand is assumed to be known, and the problem solution assigns trip requests to the available vehicles. Unassigned requests are rejected. The solution is obtained by a heuristic algorithm guided by linear programming (LP) relaxations. Through extensive numerical experiments, the authors demonstrate that the proposed approach could consistently obtain satisfactory solutions. E-vehicles may achieve a higher utilization rate compared to non-electric vehicles.

An interesting conclusion regarding the operational level is deduced by Yuan [17]. The holistic approach that they follow in their work help them to compare the value of three decision levels. The case study conducted with Changping in Beijing for 10 years showed that the rebalancing costs were 5.7% of the total cost whereas the capital cost was 79% and the maintenance cost was 15.3%. It shows that operational activities do not play as much role as the strategic and tactical decisions.

The literature focuses mainly on rebalancing operations at the operational level decisions. Both simulation and optimization methods are used to propose solutions for these operations. Since we talk about short-term decisions, the computational complexity is another burden at this level. As considering continuous time frames increases the computational complexity, the authors tend to discretize the time and use time-expanded networks.

2.2   Commercial Solution of E-Vehicle Sharing

Although scientific literature on e-vehicle sharing is broad, the authors of other works as well as the authors of this study conclude that the scientific literature currently available does not offer a model that, along with parameters such as the number, size and location of charging stations, the size of the car fleet, would also consider the dynamics of vehicle relocations and system balancing when the reserving of e-vehicles is used. The existing models [20] overview station locations either without considering vehicle relocations or assuming only a limited subset of stations corresponding to the current demand should be serviced. If vehicle relocations are modeled [20], vehicle movements costs are only considered at the end of the operating period (usually daily) and, therefore, affect the size of the available fleet [7].

According to [8] which studies an example of a city in Southern California, even 3–6 e-vehicles can be sufficient to provide 100 trips daily and achieve optimal customer waiting times. Meanwhile, about 18–24 e-vehicles would be enough to reduce the required number of e-vehicle relocations. The authors conclude that, in addition to the number of e-vehicles the relocation algorithm and the charging approach used are key factors for the successful use of such a system.

[7] highlights the importance of the service level, which, in his view, influences the access of potential users to e-vehicle stations, i.e. (1) the distance between the location of the e-vehicle and the destination resp., from the point of start and arrival of the e-vehicle, and (2) the availability of e-vehicles at stations. On the other hand, the number and size of the stations and the size and availability of the e-vehicle park at "real time" at the "particular station" are affected by the costs of establishing and operating the e-vehicle sharing system.

According to the classification of [15] the e-vehicle sharing system analyzed in this paper is:

- commercial solution as the aim is to generate maximum income,
- station-based – e-vehicles are deployed in any available parking place and the city is divided into areas - stations,
- one-directional as the customer is allowed not return the e-vehicle to the start point of the trip,
- with relocations as the service staff moves e-vehicles to potentially more favorable places in the city,
- with dynamic booked trips as an e-vehicle may be rented by the customer anywhere, at any time without prior e-vehicle reservation.

Increased profits for commercial e-vehicle sharing can be achieved by supplying vehicles to the places in a city where customers will need them with the highest probability as well as increasing the relocation efficiency. The e-vehicle sharing models proposed by other authors differ significantly from those proposed in this work.

2.3 Deployment of Shared E-Vehicle Relocations

This chapter provides a brief description of the model for shared e-vehicles that was implemented in Riga City. The model consists of several successive steps:

- dividing the city into sectors and estimating the costs of moving e-vehicles between sectors;
- determining the value of an e-vehicle in a specific sector and time;
- profitability estimation of the e-vehicle at a given moment before relocation;
- profitability estimation of the e-vehicle after relocation;
- compiling a list of profitable relocations;
- optimization of relocation plans;
- relocation of cars according to relocation plans.

According to [17] the continuous division of the transport sharing service area into the sectors (other studies referred to as stations) does not significantly affect optimization. However, division of territory into sectors must be carried out under several conditions:

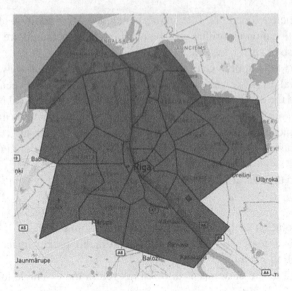

Fig. 1. Division of Riga, Latvia in sectors (using OpenStreetMap)

1. The sectors need to be relatively small to place a vehicle in the area for the client to reach within "reasonable" times (the accumulated real data set shows that customers are ready to spend up to five minutes for reaching a vehicle).
2. Secondly, the driving time between two adjacent sectors must be comparable.
3. Thirdly, within one sector, customers' behavior must be comparable, i.e., customers make trips from the respective sector uniformly frequently.

By cluster analyzing the history of trips and knowing the specific characteristics of the area, Riga was divided into sectors as can be seen in Fig. 1.

2.4 Forecasting User Trips and Estimation of Sectors' Income

While sharing e-vehicle users in Riga do not make all requests a day in advance, Certain user trips can be scheduled with high possibility, using historical trip data. Using cluster analysis, you can find "routine arcs": regular trips that consistently start and end the day from day to day in the same sectors, at approximately the same times.

The purpose of relocation is to place e-vehicle in areas where they are in demand and profits are expected accordingly. In sharing systems with booking in advance, a full estimate of demand and expected profit is known prior to the planning of relocation operations. But in our case, requests are made in real time, without prior bookings of e-vehicles. Therefore, to take tactical decisions on relocation operations, it is necessary to be able to carry out an alternative assessment to which stations to move the e-vehicles.

One potential solution that this study looks at is the modelling of expected income using historical data. The model of expected incomes describes the average expected benefits over a specific time period from a e-vehicle parked in a particular sector that can be rented by users. The expected income most probably will vary from station to station, as well as it will change over a day: In "peak hours" the expected income will be higher, in "quiet hours" less.

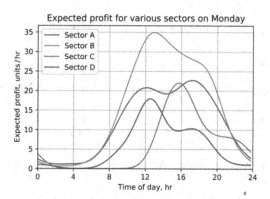

Fig. 2. Expected income for the sectors on Monday

Modelling the expected incomes may not only provide tactical support in the planning of resettlement operations, but also give general impression on the behavior of sharing e-vehicle users. Comparing the expected income at different times, different weekdays and different stations, it will be possible to draw conclusions that can also help you to make strategic, long-term decisions, such as handling different sectors or deploying charging stations.

Estimated forecasted incomes on Monday for the four sectors are summarized in Fig. 2. Data shows that there are significant differences between revenues for different sectors, as well as expected income changes by day. Moreover, some of the sectors can be very profitable only in specific time intervals and unprofitable in all others. For example, in the morning it is more convenient to move a car to sector D than to sector C, but after 1 PM a car in Sector C will be more profitable than a car parked in Sector D. These findings empirically indicate that it is essential to analyze how the expected daily income changes.

There is a difference in estimated income for a particular sector between weekdays. From simple assumptions about the behavior of e-vehicle sharing users, it can be expected that demand for sharing cars, so expected income, could vary significantly between business days and holidays.

Indeed, such a phenomenon can be observed in estimated expected income for the sector A, as shown in Fig. 3. Although there is a variation in expected income between business days, there is a very significant difference in expected income on holiday.

In other sectors, however, there is a more significant difference in expected income between other days of the week. For example, in the sector E (Fig. 3) incomes on Mondays and Sundays are slightly lower than in the rest of the week.

As there is a significant but hard-to-predict difference between weekdays, it is necessary to calculate the expected earnings for each day of the week separately.

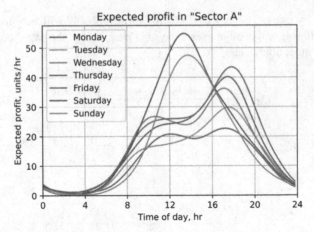

Fig. 3. Expected income in "Sector A" in different days of week

2.5 Variation in Historical Data

A related subject matter related to the modelling of forecasted income from historical data is how old historical data is effectively used. Since the number of sharing cars is final, it may be considered necessary to use a maximum history that could reduce "noise" in the data obtained. However, as a counter argument for the use of historical data, it can be mentioned that user demand for shared cars is not static but is changing in result of seasonal or other long-term processes.

This variation points to the need to find a balance between the amount of data used and the relevance of the historical data when calculating the expected income. It is also concluded that, in order to keep the calculation of the intended income used up to date, the expected in-come should be re-calculated on a regular basis.

In the definition and calculation process described above, there is an assumption that the estimated income for a particular e-vehicle parked in a sector does not depend on the total number of parked e-vehicles in that sector. If large number of e-vehicles parked in the same sector, you can see that this assumption is flawed; if the number of e-vehicles parked in the sector significantly exceeds the demand for shared e-vehicle in this sector, the average per e-vehicle income will be low.

2.6 Car-Sharing Income Optimization by E-Vehicle Relocation

Increasing income is possible by moving the cars from low-income sectors to higher-potential sectors, but of course taking into account the costs of relocation. The location of e-vehicles at a given time determines the total value of all e-vehicles. This can be increased by moving the e-vehicle between sectors and finding the optimal location with the highest possible value.

The work of optimization is primarily inspired by the Mixed-Integer Programming (MIP) model proposed by C. Gambella, E. Malaguti, F. Masini, and D. Vigo for optimizing relocation operations in electric car-sharing [23]. The parameters discussed in the previous sections are passed to the optimization algorithm and it finds a new e-vehicle location by sectors that give the highest potential revenue, as well as a relocation plan to obtain this location. An exact e-vehicle optimization model, expressed in a set of appropriate parameters is given in [22].An optimization algorithm that was matching to the task of this study is the Mixed-Integer Programming model, which maximizes profits on the assumption that next trips, the availability of fixed stations and availability of relocation staff are known.

[13] indicates that the algorithm has been tested for a relatively small number of scheduled trips and vehicles: 14 stations, 20 e-vehicles, 2 relocators, 120 trips booked on the previous day. The optimal timing, according to data provided by the algorithm's authors, has been calculated in approximately 20 min.

The model described in [13] has a deficiency from model of this study. It is designed on the assumption that future trips are known, e.g., customers order the vehicles indicating starting and ending stations and the duration of the trip. Originally, the authors examined the possibility of predicting customer trips based on the data history of many previous trips. However, the experiments failed to obtain a sufficiently reliable forecast for future trips, so this idea was rejected. On the other hand, if the trips' forecast is not sufficiently precise, the model defined by [13] does not provide a credible relocation plan, i.e., the vehicles will possibly be moved to places where customers will not need them. Although a reliable forecast of all daily trips was not obtained, it was found that up to 20% of trips could be predicted up to one hour and station accuracy. This benefit is further used in the author's solution.

Consequently, the [13] algorithm is not used directly in the study, but the authors have developed an original algorithm as a part of an optimization model.

2.7 Relocations Plan Execution

Every morning, staff carrying out e-vehicle resettlement receive a task – e-vehicle relocation plan prepared by the Q program The plan specifies the e-vehicles to be relocated, the sector from which the e-vechicle should be moved, as well as the time intervals in which the transfer is to be made. Relocations specified in the plan must be made within a short period of time (e.g., 2 h); immediately after that the service staff receives a new plan prepared during the execution of the first plan, taking into account the new deployment of e-vehicles by sectors. The plan contains two types of relocations: (1) transfers delivering e-vehicles to charging stations, (2) transfers aimed at increasing the income of the company by moving e-vehicles to "more profitable" sectors.

Two objectives have been set for a given study:

(RQ-1) assess the utility of dynamically made relocations by comparing the company's income if the transfers were not carried out at all with the income generated by dynamic relocations.

(RQ-2) assess the utility of dynamically performed transfers by comparing the company's income if the relocations were made on the basis of subjective decisions (intuition) with the income derived from relocations of e-vehicles to dynamically calculated optimized relocation plans.

The corresponding source code with data samples and the Docker container compilation file is publicly available at GitHub: https://github.com/divi-lv/share-optimize. A description of the tool using and data preparing is available in the README.md file.

3 Research Findings

The study is a continuation of the two studies carried out in the past, where the first [10] describes the shared cars system model and the algorhythm of e-vehicle relocation optimization, and the second is devoted to the architecture of the model implementation [8]. The aim of the study is to assess the effectiveness of the developed shared cars system Q. First, dynamic e-vehicle relocations to urban sectors with expected higher income are simultated and the probability of using the optimization algorithm in real time is evaluated (*RQ-1*). Assessments have been carried out in theory, simulating the functioning of the system, and practically recording data during actual use of the system (*RQ-2*).

3.1 Input Data for Cars Relocation

Four data sets serve as an input for a system that works to the described model.:

- division of territory into sectors (list of sectors);
- a list of historically occurred trips (for the assessment of possible "revenues" of the sectors);
- the current list of cars, including their localisation and battery charging levels as a percentage;
- a list of service staff with their locations according to the sectors.
  The variable parameters are:
- week day and time when the relocations are to be started;
- number of time slots during which the car relocations are to be carried out.
  Additional configuration details are:
- duration of time slots;
- the maximum number of relocations per car (may be less than the maximum number of passengers in the car);
- the percentage of the car battery at which the car is considered to be rechargeable (i.e., it must be charged before further use);
- maximum allowed calculation time (if the calculation exceeds this time, the system returns a suboptimal result).

3.2 Output of System

The system prepares and delivers:

- A relocation plan for the service staff broken down by the scheduled time slots, indicating whether the relocation staff moves the car during the time slot or not.
- A relocation plan for the cars broken down by the scheduled time slots, indicating which e-vehicles are be recharged at the end of the transfer and which not.
- An assessment of the potential "profits" of cars before and after completing the optimized relocations.
  The following data volume was used whilst running the Q system:
- the number of sectors in the area can reach 40 units;

- the maximum number of service staff: 10 people;
- the number of cars in the area: 60 units;
- only 20% of the sectors have charging capabilities.
    The following decision model for performance control was used:
- the optimization task should be solved within 15 min for an area divided into 30 sectors, eight available service people and 50 cars;
- if no optimal transfer list is found during a 15-min operation, a list of the corresponding transfers for the best possible solution found is stored (a suboptimal relocation plan).

The Q system was created as an autonomous-working docker container with input and output data files placed on a mounted storage, thereby enabling data files to be exchanged with the calculation service.

3.3 System Usage Scenario

System's operation is divided into three steps:

1. Assessment of potential "income" for sectors. The first step uses sector data and the available trips' history. Trips are arranged according to sectors, weekdays and starting time to determine the possible "income" of one car at a specified time in different sectors for each moment.
2. Creating lists of possible connections. Lists are created with possible transfers between sectors. Each connection receives a "weight" assigned representing the monetarian potential of relocations.
3. Solving of the optimization task. A MIP (Mixt-Integer Programming) optimization task is solved by using a set of SCIP tools [23].

MIP algorithm uses as input data:

- a list of sectors;
- the potential "income" of the sectors calculated in the first step;
- intersectoral coinnections created in the second step;
- available cars, indicating their localisation and battery charging levels;
- list of service staffs and their locations.
    The operation of the system results in:
- the value of vehicles' total potential income at initial time slot and maximised potential income in result of optimization;
- relocations' plan for staff;
- car relocation plan.

3.4 Results of Theoretical Assessments

The developed system is used for real car sharing service. In the first phase (*RQ-1*), the performance of the implementation of the optimization algorithm was measured and the potential results were evaluated in theory by optimizing e-vehicle transfers and measuring income growth. In the second phase (*RQ-2*), the operation of the system was assessed in real-life sutuations by relocating e -vehicles according to relocation plans proposed by the system and comparing the results obtained with historical data.

The prototype tests used the available real environmental data - initially reduced but later full-scale system data. The results of the various test data are summarised in the following table (Table 1):

Table 1. Results of test cases

Time slots	9	7	7	5
Number of cars	60	56	12	40
Number of sectors	57	30	30	30
Number of service staffs	5	7	2	5
Number of proposed relocations	22	23	9	9
Potential income (cumulated)	78156	55272	8244	50220
Potential income after relocations	95210	58350	16703	57185
Increase of potential income (%)	18%	9%	51%	12%
Calculation time in minutes	15	15	2	6

- The first experiment (see the second column of Table 1) was executed in a real-life situation with 60 cars deployed in 57 sectors, five service people and and nine time slots. After 15 min of calculating, a relocation plan with 22 proposed transfers was created thus achieving an 18% increase of the potential income.
- The other 3 columns provide 3 more experimental data: one with similar characteristics (in the third column), two with smaller numbers of cars and sectors selected.

3.5 Practical Assessment

There are several limiting factors for assessing the systems functioning in the real use environment. The first and most significant of the restrictions is that the company works seven days a week for 24 h a day. Stopping the system or restricting the service may result in loss of business and, not least, unexplainable unavailability of the service to customers.

The second restrictive factor is the total number of e-vehicles used in the system. In different periods of operation, the company has had 90 to 95 cars in total. In order to extend the approbation to the whole vehicle fleet, a significant amount of additional personnel should be involved in the relocation of cars.

Thirdly, the situation is changing from day to day, i.e. every morning 8:00 cars have been parked differently, a different number of cars are available, they have different levels of battery charging and customers are travelling different from previous days during the day. Accordingly, it is not possible to repeat directly, for example, the one-day situation and to assess with and without the use of the transfers proposed by the system.

However, comparing the results of two relocation teams was selected to assess the operation of the system.:

- both teams had the same number of members;
- each team had 20 e-vehicles for operation (relocation to specific points) during the specified day;
- one of the teams, called A-Team, makes transfers according to a relocation plan provided by the Q system; the second team, called M-Team, works according to the practices used by employees before (employees take relocation decisions according to the operational situation and their intuition);
- whereas the optimization algorithm uses the maximum number of e-vehicles, the required number of cars to be relocated was reduced in proportion to the number of e-vehicle available to teams;
- the results of teams' work are compared at the end of the day comparing the average of the potential "income" changes when following relocation plans and the average real daily income per one car.

For a specific day, the results of the two teams can be compared if the sets of e-vehicles are comparable. And the e-vehicles must be easy to identify in the information system. Therefore, in each of the test days, cars were selected in order of numbers on car number plates, i.e. the cars with numbers within specified intervals are assigned to each team. At the beginning of the day, the average potential "income" of e-vehicles is assessed for each of the teams. In cases where the M-Team (worked according to existing practices) had a lower score than the A-Team (operated using the transfers offered by the system), some of e-vehicles were ex changed to make the starting positions as similar as possible. Analogously, the charging situations for cars of both teams were matched.

Since 20 e-vehicles out of 100 is a large enough pool, only in rare cases an exchange of cars was necessary (for example, the selected e-vehicle was located in another city). The e-vehicles' total potential "incomes" were generally comparable for both teams. The same situation was with e-vehicle batteries: The most of e-vehicles were charged at the beginning of a day. Therefore, the average e-vehicle charge level for randomly selected sets of 20 e-vehicle was close.

3.6 Results of Practical Assessments

Since the assessment of potential "income" is purely indicative (i.e. this value allows a comparison of the potential income of two e-vehicle according to their "state") these figures were reduced 1000 times for practicability reasons. Therefore, the assessments of potential "income" differ so much between the theoretical examples and the practical ones.

Although the tests were carried out six times (six days), only four were considered valid because:

- in one of the days, team workers mixed up the cars assigned for relocation according to different approaches,

Table 2. Initial average "income" potential for the teams

Test date	A-Team	M-Team
2022.04.21	0.26	0.26
2022.04.27	0.26	0.25
2022.04.28	0.25	0.24
2022.05.03	0.16	0.24

- in one of the days for technical reasons, two of the cars were not available for one of the teams.

The tests carried out on 21, 27, and 28 April 2022 and 3 May 2022 were accepted for use. The initial potential income of test days is given in the following table (Table 2).

As can be seen in Table 3, regardless of the initial state, A-Team has shown better results during the day, i.e. the change of a potential "income" has been higher for the cars relocated by the A-Team. Similarly, the distance of transfers has generally been shorter and also fewer relocations have been made.

It is important to note that during the first days of the tests, M-Team did not know the potential income ratings of the city's sectors, but as of April 27, that data was available to all teams. At the same time, it should be said that sectoral assessment is naturally predictable: in the city centre, the potential "income" is higher than on the outskirts. However, there are also specific sector characteristics. In Old Riga, for example, the potential "income" ir low until 3 PM but ir grows rapidly until 6 PM. It was possible to use this knowledge when planning transfers and cars' locations, but this knowledge did not improve the outcome of M-Team's activities.

Table 3. Assessments of relocations by days and teams

Date	Team	Average change of potential "income" per relocation	Average relocation distance	Number of relocations
2022.04.21	A-Team	0.17	6.72	22
	M-Team	0.12	7.03	24
2022.04.27	A-Team	0.23	8.61	21
	M-Team	0.14	10.53	24
2022.04.28	A-Team	0.18	7.16	20
	M-Team	0.1	10.26	23
2022.05.03	A-Team	0.23	8.73	16
	M-Team	0.13	8.7	23

At the end of each test day, the daily car incomes were also identified, i.e. how much money the company's customers paid for using e-vehicles. The finansial results show a more successful performance of A-Team as in all test days A-Team generated a 20% higher income than M-Team.

We can also conclude that simply the knowledge of "valuable" sectors is not sufficient to manage e-vehicle sharing successfully - the value of the sectors changes during a day and different days of a week. It is difficult to track tracking the changes of situation and evaluate future valuable relocations manually.

However, in spite of the success of the prototyping process, it should be acknowledged that planning for each next two hours (or even shorter periods) for the company's fleet (90–100 cars) is not fast enough for 6 concurrently working relocation people and 57 urban sectors. The mechanism can be well applied in nights after 10 PM. 00 when when the use of e-vehicle is declining rapidly and a longer period of time may be available for calculation. Savukārt, efektīvai plānošanai dienas laikā būtu svarīgi uzlabot aprēķinu ātrumu, lai pārvietojumu plāns varētu tikt iegūts piecu minūšu laikā. It would be important to improve the calculation rate during the day for effective scheduling so that the relocation plan can be obtained within five minutes.

4   Discussion on Research Findings

4.1   Usage of Historical Data

The described method for calculating of expected income is based on the existence of historical data. Unlike demographic-based models, the described model cannot be used when starting a sharing e-vehicle rental system in a new city, or by expanding operations into new sectors.

Reliance on historical data prevents a model from repid responding to changes in demand for shared e-vehicle, or to price policies. The described expected income estimation algorithm will work most accurately if variations in the shared e-vehicle system are minimal.

Small sectors may lack data to adequately calculate expected income due to data noise. This phenomenon limits the lower size of sectors, thereby affecting the constructing of sectors.

4.2   Models of Car Sharing and Performance Requirements

The vehicle sharing model proposed in the study is considered to be only one step in reaching an optimal solution. The model only partly describes real-life processes, such as e-vehicle can vary between battery capacity and technical parameters. It was assumed that all e-vehicles are similar.

The study offers an algorithm that optimizes expected income by offering appropriate e-vehicle transfers. When implementing an algorithm, special attention should be paid to its performance as optimization must be performed dynamically, with a few hours interval.

5 Conclusion

The study offers a model for the use of sharing e-vehicles, described as a commercial system with one-way trips and the dynamic relocations of e-vehicles between city sectors, without pre-booked trips. The model uses the following set of parameters: breakdown of the city in sectors, maximal number of available e-vehicle, number of e-vehicle per sector, set of possible relocations, parameters characterizing e-vehicle relocations, number of available relocators.

Simulation and practical application of the system shall give the following conclusions [30]:

- e-vehicle dynamic relocation to higher-yielding sectors deliver an income growth between 9% and 18%. This assessment is obtained by relocating 60 e-vehicles between 57 sectors of Riga City by five service people. The assessment depends on many factors - time components (hours, days, seasons, etc.), e-vehicle placement sectors beforetheir relocation, number and capacity of charging stations etc. Therefore, the assessment obtained is approximate.
- The implementation of the optimization algorithm by allowing a new relocation plan to be generated for a maximum of 15 min shall ensure that the system is used with a dynamically performed e-vehicle relocation relocation plan re-generated every 2 h.
- The study compares the potential income in two cases: where e-vehicles are moved to more profitable sectors based on the experience (intuition), and when a system-generated optimized relocation plans are used. Experiments carried out show that potential revenue in the second case is 29% to 52% higher. The assessments obtained, like above, are approximately.

The vehicle sharing model proposed in the study is only one step in reaching an optimal solution. The model only partly describes real-life processes, such as e-vehicle can vary between battery capacity and technical parameters and prices. These parameters have not been considered in the given model, and their research may be the content of further studies.

Acknowledgements. This work has been supported by University of Latvia project AAP2016/B032 "Innovative information technologies".

References

1. Aguilera-García, A., Gomez, J., Sobrino, N.: Exploring the adoption of moped scooter-sharing systems in Spanish urban areas. J. Cities **96**, 102424 (2020). https://doi.org/10.1016/j.cities.2019.102424
2. Ashqar, H.I., Elhenawy, M., Rakha, H.A.: Modeling bike counts in a bike-sharing system considering the effect of weather conditions. Case Stud. Transp. Policy **7**, 261–268 (2019). https://doi.org/10.1016/j.cstp.2019.02.011
3. Bicevskis, J., Nikiforova, A., Karnitis, G., Oditis, I., Bicevska, Z.: Optimization of processes for shared cars. In: Proceedings of the 17th Conference on Computer Science and Intelligence Systems. ACSIS, vol. 30, pp. 763–767 (2022). https://doi.org/10.15439/2022F87

4. Bicevskis, J., Nikiforova, A., Karnitis, G., Oditis, I., Bicevska, Z.: Risks of concurrent execution in e-commerce processes. In: Proceedings of the 16th Conference on Computer Science and Intelligence Systems. ACSIS, vol. 25, pp. 447–451 (2021). https://doi.org/10.15439/202 1F70

5. Bicevskis, J., Karnitis, G., Bicevska, Z., Oditis, I.: Analysis of concurrent processes in internet of things solutions. In: Ziemba, E., Chmielarz, W. (eds.) FedCSIS-AIST/ISM-2021. LNBIP, vol. 442, pp. 26–41. Springer, Cham (2022). https://doi.org/10.1007/978-3-030-98997-2_2

6. Ivo, O, Viesturs, S, Janis, B: Optimization of relocation processes for shared e-vehicles. Baltic J. Mod. Comput. **10**(2), 185–204 (2022). https://doi.org/10.22364/bjmc.2022.10.2.07

7. Boyacı, H., Zografos, K.G., Geroliminis, N.: An optimization framework for the development of efficient one-way car-sharing systems. Eur. J. Oper. Res. **240**(3), 718–733 (2015). https://doi.org/10.1016/j.ejor.2014.07.020

8. Brandstätter, G., et al.: Overview of optimization problems in electric car-sharing system design and management. In: Dawid, H., Doerner, K.F., Feichtinger, G., Kort, P.M., Seidl, A. (eds.) Dynamic Perspectives on Managerial Decision Making. DMEEF, vol. 22, pp. 441–471. Springer, Cham (2016). https://doi.org/10.1007/978-3-319-39120-5_24

9. Burkart, K.: Environment & Sustanaibility. https://www.ioes.ucla.edu/person/karl-burkart/. Accessed 15 Dec 2022

10. Ciari, F., Schuessler, N., Axhausen, K.W.: Estimation of carsharing demand using an activity-based microsimulation approach: model discussion and some results. J. Sustain. Transport. **7**, 70–84 (2013). https://doi.org/10.1080/15568318.2012.660113

11. Crane, K., Ecola, L., Hassell, S., Natarah, S.: An alternative approach for identifying opportunities to reduce emissions of greenhouse gases. Technical report, RAND Corporation (2012). https://www.rand.org/pubs/technical_reports/TR1170.html

12. Çelebi, D., Yörüsün, A., Işık, H.: Bicycle sharing system design with capacity allocations. J. Transp. Res. Part B Methodol. **114**, 86–98 (2018). https://doi.org/10.1016/j.trb.2018.05.018

13. Gambella, C., Malaguti, E., Masini, F., Vigo, D.: Optimizing relocation operations in electric car-sharing. Omega **81**, 234–245 (2018). https://doi.org/10.1016/j.omega.2017.11.007

14. Huang, K., An, K., de Almeida Correia, G.H.: Planning station capacity and fleet size of one-way electric carsharing systems with continuous state of charge functions. Eur. J. Oper. Res. **287**, 1075–1091 (2020). https://doi.org/10.1016/j.ejor.2020.05.001

15. Illgen, S., Höck, M.: Literature review of the vehicle relocation problem in one-way car sharing networks. J. Transport. Res. Part B Methodol. **120**, 193–204 (2019). https://doi.org/10.1016/j.trb.2018.12.006

16. Jin, F., Yao, E., An, K.: Analysis of the potential demand for battery electric vehicle sharing: mode share and spatiotemporal distribution. J. Transport. Geogr. **82**, 102630 (2020). https://doi.org/10.1016/j.jtrangeo.2019.102630

17. Yuan, M., Zhang, Q., Wang, B., Liang, Y., Zhang, H.: A mixed integer linear programming model for optimal planning of bicycle sharing systems: a case study in Beijing. Sustain. Cities Soc. **47**, 101515 (2019). https://doi.org/10.1016/j.scs.2019.101515

18. Kutela, B., Teng, H.: The influence of campus characteristics, temporal factors, and weather events on campuses-related daily bike-share trips. J. Transport. Geogr. **78**, 160–169 (2019). https://doi.org/10.1016/j.jtrangeo.2019.06.002

19. Li, Q., Liao, F., Timmermans, H.J., Huang, H., Zhou, J.: Incorporating free-floating car-sharing into an activity-based dynamic user equilibrium model: a demand-side model. J. Transp. Res. Part B Methodol. **107**, 102–123 (2018). https://doi.org/10.1016/j.trb.2017.11.011

20. Lin, J.R., Yang, T.H.: Strategic design of public bicycle sharing systems with service level constraints. J. Transport. Res. Part E Logist. Transport. Rev. **47**(2), 284–294 (2011). https://doi.org/10.1016/j.tre.2010.09.004

21. Miao, H., Jia, H., Li, J., Qiu, T.Z.: Autonomous connected electric vehicle (ACEV)-based car-sharing system modeling and optimal planning: a unified two-stage multi-objective optimization methodology. Energy **169**, 797–818 (2019). https://doi.org/10.1016/j.energy.2018.12.066

22. de Almeida Correia, H., Antunes, A.P.: Optimization approach to depot location and trip selection in one-way carsharing systems. J. Transport. Res. Part E Logist. Transport. Rev. **48**(1), 233–247 (2012). https://doi.org/10.1016/j.tre.2011.06.003

23. SciPy documentation: Multidimensional image processing, scipy.ndimage. gaussian_filter. https://docs.scipy.org/doc/scipy/reference/generated/scipy.ndimage.gaussian_filter.html

24. Scott, D.M., Ciuro, C.: What factors influence bike share ridership? An investigation of Hamilton, Ontario's bike share hubs. Travel. Behav. Soc. **16**, 50–58 (2019). https://doi.org/10.1016/j.tbs.2019.04.003

25. Shaheen, S.A., Cohen, A.P.: Carsharing and personal vehicle services: worldwide market developments and emerging trends. Int. J. Sustain. Transport. **7**(1), 5–34 (2013). https://doi.org/10.1080/15568318.2012.660103

26. Soriguera, F., Jiménez, E.: A continuous approximation model for the optimal design of public bike-sharing systems. Sustain. Cities Soc. **52**, 101826 (2020). https://doi.org/10.1016/j.scs.2019.101826

27. Vasconcelos, A.S., Martinez, L.M., Correia, G.H., Guimarães, D.C., Farias, T.L.: Environmental and financial impacts of adopting alternative vehicle technologies and relocation strategies in station-based one-way carsharing: an application in the city of Lisbon, Portugal. J. Transport. Res. Part D Transport. Environ. **57**, 350–362 (2017). https://doi.org/10.1016/j.trd.2017.08.019

28. Vine, S.L., Sivakumar, A., Polak, J.: Traveller preferences for free-floating carsharing vehicle allocation mechanisms. J. Transport. Res. C Emerg. Technol. **102**, 1–19 (2019). https://doi.org/10.1016/j.trc.2019.02.019

29. Zhang, D., Liu, Y., He, S.: Vehicle assignment and relays for one-way electric car-sharing systems. J. Transp. Res. Part B Methodol. **120**, 125–146 (2019). https://doi.org/10.1016/j.trb.2018.12.004

30. Ziemba, E., Chmielarz, W. (eds.): ISM 2020, and FedCSIS-IST 2020. LNBIP. Springer, Cham (2020). https://doi.org/10.1007/978-3-030-71846-6

31. Zografos, K., Geroliminis, G.: An optimization framework for the development of efficient one-way car-sharing systems. Eur. J. Oper. Res. **240**, 718–733 (2015). https://doi.org/10.1016/j.ejor.2014.07.020

Students' Perception of Online Learning During the COVID-19 Pandemic: Polish and Ukrainian Perspectives

Dariusz Dymek[1] , Svitlana Didkivska[1] , Mariusz Grabowski[1] ,
Grażyna Paliwoda-Pękosz[1 (✉)] , and Tetiana Anatoliivna Vakaliuk[2]

[1] Krakow University of Economics, Rakowicka 27, Krakow, Poland
{dymekd,grabowsm,paliwodg}@uek.krakow.pl,
d2023@student.uek.krakow.pl
[2] Zhytomyr Polytechnic State University, Chudnivska St, 103, Zhytomyr, Ukraine
tetianavakaliuk@gmail.com

Abstract. The COVID-19 pandemic prompted a rapid shift to online learning at universities, leading to an acceleration of changes directed at creating more inclusive education models. The goal of this research is to explore various aspects of online learning patterns, including students' online behavior, and attitude towards online communication. The study incorporates qualitative and qualitative data analysis. Based on 1562 survey responses from Polish and Ukrainian students, it has been found that there are still differences in digital competencies between men and women, which may be rooted in traditional gender roles. The analysis of students' attitudes towards online education also identified both positive and negative aspects of this form of learning, providing insight into areas that could be improved. The main research limitation stems from the interpretative nature of the findings, which have restricted generalization power. The research findings may be useful in shaping future educational policies at Polish and Ukrainian universities.

Keywords: online education · online behavior · teaching mode · perception of online learning

1 Introduction

The COVID-19 pandemic has triggered research concerning online education and the future of education [5]. The main investigated paths include organization of online learning [3, 4], students' and teachers' attitude towards online learning [1], and students' wellbeing [12]. Online learning has the potential to deepen the equality, fairness, and inclusion among the members of the society, providing these opportunities globally, including Poland [18] and Ukraine [6, 25]. It should be noted that online learning gives the opportunity for wider access to education for unprivileged people, i.e. inhabitants of rural areas, poor members of some ethnic groups and/or people with disabilities [11, 15, 22]. The issue of online activities of students and the impact of the COVID-19 pandemic

E. Ziemba et al. (Eds.): FedCSIS-AIST 2022/ISM 2022, LNBIP 471, pp. 127–147, 2023.
https://doi.org/10.1007/978-3-031-29570-6_7

on these activities (especially their impact on the learning process) has disturbed the minds of scientists around the world.

For example, a study in Egypt examines the perceptions of higher education students regarding their engagement and satisfaction with online learning during the COVID-19 lockdown. It looks at the impact of students' personal factors such as academic self-efficacy, as well as the online learning environment and teaching presence on their engagement and satisfaction. It is suggested that this might help higher education institutions in creating plans for incorporating online learning as a permanent aspect of their education system [10].

A study in Indonesia notes that the pandemic has changed the education paradigm by forcing the implementation of online learning. It points out that students have diverse perceptions of online learning during the pandemic: some students have a positive perspective and see it as an opportunity for independent learning, while other students have a negative perspective and see it as ineffective and limiting [23].

Another study on the paradigm shift in education was conducted in the USA. The research highlights several key findings related to online learning during the pandemic. These include the need for clear expectations and accountability for students who have not chosen remote instruction, the lack of engagement with professors and peers reported by students, and the need for instructors to be aware of potential increased collaboration among students to adjust assignments and grading methods accordingly, and the issue of access to reliable technology for some students [20]. In addition to studies of the impact of online learning on the level of education in the United States, attention was also paid to the impact of the changes in behavioral patterns on people's mental health [24]. Thus, a significant increase in the number of students with depression and suicidal thoughts was found, even in comparison with other results of similar studies in pandemic times, for example from China [16, 24].

However, all these works agree on one thing - the need for further research and expanding the data sample by adding information about the impact of the pandemic on students' online activities (taking into account their impact on learning goals) in other countries.

The research gap addressed in this article is the understanding of how the COVID-19 pandemic has affected students' perception of and the engagement in online activities. It aims to explore the various aspects of online activities (understood as all forms of private and professionals online engagement), students' online behavior patterns, and their attitude toward online communication and learning from the perspectives of Polish and Ukrainian students before and during the pandemic. The main motivation is the desire to compare the situation in two neighboring countries, with a similar culture but a different history and a different political and economic situation. More specifically, we would like to answer the following research question: Are there any relationships between gender, age, country and online activities before and during the pandemic? In particular we are interested whether there are any differences in:

(RQ1) perceived student wellbeing,
(RQ2) hours spent online,
(RQ3) social behavior patterns (social cycle),
(RQ4) attitudes towards online communication,

(RQ5) attitudes towards online education?

In order to answer the research questions, a joint project was undertaken by the faculty of the Krakow University of Economics (KUE), Poland, and the Zhytomyr Polytechnic State University (ZPSU), Ukraine.

The paper is organized as follows. The next section presents the research background, followed by the outline of the research methodology. Then, the research results and their discussion are presented. Final remarks are in the Conclusions section.

2 Research Background

The pandemic forced universities to switch to the online learning mode and thus provided a unique opportunity to experience this type of learning even by people who previously avoided it, despite the previous attempts to simplify electronic systems as much as possible to facilitate the adaptation of teachers and students to some online learning methods (for example, to e-Assessment Management Systems [17] or gamification methods [19]). Belan [2] has analyzed the attitudes of Polish and Ukrainian students towards online learning and teaching technologies in training teachers of vocational education. He points out that Polish experience may be used as a benchmark for Ukraine. Basing on that premise the author proposes the modernization of the Ukrainian educational system. Klapkiv and Dluchopolska [13] discuss the challenges and opportunities during the quarantine caused by COVID-19 in Poland and Ukraine. It was indicated that the Ukrainian education system was largely unprepared to tackle these challenges due to the bureaucracy, the process rather than result orientation, educational conformism, and the lack of motivation of the main stakeholders.

The influence of online education on the mental health of students has been already discussed in research works. For example, the relationship between the pandemic and the neuroticism of Polish and Ukrainian students was examined by Dlugosz and Kryvachuk [7]. The research indicates that high levels of neuroticism were observed among 61% of respondents from Poland and 47% from Ukraine. The research has also indicated that Ukrainian students better cope with quarantine and have better mental health. The problem of mental health deterioration during the pandemic has also been investigated in a broader perspective by Ochnik et al. [21]. The research outcomes indicate that the state of students' mental health is alarming, and higher education institutions (HEIs) should provide psychological support for them. There are also research works that explore a broader perspective of online education, e.g., the problem of the limitations concerning the continuation of university education [12].

3 Research Methodology

The research is part of a project undertaken by the faculty of KUE and ZPSU. The goal was to investigate multi-dimensionally the students' perspectives of online learning during the time of the pandemic. Preliminary results of the research that looked at only one country's perspective were published in [6, 8], with Ukrainian and Polish data respectively, and in [9] that provided a preliminary comparison of students' online behavior in these countries. This paper extends these studies by comparing the data and providing a multi-perspective analysis of respondents' viewpoints, including gender, age, country, and presenting the results of the analysis of the survey qualitative data.

The research methodology contained the following steps: (1) design of a questionnaire on the basis of relevant literature and authors' academic experience, (2) verification of the questionnaire through a pilot study, (3) preparing the final version of the questionnaire (see Appendix), (4) distribution of the questionnaire to students at KUE and five Ukrainian universities (convenience sample), and (5) analysis of numerical and textual data (the open question).

We gathered the data in May and June 2021 using the questionnaire. In Poland, the survey was sent to students of KUE, mainly representing business studies. 1005 completed questionnaires were received, giving a response rate of 8%. In Ukraine, the questionnaire was distributed among students of seven universities: Zhytomyr Polytechnic State University, National University of Life and Environmental Sciences, Uman State Pavel Tychyna Pedagogical University, Melitopol State Pedagogical University, Drohobych State Pedagogical University, National Pedagogical University, and the Kryvyi Rih State Pedagogical University. In total, we received 557 responses from Ukrainian students. We analyzed the quantitative data using descriptive statistics and used open coding for analyzing the answers to the open question in the questionnaire. The respondents' structure presents Table 1.

Table 1. Respondents' structure.

		Poland		Ukraine	
		No.	%	No.	%
Gender	Female	643	64%	234	42%
	Male	357	36%	305	55%
	Not specified	5	0%	18	3%
Age	Young: <20	143	14%	329	59%
	Medium: 20–24	727	72%	213	38%
	Older: 24+	135	13%	15	3%

4 Research Findings

4.1 Students' Digital Competences

As far as respondents' digital competences are concerned, about 40% of respondents from Poland and Ukraine assessed their skills as average, however only 2.4% of Poles assessed their skills as below average, while 17% of Ukrainians assess their skills as such (Fig. 1). There were visible differences between age groups. It is especially apparent in the Young group, where the results are 0.9% and 13.5%, respectively (Fig. 2). Hence, it seems that the Ukrainian student population is much more diversified as far as digital competences are concerned. In both countries men assessed their digital competences higher than women. About 9% of Ukrainians reported constant or frequent technical problems, whereas in Poland only 3% (Fig. 3). This indicates the differences between technical environments in Poland and Ukraine. In both countries, women assess their technical conditions slightly better, similarly to the Older group of respondents (Fig. 3, Fig. 4).

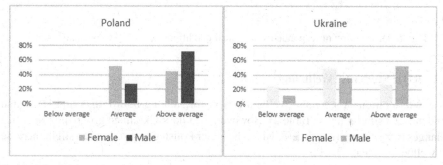

Fig. 1. Distribution of respondents' general digital competences according to gender and country.

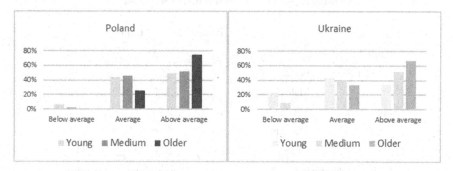

Fig. 2. Distribution of respondents' general digital competences according to age and country.

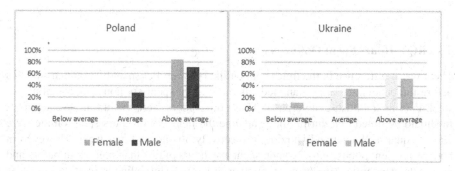

Fig. 3. Distribution of respondents' technical conditions according to gender and country.

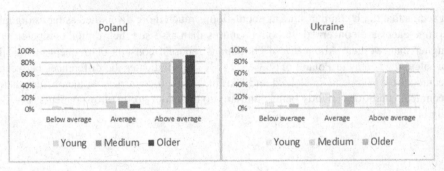

Fig. 4. Distribution of respondents' technical conditions according to age and country.

4.2 RQ1: Students' Wellbeing

The deterioration in students' wellbeing is visible among both Polish and Ukrainian students at a similar level (Table 2). However, the Older Ukrainian group did not notice changes in wellbeing (mean: 3.0), while the Older Polish group reported a slight increase in wellbeing (mean: 3.23).

Table 2. Average self-perception of wellbeing.

		Poland	Ukraine
Total		2.75	2.78
Gender	Female	2.72	2.74
	Male	2.79	2.82
Age	Young	2.73	2.77
	Medium	2.66	2.78
	Older	3.23	3.00

1 – severe deterioration, 2 – deterioration, 3 – no change, 4 – improvement, 5 – considerable improvement

4.3 RQ2: Hours Spent Online

There was a difference in the time spent online between Polish and Ukrainian students before the pandemic: Ukrainian students on average spent six hours more online per week than their Polish counterparts. These differences were visible in all categories. In should be noted that during the pandemic the numbers of hours spent online were almost equal in Poland and Ukraine, respectively 36 and 35 h per week. However, in both respondent populations, women spent less hours online than men, both before and during the pandemic. Similarly, the number of hours spent online in relation to studies before the pandemic was higher in Ukraine than in Poland, a difference visible in all categories.

Table 3, based on the changes in the number of hours spent online by students, shows the analysis of these changes in percent, taking into account the total number of hours spent online (including all private and professional engagement) and the number of hours spent online in relation to online learning. The "Increase" columns show the proportion of total activity increase to learning activity increase (100% means that all of the increase is related to online learning). The "Change" columns show in percentage the increase of online activities related to learning during the pandemic (17% shows that learning activities increased by an average of 17% points in total activity during the pandemic).

The values for Poland are close to 100%, hence it seems that the entire change was related to online learning. In the case of Ukraine, except for the Young group, the values are quite distant from 100%, for the Medium group it is 129%, which can be interpreted as online learning forcing the resignation from other online activities, while in the case of the Older group, the increase in online activity was related to activities other than learning.

Table 3. Proportion of the total online activity increase attributed to online studies and the change in the percentage of online learning in total online activities.

		Increase [%]		Change [%]	
		Poland	Ukraine	Poland	Ukraine
Total		97	*110*	*17*	8
Gender	Female	98	97	16	7
	Male	97	123	15	9
Age	Young	104	101	20	6
	Medium	96	129	16	12
	Older	103	37	15	−8

In the time spent online related to studies, it is worth noting that in Poland there was an increase in each group (although the increase gets smaller with age), which means that online learning was a significant factor in the increase in the time spent online. A similar situation was observed in the Ukrainian Young and Medium groups, but it is interesting that in the Older group we have a decrease, which means that the increase in time spent online was mostly not due to online learning, but due to other online activities. This can be related to the types of contacts – in the Older Ukrainian group the largest decrease in face-to-face contacts can be observed, with the largest increase in online contacts, which directly translated into increased online activity related not to studies, but to maintaining social contacts.

The number of hours spent online in relation to studies before the pandemic was higher in Ukraine than in Poland, a difference visible in all categories (Table 4).

Table 4. The average number of hours spent online and related to studies per week.

	Hours online						Hours online related to studies					
	Poland			Ukraine			Poland			Ukraine		
	B*	D	*Ch*	B	D	*Ch*	B	D	*Ch*	B	D	*Ch*
Total	22	36	*15*	29	35	*6*	*12*	*27*	*14*	*18*	*25*	*7*
Gender												
Female	19	36	*16*	24	33	*8*	12	28	*16*	17	25	*8*
Male	26	38	*12*	32	37	*5*	13	24	*12*	19	25	*6*
Age												
Young	23	37	*15*	29	36	*7*	12	27	*15*	19	26	*7*
Medium	21	37	*16*	29	35	*6*	12	27	*15*	16	24	*8*
Older	22	32	*11*	25	30	*5*	13	24	*11*	22	24	*2*

*B-Before, D-During, Ch-Change

4.4   RQ3: Social Pattern Behaviour

In order to capture the possible changes in students' online behavior, we assessed the number of "friends", both with respect to online and face-to-face contacts, before and during the pandemic. "Friends" are defined as people with whom respondents actively maintain contact in the private sphere.

There are visible differences in the average number of friends online between Polish and Ukrainian respondents: the average number of contacts online decreased in Poland from 13 to 12 and increased in Ukraine from 11 to 14. On average, the number of face-to-face friends decreased in both populations, however this change was more drastic in the case of Polish respondents (decrease from 16 to 8; among Ukrainian respondents the decrease was from 10 to 8) (Table 5 shows the changes).

Table 5. Change in the number of online and face-to-face friends.

		Online friends		Face-to-face friends	
		Poland	Ukraine	Poland	Ukraine
Total		*−1*	*3*	*−8*	*−2*
Gender	Female	−1	3	−9	−2
	Male	0	2	−7	−1
Age	Young	−2	3	−7	−2
	Medium	−1	2	−9	−1
	Older	2	4	−7	−5

As Fig. 5 shows, Polish respondents keep in touch with online contacts much more intensively than their Ukrainian counterparts. In both respondent groups the increase in constant online communication is visible during the pandemic, but more considerable in the case of Polish respondents (16% increase).

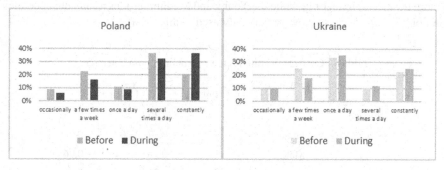

Fig. 5. Frequency of contacts online.

4.5 RQ4: Attitudes Towards Online Communication

The pandemic contributed to a more favorable perception of online communication among Ukrainian respondents (Fig. 6). Although it is difficult to notice any global differences between Poland and Ukraine in terms of age, it is interesting that in terms of communication "constantly" the increase in Ukraine is slight, while in Poland it is significant. There is an increase in the number of online contacts in Ukraine. The number of contacts is growing but their intensity is smaller, unlike in Poland, where we observed a decrease in the number of contacts, but a visible increase in their intensity.

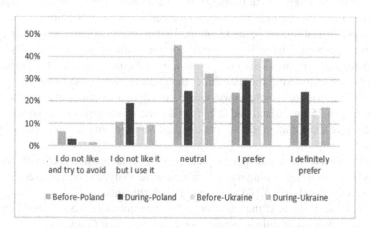

Fig. 6. Respondents' attitudes towards online communication.

In all categories, the changes in attitudes towards online communication were slightly positive, with a greater difference among women (Table 6). In both Poland and Ukraine, we saw a difference according to age: the scale of positive attitude change in the Older group was much higher than the average. This means that a significant part of this group - forced to use online communication due to the circumstances of the pandemic - gained a more positive opinion of it, while the Young and Medium groups hardly changed their opinion (perhaps because they were already used to this form).

Table 6. Changes in attitudes towards online communication.

		Poland	Ukraine
Average		*0.16*	*0.06*
Gender	Female	0.17	0.08
	Male	0.13	0.06
Age	Young	0.05	0.05
	Medium	0.15	0.07
	Older	0.30	0.27

Scale from −4 (negative) to +4 (positive), 0 – neutral

4.6   RQ5: Attitudes Towards Online Education

The amount of experience with online learning changes the attitudes toward this form of learning both in Poland and Ukraine. Table 7 presents the scale of the shift in both countries with respect to gender and age. Figures show the changes in percentage points, for instance in the case of Poland, during the pandemic 5% more students have negative (*"I do not like"*) feelings about online learning than before the pandemic (respectively 17% before and 22% during). The largest changes are in *neutral* attitude. It may result from long and total usage of online learning, what allowed students to gather experience and form an opinion. The attitude towards online learning was assessed by students on five-point scale: from −2 (strong negative) to +2 (strong positive). Comparing the attitudes before and during the pandemic, the average value of the change for all distinguished categories of recipients was calculated. In both counties the average changes were positive (0.25 for Poland and 0.13 for Ukraine, respectively), but small values of these indicators show that opinions were divided, with a slight predominance of positive opinions.

In order to get to know and understand the respondents' opinions better, their answers to the open question concerning online learning were analyzed. We received 67 and 159 comments respectively from Ukrainian and Polish students.

Based on the analysis of the answers to the open question, the following categories of the positive aspects of online learning were distinguished (Table 8).

The data shows that most of the positive responses of students relate to the overall demonstration of student satisfaction with online learning. Usually in such situations,

Table 7. Changes in attitude towards online learning (percentage points).

			I do not like [%]	Neutral [%]	I prefer [%]
Total	*Poland*		5	−20	15
	Ukraine		2	−10	8
Gender	Poland	Female	5	−23	18
		Male	3	−16	13
	Ukraine	Female	0	−12	12
		Male	3	−8	5
Age	Poland	Young	1	−14	13
		Medium	7	−23	16
		Older	3	−19	16
	Ukraine	Young	2	−9	7
		Medium	0	−7	7
		Older	7	−40	33

Table 8. Categorization of the positive aspects of online learning.

Category	Description	Polish students [%]*	Ukrainian students [%]*
General	Just satisfied with online learning	15.7	20.9
Saving time	Online learning saves them time on commuting to the university	20.1	7.5
Comfort and flexibility	Students feel more comfortable while staying at home and find it easier to deal with the flexible type of education offered by online learning	14.5	4.5
Saving money	Online learning saves them money on tickets and in some cases on accommodation near the university, as well as saving the university money on electricity and heating for classrooms	3.8	3.0

(continued)

Table 8. (*continued*)

Category	Description	Polish students [%]*	Ukrainian students [%]*
Knowledge gained	Online learning gives them the necessary skills for future work, which is likely to be in a hybrid form, and it is easier for them to understand and retain information when learning remotely	3.8	–
Teacher preparedness	Teachers are well-prepared and pay more attention to the students, showing their commitment	2.5	-
Video lessons	Lecturers might be recorded and shared in asynchronous time	0.6	3.0
Collaborative interactive methods	Many lecturers use interesting methods of teaching, such as presentations, group work, projects in social media, Moodle tasks, and quizzes	1.3	–
Lessons schedule	It is easier to manage consultations and as all classes take place on one platform it makes it easier to join any lessons	1.3	–
Motivation and concentration	It is easier to stay in a place where they will not be distracted	1.3	–
Platform for e-learning	The platform used for e-learning gives them the opportunity to test their knowledge after class and hold discussions on the subject	0.6	–

(*continued*)

Table 8. (*continued*)

Category	Description	Polish students [%]*	Ukrainian students [%]*
Equipment	Ability to work on their own IT equipment gives them wider opportunities	0.6	–
Evaluation system	In-person exams at the university are so well-prepared that cheating is almost impossible	0.6	–

*Note: Percentage of students who answered the open question.

students responded with comments from the category "I like online learning." (*"The quality is simply wonderful. I want to study a master's degree in this way!"; "Remote learning for extramural students is an optimal form of education."*).

Both Ukrainian and Polish students noticed saving time as the main advantage of online learning (*"The form of remote learning is a great way to save time on commuting to the university…"; "An additional advantage of remote classes is that I have an additional 4 h to take care of my own affairs, earlier this time was used by commuting to the university and commuting home from the university…"*) as well as the feeling of comfort during the study in the process of education (*"In addition, remote mode gives you more flexibility if you study 2 courses"; "Remote learning - especially in part-time studies - gives comfort, saves time (especially for commuters) and is effective."; "The online form of education is the most adequate and comfortable for students from many cities and different age ranges"; "Remote classes definitely reduce the stress associated with studying…"*).

The categorization of the negative aspects of online learning presents Table 9.

Table 9. Categorization of negative aspects of online learning.

Category	Description	Polish students [%]*	Ukrainian students [%]*
General	Just not satisfied with online learning	3.8	13.4
Motivation and concentration	It is harder to concentrate and stay motivated when learning from home and there is no learning atmosphere	3.1	6.0

(*continued*)

Table 9. (*continued*)

Category	Description	Polish students [%]*	Ukrainian students [%]*
Making contacts	Fewer opportunities to interact with each other during online learning	4.4	1.5
Knowledge loss	Online learning drastically reduces the effectiveness of assimilating the content presented in class	2.5	3.0
Time loss	It takes more time to prepare for lectures in online learning	3.1	0.0
Health problems	Online learning has a negative influence on different health aspects due to the long hours spent sitting in front of a computer	1.9	0.0

Note: Percentage of students who answered the open question.

As for negative aspects except of general ones (*"Nothing worse could have happened to our generation."; "Online learning is a failure. I hope that the normal form of classes will return soon."; "I insist on the complete rejection of this method"*), problems with motivation and concentration were often mentioned (*"There is no desire and motivation to learn during online learning. I consider face-to-face education to be effective and correct, so I really want them to stop introducing lockdowns and give us the opportunity to study normally"; "there's no motivation to learn as long as you're just sitting at home"; "I can't get used to remote classes, my learning quality has deteriorated significantly, I'm lazy and I don't see the point in working "for a good result". As soon as it is possible to return to full-time studies, I will do it right away".*)

Another huge problem students noticed was losing the opportunities of making contacts (*"Remote learning not only has a destructive effect on the psyche of students, but also significantly limits contacts. It should be remembered that studies are not only learning, but also making friends and making contacts. Remote teaching takes away what's best in studying at university and that's why I hope to return to the university as soon as possible"; "The first years of studies especially lose far too much when it comes to contacts with other students. It's just lack of making friends, which in many cases last for years"*).

Students also expressed their suggestions concerning the possible improvements in the education style (Table 10).

Table 10. Categorization of improvement suggestions.

Category	Description	Polish students [%]*	Ukrainian students [%]*
Combining with face-to-face	A hybrid approach, combining both face-to-face and online learning. Another option is to allow the university to offer both fully on-premise and fully remote types of learning, depending on the subject and form of study	14.5	13.4
Lessons schedule	Issues with the lessons and assignment schedule, including too many projects at the same time	9.4	7.5
Evaluation system	Extra stress from on-premise exams after online learning, a large number of large projects that take a lot of time for evaluation, the need for less knowledge for exams in online learning, the risk of easy mis-clicks while doing tests remotely, too many questions, and some students not participating in group work	10.1	4.5
Collaborative interactive tasks	The need for introducing more collaboration and interaction between students and teachers, for example with the help of puzzles, quizzes, and other interactive activities	5.7	9.0
Equipment	Issues with both teachers' and students' inadequate equipment, as well as internet quality	1.9	4.5

(continued)

Table 10. (*continued*)

Category	Description	Polish students [%]*	Ukrainian students [%]*
Comfort and flexibility	Resignation from the obligatory use of microphone and cameras - the obligatory use of cameras during online lectures is uncomfortable for students, students feel uncomfortable unmuting their microphone and asking questions during online lectures	1.3	0.0

Note: Percentage of students who answered the open question.

The most commonly mentioned improvement was the combining of online learning with face-to-face classes. Two ways of such a combination were suggested – hybrid form (*"In my opinion, after the pandemic, we can stay with the remote form, but only in the case of lectures and seminars or consultations. Project exercises or laboratories are certainly not as effective in the remote form as at the university"; "I believe that hybrid learning should be considered in the future, without switching from complete online learning to only stationary learning."*), and the option of fully remote or fully on-premise courses at the same time (*"I think that people who started studying remotely would prefer to stay with this form. However, students who started studying in full-time mode have a negative approach to remote classes"; "Remote learning is the best thing that could have happened. I save time and money. Remote learning is very conducive to flexibility. Personally, I could never physically return to the university. We are in the 21st century, technical and technological progress has gone so far that you can study many fields only through the remote form. I believe that you have to "go with the times" and remote education should be a standard, not only during a pandemic but forever. As for me, the distribution into the forms of study could be as follows: full-time studies - hybrid, extramural studies - fully remote. To sum up, I am very pleased with the remote form of classes"*).

The second most popular suggestion was an improvement in students' schedule. For example, a lot of students were complaining about an overwhelming number of tasks, and it was suggested to take control of the number of projects that students will have per one week (*"... the problem, however, is the number of projects/presentations/essays/group work assigned by the lecturers. The amount of time spent on learning and preparing for classes is greater than in the case of in-person classes. Often, even though the subject ends with an exam, a lot of other projects are assigned during the course... the number of tasks appeared to be overwhelming, especially for students in the last semester who are preparing for the defense of their thesis and often already work professionally"*). They also mentioned that in the case of hybrid learning, it would be better to have long break between stationary and online learning (*"in hybrid learning, I'm afraid that the break between remote and stationary classes will be too short to reach the apartment..."*).

Other important issue we need to work on is the evaluation system, as students have a lot of important improvement suggestions for modifying tests on the Moodle Platform (*"Moodle tests were often more of a sprint than a test of knowledge, and sharing your work on paper by scanning it and sending it via Moodle was an additional burden (as a rule, ten minutes given for proper conversion and task might not be enough in case of any problems, and delays often meant a downgrade)"*), and to include a grades explanation column in place where marks are published (*"I want all the teachers to explain what they were giving grades for"*). Also, students want more interactive and collaborative tasks, as it allows to make lessons more interesting (*"I want more frequent group work to contribute to classroom activity and to enhance student interaction, which is now severely limited"*).

5 Discussion

The differences between the digital competences of Polish and Ukrainian respondents might have three fold explanation: (1) Ukrainian youth enter higher education on average 2 years earlier than their Polish counterparts, which is a huge difference at this age; (2) differences in the level of IT education at the earlier stages, and (3) economic differences between Poland and Ukraine, resulting in lower availability of computer equipment in Ukraine. Interestingly, a much greater share of Ukrainian women than men assessed their digital competences as below average. It seems that Ukrainians are aware of some deficiencies in digital competences, and that is why actions have been taken for students to develop these skills [14, 26].

In general, Ukrainians perceive their technical conditions as worse than Poles. In Ukraine, a lot of students come from villages, without access to the Internet. Ukrainian families on average are much poorer than Polish ones; sometimes Ukrainian students do not have private computers and they can only use computers at universities, having access to the Internet via their mobile phones. Technical problems mainly concern younger Ukrainian respondents, which might be explained by their strong economic dependence on parents (for whom the Internet does not have to be a priority, especially in a generally poor economic condition).

Similarly to the findings in [12] we noticed a deterioration in students' wellbeing. However, contrary to the research results reported by [7] we did not notice considerable differences in wellbeing deterioration between Polish and Ukrainian respondents: indeed slightly more visible wellbeing deterioration was detected among Polish respondents. At the beginning of the pandemic there were severe restrictions on face-to-face communication, which may be the reason for the deterioration in the wellbeing of respondents. It should be noted that in Ukraine the survey was conducted at the time when learning at universities was on premise (contrary to Poland), hence Ukrainian respondents' memory might fade as far as bad online learning experience is concerned. The improvement in the wellbeing of the Polish Older group of respondents might be explained by the fact that this group contains students above the age of 24, including part-time students, for whom remote learning is much more attractive due to less organizational effort and resources required to study in this mode.

Some Ukrainian students have limited access to computers, which is why the pandemic has not caused such a great increase in the number of hours spent online like in the case of Polish respondents. Besides, a lot of Ukrainian students take part in online courses offered by various companies that also increase the total number of hours online. Unsurprisingly, learning activities contributed the most to the increase in the time spent online during the pandemic. In general, before the pandemic, classes in HEIs in Ukraine (with a few exceptions) were conducted on premise, in connection with which the transition to online learning caused a sharp increase in the number of hours that Ukrainian students spent online for educational purposes.

There were significant differences in online behavior patterns between Polish and Ukrainian students: in Ukraine there was a slight decrease in personal contacts and a high increase in online contacts; in Poland there was a huge decrease in face-to-face contacts and a small decrease in online contacts. The decrease in online contacts in Poland might be the result of the decrease in face-to-face contacts – when restrictions were severe and the number of face-to-face contacts decreased, then online contacts resulting from them also decreased. Pandemic regulations were similar, hence the differences between the results might be attributed to culture differences. In Ukraine, a lot of families were forced by the pandemic to buy devices that facilitate online communication, and that is why the increase in online contacts is noticeable.

Interestingly, during the pandemic almost the same numbers of face-to-face contacts were reported in both countries – 8 in Poland and 9 in Ukraine. Maybe this convergence defines the social sphere, but this topic would require further investigation. Differences in the frequency of online communication might be attributed to the differences in device ownership: Polish students usually have computers with Internet access that allow them to communicate constantly or several times a day, whereas some Ukrainian students only use computers with Internet access at campuses, which allows them to communicate online once a day or a few times a week. There is a difference in the behavior between Poles and Ukrainians: in Poland the decreases in face-to-face contacts are greater, however it seems that older students in Poland transferred some contacts from face-to-face to online. In the case of Ukraine, such an interpretation may apply to all age groups. This might be caused by the increased availability of communication equipment in Ukraine.

In Poland, most respondents were neutral towards online communication. This might be explained by the fact that they have had access to this method of communication for a long time and might be tired of it being a part of everyday life. On the contrary, in Ukraine, respondents seem to like this form of communication. Maybe they still treat it as something new that opens up more possibilities.

The quality of online learning in Ukraine might be lower than in Poland since this country has less experience in this type of teaching, however at the time of conducting the survey students had classes on premise, and that is why they might be more in favor of online learning. In Poland, the usage of online learning was more intense and some students might be fed up with it. Such a recurring difference between the members of the Older group and the other groups may result from the fact that earlier these students had no habit, or even had resistance, to online learning, and using this form, being forced to by the pandemic, could significantly change this attitude. Interestingly, women changed their attitude towards online learning to much more positive than men, similarly to older students.

6 Conclusions

The main contribution of the paper is the comprehensive, comparative and multidimensional analysis of Polish and Ukraine students' online behavior before and during the pandemic. We analyzed the students' wellbeing, online behavior patterns, and preferences concerning online learning in relation to students' gender, age, and country. The main research results suggest that there is a discrepancy between the socio-economic backgrounds of Polish and Ukrainian students, but the pandemic forced some Ukrainian students to enhance their technical conditions; this phenomenon took place in Western countries earlier. In the future, this might contribute to more inclusive education, since it seems that even after the pandemic universities might continue some form of online learning to meet the expectations and needs of some students. This might concern for example people with low economic status, who cannot afford to move to university towns or women who, in more traditional settings, need to take care of households. Online learning might attract more people to undertake studies and be convenient for some Erasmus students.

The research has some limitations mainly related to the respondent population – we used the convenience sample method to choose the respondents and that is why it is rather difficult to justify the generalization of the study results to the whole Polish and Ukrainian student populations.

In further research, we would like to investigate thoroughly different aspects of online learning, focusing mainly on its place in the future education.

Acknowledgment. The publication has been financed by the subsidy granted to the Krakow University of Economics - Project no. 032/SD/2022/PRO.

Appendix

Survey items related to the current study

1. Gender (male/female/don't want to share this information)
2. Age (<20/20–24/25–30/31+)
3. Level of digital competences (self-evaluation): (beginner/below average/average/ above average/professional)
4. Technical conditions of working place (access to the Internet and equipment: PC, laptop, tablet, smartphone, etc.): (constant problems/frequent problems/sufficient for basic needs/occasional problems/no problems)
5. The number of hours spent online per week (not counting professional work, but including studies) is approximately: (up to 15 h/16–25 h/26–35 h/36–45 h; over 45 h)

6. The number of hours per week related to online studies: (up to 10 h/11–20 h/21–30 h/31–40 h/over 40 h)
7. Estimated number of friends in regular socializing via electronic media (social media): (<5/6–15/16–30/31–50/>50)
8. Estimated number of friends in face-to-face contacts: (<5/6–15/16–30/31–50/>50)
9. The frequency of communicating with friends via electronic media: (occasionally/a few times a week/once a day/several times a day/constantly)
10. Attitude towards Internet communication: (I don't like and avoid it/I don't like, but have to use it/neutral attitude/I prefer it/I strongly prefer it)
11. Attitude towards online learning (e.g. training videos on Youtube): (I don't like and avoid it/I don't like, but have to use it/neutral attitude/I prefer it/I strongly prefer it)
12. Mental health change after switching to online learning: (significantly deteriorated/worsened/no change/improved/significantly improved)
13. Do you have any other ideas/insights/opinions regarding online learning? (Open question).

References

1. Afroz, R., Islam, N., Rahman, S., Anny, N. Z.: Students' and teachers' attitude towards online classes during COVID-19 pandemic: a study on three Bangladeshi government colleges. Int. J. Acad. Res. Bus. Soc. Sci. **10**(3), 462–476 (2021). https://doi.org/10.20525/ijrbs.v10i3.1155
2. Belan, V.: Using distance learning technologies for training future teachers of professional technical courses at the universities of the Republic of Poland and Ukraine. Prof. Pedagog. **2**(21), 145–152 (2020). https://doi.org/10.32835/2707-3092.2020.21.145-152
3. Bondar, I., Humenchuk, A., Horban, Y., Honchar, L., Koshelieva, O.: Conceptual and innovative approaches of higher education institutions (HEIs) to the model of training a successful specialist formation during a covid pandemic. J. Manag. Inf. Decis. Sci. **24**(3), 1–8 (2021)
4. Cansiz, S., Sudan, B., Ogretici, E., Aktas, M.S.: Learning from student browsing data on e-learning platforms: case study. In: Position Papers of the 2020 FedCSIS, pp. 37–44. ACSIS (2020). https://doi.org/10.15439/2020F138
5. Dhawan, S.: Online learning: a panacea in the time of Covid-19 crisis. Educ. Technol. Syst. **49**, 5–22 (2020). https://doi.org/10.1177/0047239520934018
6. Didkivska, S., Vakaliuk, T.A.: Students' opinion on the quality of distance learning during the Ukrainian pandemic reality. JELHE 2022, ID 943076 (2022). https://doi.org/10.5171/2022.943076
7. Długosz, P., Kryvachuk, L.: Neurotic generation of Covid-19 in Eastern Europe. Front. Psychiatry **12**, 1–8 (2021). https://doi.org/10.3389/fpsyt.2021.654590
8. Dymek, D., Grabowski, M., Paliwoda-Pękosz, G.: Impact of COVID-19 pandemic on students' online behavioral pattern. JELHE 2022, ID 881022 (2022). https://doi.org/10.5171/2022.881022
9. Dymek, D., Grabowski, M., Paliwoda-Pękosz, G., Didkivska, S., Vakaliuk, T.A.: Students' online behaviour in the time of the COVID-19 pandemic: insights from Poland and Ukraine. In: The Proceedings of the 17th FedCSIS, pp. 695–699. IEEE (2022). https://doi.org/10.15439/2022F134
10. El-Sayad, G., Md Saad, N.H., Thurasamy, R.: How higher education students in Egypt perceived online learning engagement and satisfaction during the covid-19 pandemic. Comput. Educ. **8**, 527–550 (2021). https://doi.org/10.1007/s40692-021-00191-y

11. Głodkowska, J., Marcinkowska, B., Wojdyła, E.: Students with disabilities in inclusive educational settings in Poland. ILEE **7**, 7–31 (2022). https://doi.org/10.1007/978-3-031-106 42-2_2

12. Kawczyńska-Butrym, Z., Pantyley, V., Butrym, M., Kisla, G., Fakeyeva, L.: Students in times of pandemic: employment, living conditions, and health. Case studies from Poland, Ukraine, and Belarus. Geogr. Pol. **94**(3), 429–440 (2021). https://doi.org/10.7163/GPol.0213

13. Klapkiv, Y., Dluhopolska, T.: Changes in the tertiary education system in pandemic times: comparison of Ukrainian and Polish universities. RREM **12**, 86–91 (2020). https://doi.org/10.18662/rrem/12.1sup2/250

14. Kovalchuk, B., Zaika, A.: Formation of digital competence of future masters of industrial training of agricultural profile. ITLT **85**(5), 118–129 (2021). https://doi.org/10.33407/itlt.v85i5.3897

15. Lee, K., Choi, H., Cho, Y.H.: Becoming a competent self: a developmental process of adult distance learning. Internet High. Educ. **41**, 25–33 (2019). https://doi.org/10.1016/j.iheduc.2018.12.001

16. Liu, X., Liu, J., Zhong, X.: Psychological state of college students during COVID-19 epidemic. SSRN Electron. J. (2020). https://doi.org/10.2139/ssrn.3552814

17. Majerník, J.: Increasing credibility of teachers in e-assessment management systems using multiple security features. In: Ziemba, E. (ed.) AITM/ISM-2018. LNBIP, vol. 346, pp. 41–52. Springer, Cham (2019). https://doi.org/10.1007/978-3-030-15154-6_3

18. Maleńczyk, I., Gładysz, B.: Academic e-learning in Poland results of a diagnostic survey. IJELR **5**, 35–59 (2019). https://doi.org/10.31261/IJREL.2019.5.1.03

19. Nguyen, D., Meixner, G.: Gamified augmented reality training for an assembly task: a study about user engagement. In: Federated Conference on Computer Science and Information Systems (FedCSIS), pp. 901–904. IEEE (2019). https://doi.org/10.15439/2019F136

20. Parker, S.W., Hansen, M.A., Bernadowski, C.: COVID-19 campus closures in the United States: American student perceptions of forced transition to remote learning. Soc. Sci. **10**(2), 62 (2021). https://doi.org/10.3390/socsci10020062

21. Ochnik, D., et al.: Mental health prevalence and predictors among university students in nine countries during the COVID-19 pandemic: a cross-national study. Sci. Rep. **11**(1), 1–13 (2021). https://doi.org/10.1038/s41598-021-97697-3

22. Tsatsou, P.: Digital inclusion of people with disabilities: a qualitative study of intra-disability diversity in the digital realm. Behav. Inf. Technol. **39**(9), 995–1010 (2020). https://doi.org/10.1080/0144929X.2019.1636136

23. Wahyu, P., et al.: Student perceptions of online learning during the COVID-19 pandemic in Indonesia: a study of phenomenology. Eur. J. Educ. Res. **10**, 1515–1528 (2021). https://doi.org/10.12973/eu-jer.10.3.1515

24. Wang, X., Hegde, S., Son, C., Keller, B., Smith, A., Sasangohar, F.: Investigating mental health of US college students during the COVID-19 pandemic: cross-sectional Survey Study. J. Med. Internet Res. **22** (2020). https://doi.org/10.2196/22817

25. Wuttke, H.-D., Parkhomenko, A., Tulenkov, A., Tabunshchyk, G., Parkhomenko, A., Henke, K.: The remote experimentation as the practical-oriented basis of inclusive engineering education. iJOE. **15**, 4 (2019). https://doi.org/10.3991/ijoe.v15i05.9752

26. Vakaliuk, T.A., Kontsedailo, V., Antoniuk, D., Korotun, V., Semerikov, S., Mintii, I.: Using game Dev Tycoon to develop professional soft competencies for future engineers-programmers. In: Sokolov, O., et al. (eds.) CEUR Workshop Proceedings, vol. 2732, pp. 808–822 (2020). https://doi.org/10.31812/123456789/4129

Methods for Improving Business and Society

The Iterative Compromise Ranking Analysis (ICRA) - The New Approach to Make Reliable Decisions

Bartosz Paradowski[1], Bartłomiej Kizielewicz[1,2], Andrii Shekhovtsov[1,2], and Wojciech Sałabun[1,2]

[1] Research Team on Intelligent Decision Support Systems,
Department of Artificial Intelligence and Applied Mathematics,
Faculty of Computer Science and Information Technology,
West Pomeranian University of Technology, Szczecin, Poland
{bartosz-paradowski,bartlomiej-kizielewicz,jakub-wieckowski,
wojciech.salabun}@zut.edu.pl
[2] National Institute of Telecommunications, Szachowa 1, 04-894 Warsaw, Poland

Abstract. In the field of multi-criteria decision-making, compromise is often sought because it is highly desirable for decision-making. However, over the years, many methods have been developed for decision-making, between which discrepancies in the final rankings are often present. For this reason, it is worth noting the possibility of a compromise between different multi-criteria decision-making methods. One such solution is the Iterative Compromise Ranking Analysis (ICRA), which, by means of an iterative evaluation of the preferences of alternatives, leads to a compromise between the methods under consideration. This work presents an example of a solution to a theoretical decision problem, for which five methods were used: TOPSIS, VIKOR, MARCOS, MABAC and EDAS. In addition, an empirical analysis of the compromise solution was carried out to check the effect of parameters on the number of iterations needed to reach a compromise and the differences between the rankings proposed by the methods and the compromise ranking. The work showed that this is an interesting tool that can find its use in the field of multi-criteria decision-making as well as can be used to analyze the behaviour of multi-criteria decision-making methods.

Keywords: Compromise · ICRA · MCDA

1 Introduction

A number of new approaches to solving multi-criteria problems have emerged over recent years. For this reason, there have been many works attempting to compare methods of multi-criteria decision-making in different fields [8] as well as attempts to empirically compare methods among themselves [3] or to present approaches to how to benchmark them. In addition, due to the number of methods available Wątróbski et al. presented a generalised framework of selection of multi-criteria decision-making method as the sole selection of a method becomes a problem in itself [28]. However, choosing one method is not necessarily the only way out, in cases where the decision maker believes that several methods can guarantee an adequate result, a compromise approach can be used.

Compromise in decision-making is a desirable phenomenon that manifests itself in this field in many forms. Virtually every method seeks to compromise through the principle of linear programming, however, some methods e.g. VlseKriterijumska Optimizacija I Kompromisno Resenje (VIKOR) [1], The Measurement Alternatives and Ranking according to COmpromise Solution (MARCOS) [25] and A Combined Compromise Solution (CoCoSo) [30] methods extend it even further. Moreover, the compromise might be sought through objective criteria weighting [20] as it provides a direct impact on criteria significance in the considered problem.

Another popular approach is the ranked voting system, which is used to establish a compromise ranking based on reference rankings. Many voting approaches were used in multi-criteria decision-making in specific practical problems such as the Borda rule and the Copeland rule for performance assessment of battery electric vehicles [7], the Copeland rule for E-commerce recommender system [2]. Moreover, Lamboray presented a comparison between available voting system [15].

However, these methods mainly focus on rankings in which it is difficult to observe slight differences between the obtained preferences of decision options. For the purpose of providing a better-suited way of obtaining a compromise, the Iterative Compromise Ranking Analysis (ICRA) was proposed by Kizielewicz et al. [13]. This new approach use evaluations of the decision alternatives obtained by the selected methods by creating a new decision matrix consisting of mentioned preference values, where the types of attributes for the newly formed matrix depend on the ranking method and iteratively seeking the compromise.

In this study, five multi-criteria decision-making methods were selected to perform the ICRA, namely the TOPSIS, the VIKOR, the MARCOS, the MABAC, and the EDAS methods. This approach makes it possible to obtain a consensus between different rankings that presents some discrepancies by means of an iterative evaluation using the multi-criteria decision-making methods considered. An example of the use of this approach to solve a specific theoretical multi-criteria problem is presented and a quantitative analysis of the influence of the factors of the course of obtaining a consensus on the number of iterations and the final consensus ranking obtained is carried out.

The rest of the article is structured as follows. Section 2 presents a literature review of different approaches to compromise in multi-criteria decision-making. In Sect. 3, preliminaries are presented that include the newly proposed method and selected methods of multi-criteria decision-making. In Sect. 4, a study case is presented in which the performance of the algorithm on five methods is presented and quantitative analysis is carried out with a discussion of the acquired results. Finally, in Sect. 5 the conclusions were drawn and a summary is presented.

2 Literature Review

Compromise is one aspect of multi-criteria decision-making that should be highly desirable. It allows the use of one of the available options which will be close to the majority, but at the same time will take into account the minority. Most multi-criteria decision-making use linear programming to provide for the aspect of compromise among considered alternatives, which often might not be enough, thus some methods tried to present a different approach. Several methods have emerged in multi-criteria decision-making that base their core principles on compromise and assess the set of considered alternatives.

The most well-known and regarded classic method is the VIKOR method presented by Serafim Opricovic [6]. This method in its assumptions proposes two rankings, which can then be aggregated using the compromise value given by the expert. This method has been used in many works, demonstrating its usefulness in various fields. In addition, the method has seen many developments, e.g. for group decision-making [10], an approach that operates in a fuzzy environment [9] and uses interval numbers [22]. Since the VIKOR method was presented, few methods have directly addressed compromise, two solutions being the relatively new, namely the combined compromise solution (COCOSO) method and the Measurement of alternatives and ranking according to the COmpromise solution (MARCOS) method. The COCOSO method was proposed by Yazdani et al. in work presented in 2018 [30], where the new method combines the weighted product method (WPM) and the weighted sum method (WSM) to provide a new equation which results in balanced compromise of those two scores in accordance to the best and the worst alternative. The MARCOS method, on the other hand, was first introduced by Željko Stević et al. in 2020 [25]. This method presented the utility functions which provided the compromise of the considered alternatives in relation to the ideal and anti-ideal solution. They presented the usage of this function in the example of sustainable supplier selection in healthcare industries.

Another approach to incorporating comparison in multi-criteria decision-making methods is to use objective criteria weighting methods. These methods do not directly address the use of comparison, but by checking the correlation between the criteria considered they provide some degree of compromise value of the importance of a criterion. Such approaches, although rarely considered, can be helpful in the case of a problem in determining the relevance of criteria. Such methods allow for a better resolution of the conflict characterizing a given decision situation. One of the best-known and also oldest methods is CRiteria Importance Through Intercriteria Correlation (CRITIC) presented by Diakoulaki et al. in 1995 [5]. This method determines the importance of a criterion through the calculation of intercriteria correlation. In 2021 Krishnan et al. presented an extension of the CRITIC method where a new distance correlation coefficient was incorporated [14]. Aggregated method of Integrated Determination of Objective CRIteria Weights (IDOCRIW) was presented by Zavadskas and Podvezko in 2016 [31] which used the assumptions of the criterion impact loss (CILOS) approach and entropy and was further extended by them into a fuzzy environment in 2020 [21]. One of the latest methods is MEthod based on the Removal Effects of Criteria (MEREC) presented by Keshavarz-Ghorabaee et al. in 2021 [11]. This method provides a new perspective on objective weighting methods as the criterion's removal effect on the performance of alternatives is presented and incorporated into the algorithm.

More relevant, from the point of view of this work, are solutions that make compromises between rankings obtained using multiple multi-criteria decision-making methods. For this purpose, the Borda count methodology was applied. Its usage in multi-criteria decision-making is prominent in many fields, for example, Roozbahani et al. presented a framework that incorporated Borda count for the final ranking calculation in Ground Water Management Based problem [23], on the other hand, Serrai et al. presented its usage for compromise ranking for a problem of web service selection [24]. This methodology was further used by Wu et al. to extend MULTIMOORA decision-making method to improve robustness in the alternatives assessment [29]. Another well-known and highly used method is the Copeland method, which execution was presented for example by Özdagoglu et al. in the case study of motorcycle selection [18] or by Lestari et al. in the performance comparison of Copeland and Borda methods in a recommender system [16]. Even though those two are most prominent in research where aggregation of rankings is considered, there are many different approaches to provide a compromise solution. There are such approaches as Kemeny's rule and Condorcet's rule which were used by Muravyov et al. [17].

In this work, we present the iterative approach to obtain a compromise solution of rankings provided by several multi-criteria decision-making methods. This approach let the decision-maker choose more than one desirable method and acquire one final ranking. Such an approach may be highly desirable in scenarios where selecting a specific method might not be considered easy.

3   Research Methodology

3.1   TOPSIS Method

Technique of Order Preference Similarity (TOPSIS) is based on the ideal solution approach for solving multi-criteria decision problems [4]. The approach evaluates decision alternatives for the distance between a positive ideal solution and a negative ideal solution. Its basic version can be presented in the following steps:

Step 1. Construct the decision matrix and determine the weight of criteria and type of it (1). Criteria can be either: profit (more is better) or cost (less is better).

$$F = \begin{bmatrix} f_{11} & f_{12} & \cdots & f_{1n} \\ f_{21} & f_{22} & \cdots & f_{2n} \\ \vdots & \vdots & \cdots & \vdots \\ f_{m1} & f_{m2} & \cdots & f_{mn} \end{bmatrix}, \tag{1}$$

where f_m denotes alternative m.

Step 2. Calculate the normalized decision matrix. This step allows the attributes to be converted to a single scale for easier comparison.

Step 3. Determine the weighted normalized decision matrix. The weighted normalized value is calculated in the following way (2):

$$
F^w = \begin{bmatrix} r_{11} \cdot w_1 & r_{12} \cdot w_2 & \cdots & r_{1n} \cdot w_n \\ r_{21} \cdot w_1 & r_{22} \cdot w_2 & \cdots & r_{2n} \cdot w_n \\ \vdots & \vdots & \cdots & \vdots \\ r_{m1} \cdot w_1 & r_{m2} \cdot w_2 & \cdots & r_{mn} \cdot w_n \end{bmatrix} = \begin{bmatrix} v_{11} & v_{12} & \cdots & v_{1n} \\ v_{21} & v_{22} & \cdots & v_{2n} \\ \vdots & \vdots & \cdots & \vdots \\ v_{m1} & v_{m2} & \cdots & v_{mn} \end{bmatrix}, \qquad (2)
$$

where r_m - normalized alternative m, w - weight corresponding to criteria.

Step 4. Calculate positive and negative ideal solution. Calculate the separation measures, using the n-dimensional Euclidean distance. The separation of each alternative from the positive ideal solution is given as (3):

$$
D_j^* = \sqrt{\sum_{i=1}^n (v_{ij} - v_i^*)^2}, \quad j = 1, \ldots, J, \qquad (3)
$$

where $v_{ij} = r_{ij} \cdot w_j$, v_i^* - positive ideal solution.

Similarly, the separation from the negative ideal solution is given as (4):

$$
D_j^- = \sqrt{\sum_{i=1}^n (v_{ij} - v_i^-)^2}, \quad j = 1, \ldots, J, \qquad (4)
$$

where $v_{ij} = r_{ij} \cdot w_j$, v_i^- - negative ideal solution.

Step 5. Calculate the relative closeness to the ideal solution. The relative closeness of the alternative a_j is defined as follows (5):

$$
C_j^* = \frac{D_j^-}{(D_j^* + D_j^-)}, \quad j = 1, \ldots, J \qquad (5)
$$

Step 6. Rank the preference order.

3.2   VIKOR Method

VlseKriterijumska Optimizacija I Kompromisno Resenje (VIKOR) is a method based on the compromise approach, which evaluates alternatives with conflicting types of criteria [1]. The compromise solution in this method is considered to be the solution that is closest to the ideal. On the other hand, compromise is achieved through mutual concessions. This method can be presented in the following steps:

Step 1. Determine the best and the worst values of all criteria - determine best and worst values in given problem for the profit type criteria (6) and cost type criteria (7).

$$f_j^* = \max_i f_{ij}, \ f_j^- = \min_i f_{ij}, \ i = 1, 2, \cdots, m, \ j = 1, 2, \cdots, n \quad (6)$$

$$f_j^* = \min_i f_{ij}, \ f_j^- = \max_i f_{ij}, \ i = 1, 2, \cdots, m, \ j = 1, 2, \cdots, n \quad (7)$$

Step 2. Compute S_i (8) **and R_i values** (9) - w_j is weight vector which describe the relevance of a given criterion.

$$S_i = \sum_{i=1}^{n} w_j \frac{(f_j^* - f_{ij})}{(f_j^* - f_j^-)}, \ i = 1, 2, \cdots, m, \ j = 1, 2, \cdots, n \quad (8)$$

$$R_i = \max_j \left[w_j \frac{(f_j^* - f_{ij})}{(f_j^* - f_j^-)} \right], \ i = 1, 2, \cdots, m, \ j = 1, 2, \cdots, n \quad (9)$$

Step 3. Compute the values of Q_i by Eq. (10) - v is introduced as a weight for the strategy of the majority of criteria, whereas 1 - v is the weight of the individual regret. These strategies could be compromised by $v = 0.5$.

$$Q_i = v \frac{(S_i - S^*)}{(S^- - S^*)} + (1 - v) \frac{(R_i - R^*)}{(R^- - R^*)}, \ i = 1, 2, \cdots, m \quad (10)$$

Step 4. Rank the alternatives - the VIKOR method provides three rankings named S, R and Q. Each of them should be ranked in ascending order. The measures of S and R are integrated into Q for a compromise solution, the base for an agreement established by mutual concessions. It is up to the decision-maker to choose a preferred solution.

3.3 MARCOS Method

The Measurement Alternatives and Ranking according to COmpromise Solution (MARCOS) method provided a new approach to solving decision problems by considering an anti-ideal and an ideal solution a the initial steps of problem-solving. It was first proposed by Željko Stević et al. in 2020 [25] where they introduced the method by solving the problem of sustainable supplier selection in healthcare industries. Moreover, they proposed a new way to determine utility functions and their further aggregation, while maintaining stability in the problems requiring a large set of alternatives and criteria.

Step 1. The initial step requires to define set of n criteria and m alternatives to create decision matrix.

Step 2. Next, the extended initial matrix X should be formed by defining ideal (AI) and anti-ideal(AAI) solution.

$$X = \begin{array}{c} AII \\ A_1 \\ A_2 \\ \cdots \\ A_m \\ AI \end{array} \begin{bmatrix} x_{aa1} & x_{aa2} & \cdots & x_{aan} \\ x_{11} & x_{12} & \cdots & x_{1n} \\ x_{21} & x_{22} & \cdots & x_{2n} \\ \cdots & \cdots & \cdots & \cdots \\ x_{m1} & x_{22} & \cdots & x_{mn} \\ x_{ai1} & x_{ai2} & \cdots & x_{ain} \end{bmatrix} \tag{11}$$

The anti-ideal solution (AAI) which is the worst alternative is defined by Eq. (12), whereas the ideal solution (AI) is the best alternative in the problem at hand defined by Eq. (13).

$$AAI = \min_{i} x_{ij} \quad \text{if } j \in B \text{ and } \max_{i} x_{ij} \quad \text{if } j \in C \tag{12}$$

$$AI = \max_{i} x_{ij} \quad \text{if } j \in B \text{ and } \min_{i} x_{ij} \quad \text{if } j \in C \tag{13}$$

where B is a benefit group of criteria and C is a group of cost criteria.

Step 3. After defining anti-ideal and ideal solutions, the extended initial matrix X needs to be normalized, by applying Eqs. (14) and (15) creating normalized matrix N.

$$n_{ij} = \frac{x_{ai}}{x_{ij}} \quad \text{if } j \in C \tag{14}$$

$$n_{ij} = \frac{x_{ij}}{x_{ai}} \quad \text{if } j \in B \tag{15}$$

Step 4. The weight for each criterion needs to be defined to present its importance in accordance with others. The weighted matrix V needs to be calculated by multiplying the normalized matrix N with the weight vector through Eq. (16).

$$v_{ij} = n_{ij} \times w_j \tag{16}$$

Step 5. Next, the utility degree K of alternatives in relation to the anti-ideal and ideal solutions needs to be calculated by using Eqs. (17) and (18).

$$K_i^- = \frac{\sum_{i=1}^{n} v_{ij}}{\sum_{i=1}^{n} v_{aai}} \tag{17}$$

$$K_i^+ = \frac{\sum_{i=1}^{n} v_{ij}}{\sum_{i=1}^{n} v_{ai}} \tag{18}$$

Step 6. The utility function f of alternatives, which is the compromise of the observed alternative in relation to the ideal and anti-ideal solution, needs to be determined. Its done using Eq. (19).

$$f\left(K_i\right) = \frac{K_i^+ + K_i^-}{1 + \frac{1-f\left(K_i^+\right)}{f\left(K_i^+\right)} + \frac{1-f\left(K_i^-\right)}{f\left(K_i^-\right)}} \tag{19}$$

where $f\left(K_i^-\right)$ represents the utility function in relation to the anti-ideal solution and $f\left(K_i^+\right)$ represents the utility function in relation to the ideal solution.

Utility functions in relation to the ideal and anti-ideal solution are determined by applying Eqs. (20) and (21).

$$f\left(K_i^-\right) = \frac{K_i^+}{K_i^+ + K_i^-} \tag{20}$$

$$f\left(K_i^+\right) = \frac{K_i^-}{K_i^+ + K_i^-} \tag{21}$$

Step 7. Finally, rank alternatives accordingly to the values of the utility functions. The higher the value the better an alternative is.

3.4   MABAC Method

The Multi-Attributive Border Approximation Area Comparison (MABAC) is a multi-criteria decision-making method introduced by Pamučar and Ćirović in 2015 [19] on the problem of selection of transport and handling resources in logistics centres. This method's approach was to determine the distance measures between each possible alternative and the boundary approximation area (BAA). Moreover, this method has seen many developments such as extensions into hesitant fuzzy linguistic [26] or q-rung orthopair fuzzy environments [27]. Its original version can be presented in the following steps:

Step 1. Define a decision matrix of dimension $n \times m$, where n is the number of alternatives, and m is the number of criteria (22).

$$x_{ij} = \begin{bmatrix} x_{11} & x_{12} & \dots & x_{1m} \\ x_{21} & x_{22} & \dots & x_{2m} \\ \dots & \dots & \dots & \dots \\ x_{n1} & x_{n2} & \dots & x_{nm} \end{bmatrix} \tag{22}$$

Step 2. Normalization of the decision matrix, where for criteria of type profit use Eq. (23) and for criteria of type cost use Eq. (24).

$$n_{ij} = \frac{x_{ij} - \min x_i}{\max x_i - \min x_i} \tag{23}$$

$$n_{ij} = \frac{x_{ij} - \max x_i}{\min x_i - \max x_i} \tag{24}$$

Step 3. Create a weighted matrix based on the values from the normalized matrix according to the formula (25).

$$v_{ij} = w_i \cdot (n_{ij} + 1) \tag{25}$$

Step 4. Boundary approximation area (G) matrix determination. The Boundary Approximation Area (BAA) for all criteria can be determined using the formula (26).

$$g_i = \left(\prod_{j=1}^{m} v_{ij} \right)^{1/m} \tag{26}$$

Step 5. Distance calculation of alternatives from the boundary approximation area for matrix elements (Q) by Eq. (27).

$$Q = \begin{bmatrix} v_{11} - g_1 & v_{12} - g_2 & \cdots & v_{1n} - g_n \\ v_{21} - g_1 & v_{22} - g_2 & \cdots & v_{2n} - g_n \\ \cdots & \cdots & \cdots & \cdots \\ v_{m1} - g_1 & v_{m2} - g_2 & \cdots & v_{mn} - g_n \end{bmatrix} = \begin{bmatrix} q_{11} & q_{12} & \cdots & q_{1n} \\ q_{21} & q_{22} & & q_{2n} \\ \cdots & \cdots & \cdots & \cdots \\ q_{m1} & q_{m2} & \cdots & q_{mn} \end{bmatrix} \tag{27}$$

The membership of a given alternative A_i to the approximation area $(G, G^+$ or $G^-)$ is established by (28).

$$A_i \in \begin{cases} G^+ & \text{if } q_{ij} > 0 \\ G & \text{if } q_{ij} = 0 \\ G^- & \text{if } q_{ij} < 0 \end{cases} \tag{28}$$

Step 6. Ranking the alternatives according to the sum of the distances of the alternatives from the areas of approximation of the borders (29).

$$S_i = \sum_{j=1}^{n} q_{ij}, \quad j = 1, 2, \ldots, n, \quad i = 1, 2, \ldots, m \tag{29}$$

3.5   EDAS Method

The Evaluation based on Distance from Average Solution (EDAS) method was proposed by Keshavarz et al. in 2015 [12] and its main aim was to design a method which would be useful when conflicting criteria are present. This method utilizes two different measures, the positive distance from average (PDA), and the negative distance from average (NDA) which can show the difference between each alternative and the average solution. The higher the PDA values are or the lower the NDA values are, the better is the alternative in comparison to the average solution. This method can be executed by following steps:

Step 1. Define a decision matrix of dimension $n \times m$, where n is the number of alternatives, and m is the number of criteria (30).

$$X_{ij} = \begin{bmatrix} x_{11} & x_{12} & \cdots & x_{1m} \\ x_{21} & x_{22} & \cdots & x_{2m} \\ \cdots & \cdots & \cdots & \cdots \\ x_{n1} & x_{n2} & \cdots & x_{nm} \end{bmatrix} \tag{30}$$

Step 2. Calculate the average solution for each criterion according to the formula (31).

$$AV_j = \frac{\sum_{i=1}^{n} X_{ij}}{n} \tag{31}$$

Step 3. Calculating the positive distance from the mean solution and the negative distance from the mean solution for the alternatives. When the criterion is of profit type, the negative distance and the positive distance are calculated using Eqs. (32) and (33), while when the criterion is of cost type, the distances are calculated using formulas (34) and (35).

$$NDA_{ij} = \frac{\max\left(0, (AV_j - X_{ij})\right)}{AV_j} \tag{32}$$

$$PDA_{ij} = \frac{\max\left(0, (X_{ij} - AV_j)\right)}{AV_j} \tag{33}$$

$$NDA_{ij} = \frac{\max\left(0, (X_{ij} - AV_j)\right)}{AV_j} \tag{34}$$

$$PDA_{ij} = \frac{\max\left(0, (AV_j - X_{ij})\right)}{AV_j} \tag{35}$$

Step 4. Calculate the weighted sums of PDA and NDA for each decision variant using Eqs. (36) and (37).

$$ASP_i = \sum_{j=1}^{m} w_j PDA_{ij} \tag{36}$$

$$SN_i = \sum_{j=1}^{m} w_j NDA_{ij} \tag{37}$$

Step 5. Normalize the weighted sums of negative and positive distances using Eqs. (38) and (39).

$$NSN_i = 1 - \frac{SN_i}{\max_i (SN_i)} \tag{38}$$

$$NSP_i = \frac{SP_i}{\max_i (SP_i)} \tag{39}$$

Step 6. Calculate the evaluation score (AS) for each alternative using the formula (40). A higher point value determines a higher ranking alternative.

$$AS_i = \frac{1}{2} (NSP_i + NSN_i) \tag{40}$$

3.6   Weighted Spearman's Correlation Coefficient

Correlation coefficients are used to represent the similarity of compared rankings in a quantifiable way. The weighted Spearman's correlation coefficient is one of the most commonly used coefficients. It was designed to consider the most relevant alternatives which are the ones that were rated the best. This coefficient is presented in Eq. (41).

$$r_w = 1 - \frac{6 \cdot \sum_{i=1}^{n} (x_i - y_i)^2 \left((N - x_i + 1) + (N - y_i + 1)\right)}{n \cdot (n^3 + n^2 - n - 1)} \tag{41}$$

4   Research Findings and Discussion

The Iterative Compromise Ranking Approach (ICRA) main aim is to provide a way of compromising rankings obtained through different multi-criteria decision-making methods. A need arose as many methods are proposed which provided a new way of evaluating the alternatives. However, this creates a problem in which the best decision-making method must be picked for the final evaluation of alternatives, which might not be an easy case in some situations, thus such a compromise approach might be better suited. To carry out this approach, the following steps are required:

Step 1. Evaluate formed decision matrix by n MCDM methods

Step 2. Create a decision matrix based on the preference value calculated by MCDM methods. Criteria types are determined based on the method's ranking type.

Step 3. Return to step 1 until rankings provided by all selected methods are the same. For the purpose of comparison correlation coefficient usage is preferred and in this work, the weighted Spearman's correlation coefficient was used.

The study of the solution was carried out by demonstrating the use of ICRA on a randomly generated example, and by analyzing the influence of factors on the course of the solution by generating one hundred random decision matrices, and then changing the research factor, whose influence was shown on boxen plots.

4.1   Theoretical Example

In the first approach, a decision matrix with ten alternatives and eight criteria was generated. The types of criteria were set as follows: C_1 - Cost, C_2 - Cost, C_3 - Profit, C_4 - Cost, C_5 - Profit, C_6 - Profit, C_7 - Cost, C_8 - Cost. The matrix was randomly generated, where the values fell within the normal distribution $[0, 1]$. For the use of multi-criteria decision-making methods, the weights were divided evenly, i.e. each criterion had the same significance. The matrix is shown in Table 1.

The Spearman weighted correlation values of ranking i with ranking $i-1$ are shown in Table 2. From the values shown, we can see that the TOPSIS method stabilised the fastest, followed by the MABAC method, the EDAS method and

Table 1. Generated theoretical problem decision matrix.

A_i	C_1	C_2	C_3	C_4	C_5	C_6	C_7	C_8
A_1	0.695342	0.537567	0.817879	0.590484	0.669001	0.06372	0.224616	0.936154
A_2	0.191504	0.485942	0.041557	0.288029	0.011213	0.981233	0.312331	0.222928
A_3	0.30724	0.320894	0.453718	0.573191	0.711328	0.314716	0.365802	0.893979
A_4	0.947824	0.307941	0.537124	0.961897	0.089169	0.698669	0.976673	0.465632
A_5	0.121483	0.376043	0.571574	0.292358	0.728113	0.739274	0.958435	0.836585
A_6	0.741406	0.482223	0.844639	0.254446	0.509148	0.429902	0.490728	0.308689
A_7	0.170687	0.433029	0.030963	0.932767	0.7613	0.930262	0.54715	0.038406
A_8	0.734518	0.738879	0.572844	0.649799	0.812476	0.85712	0.832846	0.181159
A_9	0.729182	0.103717	0.92813	0.532178	0.442577	0.298785	0.293263	0.050323
A_10	0.82726	0.327959	0.759711	0.407212	0.848137	0.578501	0.307067	0.854799
$Type$	$Cost$	$Cost$	$Profit$	$Cost$	$Profit$	$Profit$	$Cost$	$Profit$

Table 2. Spearman's weighted coefficient r_w values for subsequent iterations.

Iteration	Methods				
	TOPSIS	VIKOR	MARCOS	MABAC	EDAS
i = 2	1.0	0.906336	0.850137	0.987878	0.990082
i = 3	1.0	0.960330	0.940495	1.0	0.966942
i = 4	1.0	0.987878	1.0	1.0	1.0
i = 5	1.0	1.0	1.0	1.0	1.0

the MARCOS method, and finally the VIKOR method, where in the case of the VIKOR method five iterations were needed to obtain the final compromise. It is interesting case that the TOPSIS method ranking in this case did not require any modification.

The rankings obtained in each iteration for each method are shown in Fig. 1. As can be seen, the TOPSIS method showed no changes, MABAC and EDAS have slightly visible changes, but the largest changes in rankings are seen for the MARCOS and VIKOR methods. For the MABAC method, the most significant changes are the positions of the sixth and ninth alternatives, where they have swapped positions, but this is not a change at the podium of the ranking so it is not that significant. In the case of the EDAS method, the situation is similar, except that there are more changes, namely for the second, sixth and ninth alternatives, but these are also not significant changes as these alternatives are more or less in the middle of the ranking. In the case of the MARCOS and VIKOR methods, changes are evident not only in the middle of the ranking but also in the podium, which means that the initial ranking differs quite significantly compared to the compromise ranking.

In Fig. 2 the preferences in consecutive iterations are presented for each of the considered methods. Even though, the ranking for the TOPSIS method did not change the preferences changed significantly, more precisely the range and

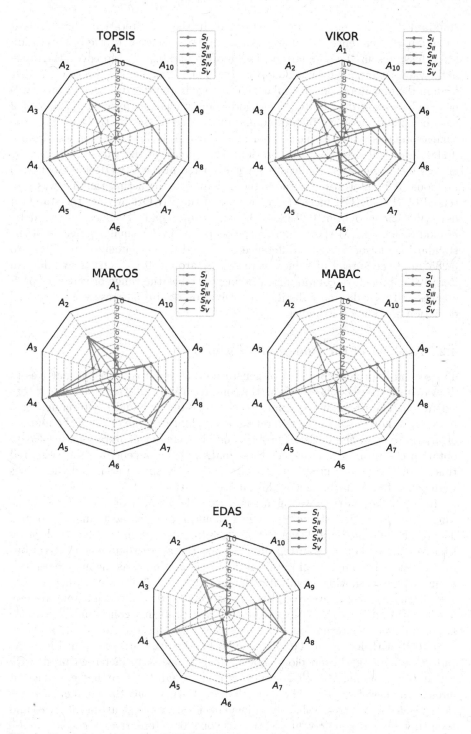

Fig. 1. Obtained rankings for TOPSIS, VIKOR, MARCOS, MABAC, and EDAS methods in subsequent iterations.

standard deviation of values have changed. In the first iteration, the standard deviation of preference values was around 0.0885, whereas in the last iteration the values presented a standard deviation of around 0.2987. Moreover, the range of the values extended from $[0.3658, 0.6679]$ to $[0, 1]$, making the spread 0.7 higher than in the first iteration. A similar high change in the standard deviation of values can be seen in the MARCOS method where it changed from 0.0917 to 0.3372 and the spread increased by around 0.8. In the case of the MABAC method, the changes are less visible as the standard deviation in the first iteration was around 0.1189 and 0.2988 in the last iteration. The spread of the values increased by around 0.595. However, the least change occurred in the VIKOR and the EDAS methods. It is interesting as the highest change in the actual ranking was presented by the VIKOR method. In the case of the VIKOR method the standard deviation changed from 0.2888 to 0.3 and the spread of values increased by around 0.065. The MABAC method presented a similar small change as in the standard deviation it was a difference of around 0.038, namely from 0.2473 to 0.2853 and the spread of values increased by around 0.13. This shows that an iterative approach to compromise ranking stretches the range of values of preferences and provides more distinctive evaluation of alternatives as the standard deviation and spread is higher.

4.2   Analysis of the Compromise Approach

The second approach consisted of generating one hundred decision matrices to draw quantitative conclusions from the compromise ranking approach under consideration. The research was conducted on the same five multi-criteria decision-making methods used in the theoretical example. First, the effect of the number of alternatives in the decision problem on the number of iterations needed to obtain a compromise was tested. Each matrix size was generated one hundred times, where the matrix size was n alternatives by six criteria, and the values were generated from the normal distribution $[0, 1]$.

Initially, the matrices were generated with the number of alternatives in the range $[10, 100]$ with a step of 10, which should represent most small problems. The results obtained are shown in the Fig. 3. It can be seen that for small problems i.e. those that contain ten alternatives, the average number of iterations remains at 4. The number of iterations increases gradually as the number of iterations increases, slowing down with a larger number of alternatives, whereas with 100 alternatives, an average of 9 iterations were needed to reach a compromise.

The second case that was considered was problems consisting of a much larger number of alternatives. The sizes that were checked are in the range of $[100, 1000]$ with a step of 100. The results for this case are shown in Fig. 4. As can be seen in the boxen plots shown, the values slowly increased until, with a matrix containing 700 alternatives, it grew rapidly, but at higher values, it already increased slightly. This behaviour may show that the number of iterations needed can increase sharply in huge decision problems at specific sizes and then stay within a single value. In the case of 1000 alternatives, the compromise was obtained after 22 iterations on average, which, looking at the size of the

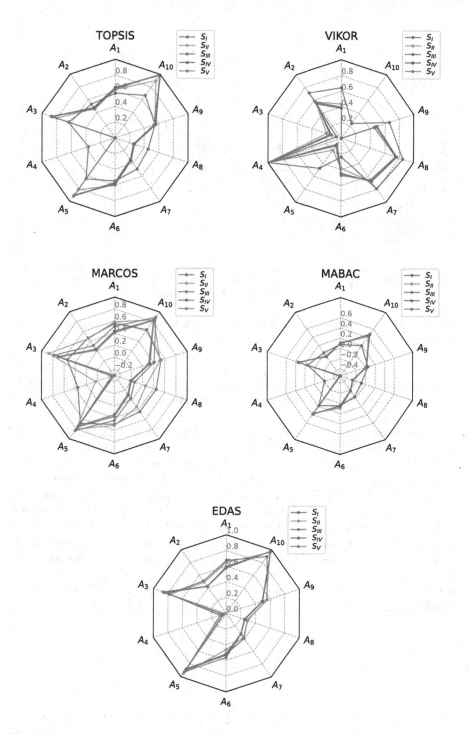

Fig. 2. Obtained preference for TOPSIS, VIKOR, MARCOS, MABAC, and EDAS methods in subsequent iterations.

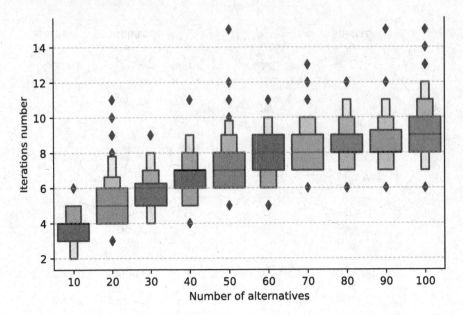

Fig. 3. Influence of number of alternatives on the number of iterations in small decision problems.

problem, does not seem to be a large value, because as the number of alternatives in a decision problem increases, the difficulty of decision-making increases significantly.

For each method considered, it was checked how the ranking proposed in the first step by methods changes in relation to the compromise ranking obtained. A hundred matrices were generated with values from the normal distribution $[0, 1]$ with the size of ten alternatives and six criteria. The values were visualized in Fig. 5. The TOPSIS method in this chart proposed rankings closest to the compromise rankings, followed by the MABAC method, MARCOS, EDAS, and finally VIKOR. In the case of the VIKOR method, there were the greatest discrepancies in the compromise rankings relative to the initial rankings. It can be said in this case that all methods except VIKOR proposed similar rankings. In such cases, the compromise approach can prove to be a good solution, as it takes into account how the majority opined, given the rating, which differed significantly.

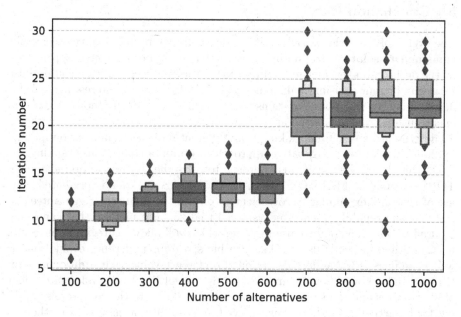

Fig. 4. Influence of number of alternatives on the number of iterations in big decision problems.

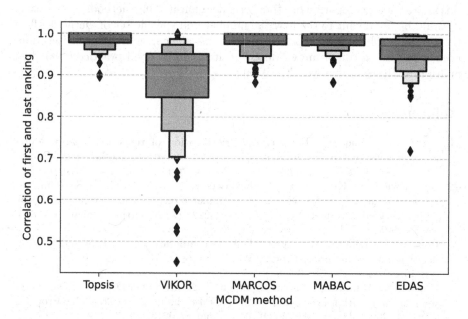

Fig. 5. Correlation between first ranking provided by a method and compromise ranking.

5 Conclusion

The ever-evolving field of multi-criteria decision-making requires the search for non-standard solutions to produce a result that could be considered appropriate by the decision-maker. One of the important problems is obtaining a compromise between different decision-making methods. While these are interesting tools for determining the set of best solutions to the problem under consideration, discrepancies in final rankings often arise between the results from different methods. To determine a single final ranking from different multi-criteria decision-making methods, we can use an iterative approach to obtain a compromise ranking.

In this study, the use of this approach to solve the theoretical problem using TOPSIS, VIKOR, MARCOS, MABAC, and EDAS methods is presented. The use of the ranking similarity coefficient to obtain the final result guarantees its stability and reliability. The study showed that this is a method that can easily be used to obtain a compromise ranking, which will allow aggregation of results from multiple methods using a larger value space for preference evaluation, as well as an increased standard deviation of preference values. An additional quantitative study showed how the method behaves according to the different number of alternatives and the similarity of the initial rankings to the compromise ranking for a particular method. This shows the feasibility of using this method to compare multi-criteria decision-making methods as well as the simplicity and fast execution of using this approach.

In future studies, it would be worthwhile to test the broader applicability of this approach for comparing multi-criteria decision-making methods. In addition, it would be important to see how the number and specific set of methods affect the resulting solution, and to what extent this affects the number of iterations needed to reach a compromise. Moreover, it would be good practice to conduct multiple analyses of real-world problems.

References

1. Abdul, D., Wenqi, J., Tanveer, A.: Prioritization of renewable energy source for electricity generation through AHP-VIKOR integrated methodology. Renew. Energy **184**, 1018–1032 (2022). https://doi.org/10.1016/j.renene.2021.10.082
2. Bączkiewicz, A., Kizielewicz, B., Shekhovtsov, A., Wątróbski, J., Sałabun, W.: Methodical aspects of MCDM based e-commerce recommender system. J. Theor. Appl. Electron. Commer. Res. **16**(6), 2192–2229 (2021). https://doi.org/10.3390/jtaer16060122
3. Ceballos, B., Lamata, M.T., Pelta, D.A.: A comparative analysis of multi-criteria decision-making methods. Progr. Artif. Intell. **5**(4), 315–322 (2016). https://doi.org/10.1007/s13748-016-0093-1
4. Chodha, V., Dubey, R., Kumar, R., Singh, S., Kaur, S.: Selection of industrial arc welding robot with topsis and entropy MCDM techniques. Mater. Today Proc. **50**, 709–715 (2022). https://doi.org/10.1016/j.matpr.2021.04.487
5. Diakoulaki, D., Mavrotas, G., Papayannakis, L.: Determining objective weights in multiple criteria problems: the critic method. Comput. Oper. Res. **22**(7), 763–770 (1995). https://doi.org/10.1016/0305-0548(94)00059-H

6. Duckstein, L., Opricovic, S.: Multiobjective optimization in river basin development. Water Resour. Res. **16**(1), 14–20 (1980). https://doi.org/10.1029/WR016i001p00014

7. Ecer, F.: A consolidated MCDM framework for performance assessment of battery electric vehicles based on ranking strategies. Renew. Sustain. Energy Rev. **143**, 110916 (2021). https://doi.org/10.1016/j.rser.2021.110916

8. Ghaleb, A.M., Kaid, H., Alsamhan, A., Mian, S.H., Hidri, L.: Assessment and comparison of various MCDM approaches in the selection of manufacturing process. Adv. Mater. Sci. Eng. **2020**, 1–16 (2020). https://doi.org/10.1155/2020/4039253

9. Gul, M., Celik, E., Aydin, N., Gumus, A.T., Guneri, A.F.: A state of the art literature review of VIKOR and its fuzzy extensions on applications. Appl. Soft Comput. **46**, 60–89 (2016). https://doi.org/10.1016/j.asoc.2016.04.040

10. Ju, Y., Wang, A.: Extension of VIKOR method for multi-criteria group decision making problem with linguistic information. Appl. Math. Model. **37**(5), 3112–3125 (2013). https://doi.org/10.1016/j.apm.2012.07.035

11. Keshavarz-Ghorabaee, M., Amiri, M., Zavadskas, E.K., Turskis, Z., Antucheviciene, J.: Determination of objective weights using a new method based on the removal effects of criteria (MEREC). Symmetry **13**(4), 525 (2021). https://doi.org/10.3390/sym13040525

12. Keshavarz Ghorabaee, M., Zavadskas, E.K., Olfat, L., Turskis, Z.: Multi-criteria inventory classification using a new method of evaluation based on distance from average solution (EDAS). Informatica **26**(3), 435–451 (2015)

13. Kizielewicz, B., Shekhovtsov, A., Sałabun, W.: A novel iterative approach to determining compromise rankings. In: 2022 17th Conference on Computer Science and Intelligence Systems (FedCSIS), pp. 783–787. IEEE (2022). https://doi.org/10.15439/2022F255

14. Krishnan, A.R., Kasim, M.M., Hamid, R., Ghazali, M.F.: A modified critic method to estimate the objective weights of decision criteria. Symmetry **13**(6), 973 (2021). https://doi.org/10.3390/sym13060973

15. Lamboray, C.: A comparison between the prudent order and the ranking obtained with Borda's, Copeland's, slater's and Kemeny's rules. Math. Soc. Sci. **54**(1), 1–16 (2007). https://doi.org/10.1016/j.mathsocsci.2007.04.004

16. Lestari, S., Adji, T.B., Permanasari, A.E.: Performance comparison of rank aggregation using Borda and Copeland in recommender system. In: 2018 International Workshop on Big Data and Information Security (IWBIS), pp. 69–74. IEEE (2018). https://doi.org/10.1109/IWBIS.2018.8471722

17. Muravyov, S.V., Emelyanova, E.Y.: Kemeny rule for preference aggregation: reducing all exact solutions to a single one. Measurement **182**, 109403 (2021). https://doi.org/10.1016/j.measurement.2021.109403

18. Özdağoğlu, A., Keleş, M.K., Altınata, A., Ulutaş, A.: Combining different MCDM methods with the Copeland method: an investigation on motorcycle selection. J. Process. Manag. New Technol. **9**(3–4), 13–27 (2021). https://doi.org/10.5937/jpmnt9-34120

19. Pamučar, D., Ćirović, G.: The selection of transport and handling resources in logistics centers using multi-attributive border approximation area comparison (MABAC). Expert Syst. Appl. **42**(6), 3016–3028 (2015). https://doi.org/10.1016/j.eswa.2014.11.057

20. Paradowski, B., Shekhovtsov, A., Bączkiewicz, A., Kizielewicz, B., Sałabun, W.: Similarity analysis of methods for objective determination of weights in multi-criteria decision support systems. Symmetry **13**(10), 1874 (2021). https://doi.org/10.3390/sym13101874

21. Podvezko, V., Zavadskas, E.K., Podviezko, A.: An extension of the new objective weight assessment methods CILOS and IDOCRIW to fuzzy MCDM. Econ. Comput. Econ. Cybern. Stud. Res. **54**(2) (2020). https://doi.org/10.24818/18423264/54.2.20.04

22. Qin, J., Liu, X., Pedrycz, W.: An extended VIKOR method based on prospect theory for multiple attribute decision making under interval type-2 fuzzy environment. Knowl.-Based Syst. **86**, 116–130 (2015). https://doi.org/10.1016/j.knosys.2015.05.025

23. Roozbahani, A., Ebrahimi, E., Banihabib, M.E.: A framework for ground water management based on Bayesian network and MCDM techniques. Water Resour. Manag. **32**(15), 4985–5005 (2018). https://doi.org/10.1007/s11269-018-2118-y

24. Serrai, W., Abdelli, A., Mokdad, L., Hammal, Y.: Towards an efficient and a more accurate web service selection using MCDM methods. J. Comput. Sci. **22**, 253–267 (2017). https://doi.org/10.1016/j.jocs.2017.05.024

25. Stević, Ž, Pamučar, D., Puška, A., Chatterjee, P.: Sustainable supplier selection in healthcare industries using a new MCDM method: measurement of alternatives and ranking according to compromise solution (MARCOS). Comput. Industr. Eng. **140**, 106231 (2020). https://doi.org/10.1016/j.cie.2019.106231

26. Sun, R., Hu, J., Zhou, J., Chen, X.: A hesitant fuzzy linguistic projection-based MABAC method for patients' prioritization. Int. J. Fuzzy Syst. **20**(7), 2144–2160 (2017). https://doi.org/10.1007/s40815-017-0345-7

27. Wang, J., Wei, G., Wei, C., Wei, Y.: MABAC method for multiple attribute group decision making under q-rung orthopair fuzzy environment. Defence Technol. **16**(1), 208–216 (2020). https://doi.org/10.1016/j.dt.2019.06.019

28. Wątróbski, J., Jankowski, J., Ziemba, P., Karczmarczyk, A., Zioło, M.: Generalised framework for multi-criteria method selection. Omega **86**, 107–124 (2019). https://doi.org/10.1016/j.omega.2018.07.004

29. Wu, X., Liao, H., Xu, Z., Hafezalkotob, A., Herrera, F.: Probabilistic linguistic multimoora: a multicriteria decision making method based on the probabilistic linguistic expectation function and the improved Borda rule. IEEE Trans. Fuzzy Syst. **26**(6), 3688–3702 (2018). https://doi.org/10.1109/TFUZZ.2018.2843330

30. Yazdani, M., Zarate, P., Zavadskas, E.K., Turskis, Z.: A combined compromise solution (COCOSO) method for multi-criteria decision-making problems. Manag. Decis. **57**(9), 2501–2519 (2018). https://doi.org/10.1108/MD-05-2017-0458

31. Zavadskas, E.K., Podvezko, V.: Integrated determination of objective criteria weights in MCDM. Int. J. Inf. Technol. Decis. Making **15**(02), 267–283 (2016). https://doi.org/10.1142/S0219622016500036

Temporal SWARA-SPOTIS for Multi-Criteria Assessment of European Countries Regarding Sustainable RES Exploitation

Aleksandra Bączkiewicz[1,2(✉)] [iD]

[1] Institute of Management, University of Szczecin, ul. Cukrowa 8, 71-004 Szczecin, Poland
aleksandra.baczkiewicz@phd.usz.edu.pl

[2] Doctoral School of University of Szczecin, ul. Mickiewicza 16, 70-383 Szczecin, Poland

Abstract. This paper aims to introduce a novel Temporal SWARA-SPOTIS method for multi-criteria temporal performance evaluation of alternatives. The proposed method combines the Step-Wise Weights Assessment Ratio Analysis (SWARA) method for determining the significance values of particular periods and the Stable Preference Ordering Towards Ideal Solution (SPOTIS) method for the multi-criteria assessment of alternatives. The developed method was applied to construct a framework for assessing the sustainable use of renewable energy sources (RES) by European countries in various branches of the economy and industry, considering multiple criteria and the dynamics of change of the obtained results over time. The application of the proposed method is presented in an illustrative example covering the assessment of 30 selected European countries over the five years 2015–2019 with data from Eurostat. The presented approach proved its usefulness in the problem investigated and allowed obtaining reliable and straightforward results indicating that the best-scored countries regarding sustainable use of RES are dominantly the Nordic countries.

Keywords: Temporal SWARA-SPOTIS · MCDA · renewable energy sources · sustainability

1 Introduction

Renewable energy sources (RES) play an essential role in the sustainable economy of countries. Therefore, the sustainable use of RES in various economic and industrial sectors has an important place in the long-term energy policy planning strategy [27]. The increase in RES participation in various domains contributes to limiting greenhouse gas emissions and atmospheric pollutants and reducing countries' dependence on imports of non-renewable energy sources [37]. Furthermore, the popularity of RES allows for a decrease in the exploitation of reserves

© The Author(s), under exclusive license to Springer Nature Switzerland AG 2023
E. Ziemba et al. (Eds.): FedCSIS-AIST 2022/ISM 2022, LNBIP 471, pp. 171–191, 2023.
https://doi.org/10.1007/978-3-031-29570-6_9

of non-renewable energy sources. Thus, it is possible to improve energy security and reduce the harmful impact of the economy and industry on the environment [9, 30]. The efforts to increase the share of RES cover many different dimensions. Among them is electricity generation from RES such as Hydro, Wind, Solar, Biomass, Geothermal, and Wave (tidal). Besides, energy policies promoting the use of RES include increasing the share of RES in energy consumption in sectors such as transportation, heating and cooling, and many others [23, 25]. Furthermore, due to the relevance of the sustainable use of RES by governments, appropriate measurement methods and tools are necessary to assess the achievement of planned goals, evaluate a selected region against other regions, and construct rankings of considered cities, regions, or countries [7, 24, 29, 31]. A reliable assessment of sustainable development problems often requires considering the performance dynamics of the evaluated alternatives over the observed time. It enables assessment of the improvement or worsening of the considered alternatives [21]. For this purpose, special methods are required that make it possible to aggregate the variability of performances over time and incorporate it into the final results.

This paper introduces a newly developed Temporal SWARA-SPOTIS method designed for multi-criteria temporal evaluation. The proposed method could find application in information systems supporting multi-criteria sustainability assessment and comparing alternatives over a given time range. The application of the proposed method is presented in the example of a temporal multi-criteria assessment of selected European countries in terms of RES use in various branches of the economy and industry. Considered evaluation criteria include, but are not limited to, electricity generation from RES and consumption of energy from RES in transport and heating and cooling. The significance values of the evaluation criteria were determined using the CRiteria Importance Through Inter criteria Correlation (CRITIC) objective weighting method [35]. The applied weighting technique ensures the objectivity of the evaluation and contributes to the automation of the system in which the proposed approach can be used. It is because the weights are determined based on the performance values in the decision matrix without the need to involve an expert with specialized knowledge of the problem being solved. For comparison purposes, the Stable Preference Ordering Towards Ideal Solution (SPOTIS) results obtained for each year were compared with results provided by the well-known and widely used Technique for Order of Preference by Similarity to Ideal Solution (TOPSIS) method [39].

In the proposed approach, scores obtained with the SPOTIS method for each year are aggregated in a temporal decision matrix and re-evaluated by SPOTIS. In this stage, periods play the role of criteria. Therefore, the Step-Wise Weights Assessment Ratio Analysis (SWARA) method was adapted to determine the significance of particular periods. The SPOTIS method is an innovative method developed in 2020 [10]. Its main advantage is resistance to the rank reversal paradox, which appears as ranking reversal when changes in the evaluated set of alternatives are made [18]. Another feature of the SPOTIS method is identifying a full domain model, which is an important advantage for sustainability assessment. The SWARA method is a technique for subjectively determining the weights of criteria to evaluate using Multi-Criteria Decision Analysis (MCDA) methods [45]. This method is easier to apply than other known subjective weighting techniques such as AHP or Simple Multi-Attribute Rating Technique (SMART). SWARA requires the decision-maker to rank the evaluation criteria starting with the most important and assign comparative importance ratio values representing percentage differences between their importance [26].

The rest of the paper is organized as follows. Section 2 provides literature review. Section 3 gives the background and formulas for all methods used in this research and describes the practical problem of sustainability assessment focused on RES exploitation by European countries is introduced. The next Sect. 4 presents research results which are discussed in Sect. 5. Finally, in the lat Sect. 6 conclusions are provided, and future work directions are drawn.

2   Literature Review

Reliable assessment of sustainable use of RES requires simultaneous consideration of multiple dimensions such as economic, environmental, and social [29]. In addition, the assessment methodology for multi-criteria RES problems should consider different aspects of the assessment, such as various types of RES, several attributes of the location for RES-generating infrastructures, and different sectors in which RES are produced or produced or used consumed [1]. These requirements are fulfilled by multi-criteria decision analysis methods (MCDA), which allow simultaneous consideration of multiple, often conflicting criteria and different interest groups and stakeholders [13,42–44]. With the application of MCDA methods, it is possible to consider the significance values of evaluation criteria called criterion weights, representing the preferences of individual decision-makers or groups of decision-makers [19,33]. Criteria weights may be determined using subjective methods that require the participation of decision-makers and their knowledge of the problem being evaluated [28]. However, objective weighting methods are also available besides subjective methods for determining weights. These techniques allow the calculation of criteria weights based on the performance values of the alternatives relative to the evaluation criteria in the decision matrix [41]. Their feature is that they are automated and do not require the active involvement of the decision-maker, which is an advantage in the absence of experts with specialized knowledge of the decision problem in a given situation [4].

Many research papers are available in the literature focused on evaluating RES issues with multiple criteria. It is worth mentioning research whose subject was the multi-criteria assessment of selected fourteen different countries in terms of preparation for the sustainable energy transition. This study used the analysis conducted using two MCDA methods, namely Preference Ranking Organization METHod for Enrichment of Evaluation (PROMETHEE) II and Analytical Hierarchy Process (AHP), to obtain the results [29]. A comparative analysis employing four MCDA methods, including Characteristic Objects

METhod (COMET), Technique for Order of Preference by Similarity to Ideal Solution (TOPSIS), Vise Kriterijumska Optimizacija I Kompromisno Resenje (VIKOR), and PROMETHEE II, was performed to reliably assess the European countries in terms of energy consumption with particular attention to RES share [2]. MCDA methods have also been successfully applied to evaluate infrastructure and technologies for generating electricity from RES. For example, two multi-criteria rank reversal free methods, including COMET and Stable Preference Ordering Towards Ideal Solution (SPOTIS), were used to evaluate solar panel alternatives regarding selected technical attributes of assessed options [4].

The literature review confirms the usefulness of MCDA methods in the multi-dimensional evaluation of RES, considering multiple aspects for a given moment. However, a clear and interesting research gap is visible, including the lack of simultaneous respect for the performance variability over the time analyzed in the evaluating procedure. Several attempts of temporal approach in multi-criteria evaluation using MCDA methods can be found in the literature. For example, an approach involving an adaptation of the TOPSIS method for evaluation that considers the variability of results over time can be mentioned [14]. The proposed approach considers evaluating alternatives using the TOPSIS method performed individually for each analyzed year. Then, a temporal decision matrix is created containing utility function values of alternatives calculated for successive years. The created matrix is evaluated using the TOPSIS method in the next stage. The role of criteria is played by years in this step. For particular years significance values called confidence levels are assigned. Most recent years have the highest significance. The proposed approach has been applied to the multi-criteria temporal evaluation of forest management. The presented method demonstrates a high potential for usefulness in temporal multi-criteria evaluation. However, it is a preliminary approach requiring further development because the paper does not provide clear and straightforward rules for determining the significance levels of individual periods. The authors of another research adapted the PROMETHEE II method to perform a multi-criteria evaluation of temporal sustainable forest management [36]. The approach introduced in this paper involves aggregating the results of comparing pairs of criteria in each period. The rank relations are converted to preference relations for each pair of alternatives and each period in the next stage. However, the procedure described is complex, making it difficult to apply to complex hierarchical models containing multiple criteria. Another paper presents research in which the dynamics of results achieved by European countries regarding sustainable cities and communities were aggregated using the Gini coefficient as a measure of variability and evaluated using TOPSIS [40].

The development of a multi-criteria temporal approach in sustainability assessment is justified because one of the aspects of reliable sustainability assessment is the consideration of the achievement of long-term goals and the progress of alternatives. The limitations in multi-criteria temporal evaluation studies discussed above became the motivation for developing a new approach that aggregates the evaluated alternatives' results in successive periods and evaluates them using the significance values assigned to the analyzed periods.

3 Research Methodology

The first step of the proposed Temporal SWARA-SPOTIS method is to generate vectors containing the utility function values of all evaluated alternatives using the classic SPOTIS method [10] for each year in the analysis period. For this purpose, it is necessary to determine the significance values of the evaluation criteria using a subjective or objective weighting method. In this research, the objective weighting method called CRITIC was applied. CRITIC allows the significance of the criteria, namely criteria weights, to be calculated from the performance values in the decision matrices [3]. Then the new temporal decision matrix is constructed, which includes vectors with SPOTIS utility function values placed in subsequent columns according to the following years. Then the new temporal decision matrix is built, which includes vectors with SPOTIS utility function values set in subsequent columns according to the following years, which play the evaluation criteria role. The next step involves determining the significance values or weights for each year using the SWARA method. The temporal decision matrix is then evaluated using the SPOTIS method. The evaluation requires a vector of weights for years and criteria types. In the SPOTIS method, the best-scored alternatives have the lowest utility function value, and SPOTIS ranking is generated based on them by ranking the options in ascending order. It implies that the criteria years are of the cost type since low values indicate better performance.

3.1 The SPOTIS Method

The following steps of the SPOTIS (Stable Preference Ordering Towards Ideal Solution) method, which has the main contribution to the proposed Temporal SWARA-SPOTIS method, are provided below, based on [10].

Step 1. Specify the MCDA problem by establishing the bounds including the minimum and maximum performance values included in assessed decision matrix $S = [s_{ij}]_{m \times n}$ for each attribute, namely criterion. The minimum and maximum bounds for each criterion $C_j (j = 1, 2, \ldots, n)$ are established accordingly by S_j^{min} and S_j^{max}.

Step 2. The aim of this step is determination of the Ideal Solution Point (ISP) denoted by S^*. When for the attribute C_j higher score value is favored, then the ISP for attribute C_j is determined as $S_j^* = S_j^{max}$. In another situation, when for the attribute C_j lower score value is preferable, then the ISP for attribute C_j is denoted by $S_j^* = S_j^{min}$. The ideal multi-criteria best solution S^* is represented by values $(S_1^*, S_j^*, \ldots, S_n^*)$.

Step 3. Calculate the normalized distance values d_{ij} considering ISP for each evaluated alternative A_i as Eq. (1) presents.

$$d_{ij}(A_i, s_j^\star) = \frac{|S_{ij} - S_j^\star|}{|S_j^{max} - S_j^{min}|} \tag{1}$$

Step 4. Compute of the weighted normalized averaged distance values for each alternative A_i according to Eq. (2)

$$d(A_i, s^*) = \sum_{j=1}^{n} w_j d_{ij}(A_i, s_j^\star) \tag{2}$$

where w_j denotes the weight value of jth attribute.

Step 5. Generate ranking of assessed options by sorting $d(A_i, s^*)$ values in ascending order. The best-scored option is alternative which has the lowest $d(A_i, s^*)$ value.

3.2 The TOPSIS Method

The successive steps of the TOPSIS (Technique for Order of Preference by Similarity to Ideal Solution) method, which was employed as the benchmarking approach [17] to the TOPSIS method in this research, are demonstrated as follows, based on [5].

Step 1. This step aims to normalize the decision matrix containing performance values with the selected normalization method. It may be the Minimum-Maximum normalization method, like in the presented research. Another type of normalization method may also be applied. The Minimum-Maximum normalization calculates r_{ij} normalized values of decision matrix according to Eq. (3) for profit attributes and (4) for cost attributes.

$$r_{ij} = \frac{x_{ij} - min_j(x_{ij})}{max_j(x_{ij}) - min_j(x_{ij})} \tag{3}$$

$$r_{ij} = \frac{max_j(x_{ij}) - x_{ij}}{max_j(x_{ij}) - min_j(x_{ij})} \tag{4}$$

where $X = [x_{ij}]_{m \times n}$ denotes the decision matrix including performance values of m alternatives in relation to n attributes considered.

Step 2. Compute the values of weighted normalized decision matrix using Eq. (5)

$$v_{ij} = w_j r_{ij} \tag{5}$$

where w_j represents jth attribute weight values.

Step 3. Calculate the Positive Ideal Solution (PIS) with Eq. (6) and Negative Ideal Solution (NIS) using Eq. (7). PIS contains the maximum values of the weighted normalized decision matrix, and NIS includes minimal values. Because the normalization of the decision matrix was performed in step 1, dividing attributes into profit and cost types is not necessary.

$$v_j^+ = \{v_1^+, v_2^+, \ldots, v_n^+\} = \{max_j(v_{ij})\} \tag{6}$$

$$v_j^- = \{v_1^-, v_2^-, \ldots, v_n^-\} = \{min_j(v_{ij})\} \tag{7}$$

Step 4. Compute the distance from PIS (8) and NIS (9) of every evaluated option. The measure determining distance used primarily in the TOPSIS method is Euclidean distance.

$$D_i^+ = \sqrt{\sum_{j=1}^{n}(v_{ij} - v_j^+)^2} \tag{8}$$

$$D_i^- = \sqrt{\sum_{j=1}^{n}(v_{ij} - v_j^-)^2} \tag{9}$$

Step 5. Compute the utility function value for every assessed option according to Eq. (10). The C_i value is between 0 to 1. The option, which has the highest C_i value assigned, is the most favored. Thus, the ranking of the TOPSIS method is built by sorting options descendingly, considering their utility function values.

$$C_i = \frac{D_i^-}{D_i^- + D_i^+} \tag{10}$$

3.3   The CRITIC Method

This section provides the basics and formulas required for determining criteria weights by the CRITIC objective weighting method. This technique was applied in the presented research to calculate the significance values of the considered criteria. For performing MCDA evaluation of the decision problem, the decision matrix $X = [x_{ij}]_{m \times n}$ is necessary. Decision matrix includes m alternatives, n criteria, and x_{ij} denotes the performance measure of ith alternative in relation to j^{th} criterion. To determine the jth criterion weight w_j using CRITIC, the following formulas have to be applied [16].

Step 1. Normalization of the decision matrix using Eq. (3) for profit criteria and Eq. (4) for cost criteria, which are provided in Sect. 3.2.

Step 2. Calculate the Pearson correlation coefficient values between compared criteria pairs according to Eq. (11).

$$\rho_{jk} = \frac{\sum_{i=1}^{m}(r_{ij} - \overline{r}_j)(r_{ik} - \overline{r}_k)}{\sqrt{\sum_{i=1}^{m}(r_{ij} - \overline{r}_j)^2 \sum_{i=1}^{m}(r_{ik} - \overline{r}_k)^2}}. \tag{11}$$

Step 3. Calculate criteria weights with Eqs. (12) and (13),

$$c_j = \sigma_j \sum_{k=1}^{n}(1 - \rho_{jk}); \tag{12}$$

$$w_j = \frac{c_j}{\sum_{k=1}^{n} c_k},$$ (13)

where $i = 1, 2, \ldots, m$; $j, k = 1, 2, \ldots, n$. In given equations c_j denotes the quantity of information included in j^{th} criterion, σ_j represents the standard deviation of the jth criterion and ρ_{jk} denotes the correlation coefficient between the jth and k^{th} criteria. High correlation weight is implied by high values of standard deviation and low values of correlation between a given criterion and the others. Therefore, a high value of C_j delivers more information from the criterion under consideration [35].

3.4   The Weighted Spearman Rank Correlation Coefficient

The r_w correlation coefficient is calculated by Eq. (14) to compare both rankings x and y. N represents a number of rank values x_i and y_i [4].

$$r_w = 1 - \frac{6 \sum_{i=1}^{N} (x_i - y_i)^2 ((N - x_i + 1) + (N - y_i + 1))}{N^4 + N^3 - N^2 - N}$$ (14)

3.5   The Spearman Rank Correlation Coefficient

The Spearman Rank Correlation Coefficient is calculated to determine the correlation value between two rankings x and y as Eq. (15) shows,

$$r_s = 1 - \frac{6 \cdot \sum_{i=1}^{N} (x_i - y_i)^2}{N \cdot (N^2 - 1)}$$ (15)

where N represents size of vector x and y [32].

3.6   The Temporal SWARA-SPOTIS Method

Step 1. Create the temporal decision matrix $S = [s_{ip}]_{m \times t}$ including in following columns the utility function values (namely weighted normalized average distance values) calculated with SPOTIS for each ith assessed option $i = 1, 2, \ldots, m$ in pth periods analysed, where $p = 1, 2, \ldots, t$. Utility function values are final SPOTIS method scores.

Step 2. This step starts the SWARA procedure of determining the significance of particular periods considered [20]. Rank analyzed periods of time in descending order according to their significance. Period p_1 is regarded as the most significant.

Step 3. Establish comparative importance ratio c among investigated periods. Start with the period p_2 and define how much period p_1 is more significant than p_2. Determine c_p ratio using values in the range from 0 to 1, analogously to percentage. Value of comparative importance ration c_1 is determined for periods p_1 and p_2. Then, identical procedure is followed up to period p_t. Comparative importance determined between p_{t-1} and p_t is denoted by c_{t-1}, where t represents number of all periods to investigate.

Step 4. Compute the coefficient k_p values according to Eq. (16), where p represents periods ranked in descending order according to their importance.

$$k_p = \begin{cases} 1, & p = 1 \\ c_p + 1, & p > 1 \end{cases} \tag{16}$$

Step 5. Calculate initial weights v_p for particular periods as Eq. (17) presents.

$$v_p = \begin{cases} 1, & p = 1 \\ \frac{v_{p-1}}{k_p}, & p > 1 \end{cases} \tag{17}$$

Step 6. Determine final SWARA weights w_p for each period according to Eq. (18).

$$w_p = \frac{v_p}{\sum_{p=1}^{t} v_p} \tag{18}$$

Step 7. The three final stages involve the Temporal SWARA-SPOTIS assessment of matrix S including SPOTIS utility function values s in the form of weighted average distance values calculated for alternatives for each period p. First step includes determination of the normalized distances d_{ip} for each alternative A_i from Ideal Solution Point $S^\star$ according to Eq. 19. $S^\star$ is represented by S^{min} in this case since the SPOTIS creates rankings by sorting alternatives in ascending order, considering utility function values received by alternatives in each period. Due to this, the option with the lowest utility function value is regarded as the best-evaluated option.

$$d_{ip}(A_i, s_p^\star) = \frac{|s_{ip} - s_p^\star|}{|s_p^{max} - s_p^{min}|} \tag{19}$$

Step 8. Compute the final temporal utility function values for each alternative as Equation (20) shows

$$d(A_i, s^\star) = \sum_{p=1}^{t} w_p d_{ip}(A_i, s_p^\star) \tag{20}$$

where w_p represents SWARA weights assigned for particular periods of analyzed time.

Step 9. Generate the final Temporal SWARA-SPOTIS ranking of evaluated alternatives involving the full investigated time by sorting values $d(A_i, s^\star)$ obtained in the previous step in increasing order following the principles of the SPOTIS method. The best-evaluated option has the lowest $d(A_i, s^\star)$ value.

3.7 The Practical Problem of European Countries' Multi-criteria Assessment in Terms of RES Exploitation Considering Temporal Variability

This paper aims to present a framework for a multi-criteria evaluation of sustainable exploitation of renewable energy sources by selected European countries, taking into account performance variability over investigated time. The designed framework is based on annual data made available by Eurostat in a database collected with the SHARES (SHort Assessment of Renewable Energy Sources) tool [12]. This tool is intended to calculate the annual share of energy from renewable sources in various branches of the economy and industry. In the conception of the framework, 15 criteria were included as measures of RES use in different economic and industrial sectors. Particular criteria are included in Table 1.

Table 1. Criteria representing the framework for sustainable RES using assessment.

C_j	Criterion name	Aim	Unit
C_1	Annual electricity generation from Hydro	↑	[% of E]
C_2	Annual electricity generation from Wind	↑	[% of E]
C_3	Annual electricity generation from Solar	↑	[% of E]
C_4	Annual electricity generation from Solid biofuels	↑	[% of E]
C_5	Annual electricity generation from all other renewables	↑	[% of E]
C_6	Annual consumption of renewable electricity in road transport	↑	[% of T]
C_7	Annual consumption of renewable electricity in rail transport	↑	[% of T]
C_8	Annual consumption of renewable electricity in all other transport modes	↑	[% of T]
C_9	Annual consumption of renewable electricity from compliant biofuels in transport	↑	[% of T]
C_{10}	Annual final energy consumption in heating and cooling	↑	[% of H&C]
C_{11}	Annual derived RES based heat in heating and cooling	↑	[% of H&C]
C_{12}	Annual derived RES based heat in heating and cooling for heat pumps	↑	[% of H&C]
C_{13}	Gross final consumption of energy from renewable sources in electricity	↑	[% of G]
C_{14}	Gross final consumption of energy from renewable sources in heating and cooling	↑	[% of G]
C_{15}	Gross final consumption of energy from renewable sources in transport	↑	[% of G]

There are criteria covering generation of electricity from RES (C_1–C_5) and its consumption (C_6–C_{15}). Data in the mentioned database are available in the unit KTOE (Thousand tonnes of oil equivalent). However, in an attempt to more reliably and objectively assess countries against the use of RES, this research employed percentage data representing the share of each measure in each sector using RES. This approach enables the reduction of inequalities between the compared countries caused by non-modifiable factors such as area, geographical location, and population, which objectifies the assessment.

Therefore, this framework considers RES percentage share in particular sectors, considering all energy sources, such as electricity production (E), energy consumption in transport (T), heating and cooling (H&C), and gross final energy consumption (G). The goal of each criterion is maximization because the assumption of sustainable development is to increase the share of RES in all economic and industrial sectors. Thus, each criterion considered in the developed framework is profit type.

Performance values in the form of percentages of criteria representing the use of RES in particular sectors for the most recent year investigated, 2019, are displayed in Table 2. Analogous decision matrices were created for four previous years analyzed, namely 2015–2018. They are available in the GitHub repository at [11]. The results of the procedures to perform a multi-criteria temporal assessment of countries concerning sustainable RES are presented in the following Sect. 4.

Table 2. Decision matrix with criteria performance values for 2019.

A_i	Country	C_1	C_2	C_3	C_4	C_5	C_6	C_7	C_8	C_9	C_{10}	C_{11}	C_{12}	C_{13}	C_{14}	C_{15}
A_1	Belgium	0.33	10.07	4.67	3.62	2.14	0.03	0.49	0.00	5.23	7.43	0.29	0.59	4.36	4.18	1.39
A_2	Bulgaria	11.23	3.70	3.79	4.06	0.72	0.03	0.29	0.01	5.20	28.82	4.02	2.67	7.05	13.04	1.47
A_3	Czechia	3.06	0.89	3.18	3.30	3.62	0.03	0.66	0.02	5.19	19.46	1.73	1.46	3.10	11.71	1.44
A_4	Denmark	0.05	45.23	2.73	12.32	5.03	0.07	0.50	0.00	5.07	17.90	26.74	3.38	12.82	22.86	1.55
A_5	Germany	3.47	20.37	8.13	1.95	6.89	0.02	0.64	0.00	4.87	11.65	1.75	1.15	8.85	7.12	1.38
A_6	Estonia	0.27	7.04	0.75	12.89	1.05	0.06	0.04	0.09	4.02	27.45	19.70	5.13	5.75	25.06	1.08
A_7	Greece	9.36	13.21	7.99	0.04	0.68	0.01	0.09	0.00	3.09	23.17	0.00	7.02	9.19	9.45	1.03
A_8	Spain	10.52	19.02	5.39	1.39	0.61	0.02	0.36	0.03	5.91	15.91	0.00	2.95	9.94	6.28	2.14
A_9	France	11.76	6.38	2.40	0.76	1.08	0.02	0.52	0.08	7.31	14.71	2.98	4.77	6.18	8.90	2.25
A_{10}	Croatia	36.71	7.47	0.44	2.54	2.62	0.00	0.44	0.06	2.92	33.65	2.69	0.45	11.06	16.38	1.03
A_{11}	Ireland	2.37	31.34	0.07	1.11	1.61	0.02	0.03	0.00	4.65	5.26	0.00	1.06	7.99	2.44	1.55
A_{12}	Italy	14.25	5.80	7.17	1.28	6.46	0.01	0.51	0.54	4.12	13.22	1.85	4.63	7.97	8.84	1.38
A_{13}	Cyprus	0.00	4.38	4.25	0.00	1.13	0.00	0.00	0.00	1.66	26.15	0.23	8.71	2.49	10.65	0.65
A_{14}	Latvia	39.13	1.97	0.04	7.61	4.66	0.18	0.30	0.03	3.42	42.22	15.52	0.03	8.01	31.99	0.98
A_{15}	Lithuania	3.50	10.38	0.72	2.60	1.59	0.05	0.02	0.03	3.72	24.72	21.88	0.77	3.51	20.61	1.33
A_{16}	Luxembourg	1.50	3.47	1.88	2.29	1.72	0.00	0.18	0.00	5.89	2.97	5.56	0.19	1.48	2.35	3.22
A_{17}	Hungary	0.51	1.47	3.20	3.78	1.02	0.02	0.62	0.01	4.03	16.31	1.68	0.13	1.93	9.47	1.21
A_{18}	Malta	0.00	0.00	7.80	0.00	0.24	0.02	0.00	0.00	4.39	9.46	0.03	16.21	3.14	3.49	1.86
A_{19}	Netherlands	0.08	8.84	4.38	2.33	2.60	0.19	0.40	0.00	5.90	4.42	1.67	0.99	3.68	3.70	1.39
A_{20}	Austria	57.11	9.32	2.30	5.10	1.31	0.01	1.37	0.88	5.40	23.86	7.24	2.69	15.63	15.67	2.33
A_{21}	Poland	1.34	8.19	0.41	3.70	0.71	0.00	0.41	0.03	5.03	14.12	1.16	0.70	2.78	7.87	1.51
A_{22}	Portugal	21.60	23.24	2.43	4.99	1.50	0.01	0.39	0.00	4.96	30.84	0.00	10.80	14.19	14.71	1.72
A_{23}	Romania	26.94	11.04	2.91	0.74	0.09	0.02	0.56	0.01	6.34	25.17	0.56	0.00	8.58	13.92	1.79
A_{24}	Slovenia	29.07	0.04	1.95	0.97	0.61	0.00	0.32	0.01	4.91	27.79	2.20	2.17	8.47	11.53	1.98
A_{25}	Slovakia	14.35	0.02	1.95	3.75	1.87	0.02	0.45	0.07	5.84	16.69	2.37	0.63	4.81	10.64	1.44
A_{26}	Finland	16.27	6.63	0.17	13.89	1.11	0.05	0.58	0.00	10.42	40.87	13.12	3.50	10.88	30.48	1.72
A_{27}	Sweden	46.98	14.59	0.48	7.89	1.25	0.21	2.02	0.00	19.88	35.22	21.07	9.83	24.92	28.44	4.50
A_{28}	United Kingdom	1.47	18.41	3.77	7.58	3.54	0.02	0.34	0.00	4.48	6.53	0.22	1.09	7.57	3.29	1.47
A_{29}	Iceland	69.72	0.04	0.00	0.00	30.88	0.53	0.00	0.00	6.00	7.14	72.30	0.00	51.18	26.34	0.68
A_{30}	Norway	106.10	4.52	0.01	0.02	0.17	1.78	1.21	0.00	10.69	18.16	5.88	11.77	61.11	8.25	2.79

4 Research Findings

The following procedures were conducted to evaluate countries against sustainable RES usage temporally. First, from the decision matrices containing performance values for each analyzed year, the significance values of the evaluation criteria were determined using the CRITIC objective weighting method. Then, each decision matrix was evaluated by applying the SPOTIS method, obtaining utility function values for each alternative. Based on them, SPOTIS rankings of countries for each year were generated. Next, a decision matrix containing utility function values obtained by countries for each year was created. The next step was to determine the significance values for each period of time considered in the assessment with the SWARA technique. Then, a decision matrix including SPOTIS utility function values for each year was evaluated using the SWARA weights for each year. The resulting vector with Temporal SWARA-SPOTIS utility function values for each country aggregates the results from each year into a single score. The obtained Temporal SWARA-SPOTIS utility function values were then ranked in ascending order, according to the SPOTIS rule. The criteria weights determined by the CRITIC method for each year are included in Table 3.

Table 3. CRITIC weights assigned for criteria in each investigated year.

Year	C_1	C_2	C_3	C_4	C_5	C_6	C_7	C_8	C_9	C_{10}	C_{11}	C_{12}	C_{13}	C_{14}	C_{15}
2015	0.0550	0.0719	0.1161	0.0698	0.0554	0.0555	0.0545	0.0604	0.0588	0.0819	0.0526	0.0740	0.0525	0.0767	0.0648
2016	0.0545	0.0715	0.1190	0.0771	0.0557	0.0524	0.0520	0.0627	0.0456	0.0885	0.0536	0.0764	0.0518	0.0822	0.0571
2017	0.0544	0.0722	0.1178	0.0791	0.0560	0.0506	0.0540	0.0647	0.0462	0.0853	0.0541	0.0828	0.0509	0.0779	0.0540
2018	0.0561	0.0729	0.1163	0.0850	0.0555	0.0519	0.0539	0.0645	0.0426	0.0842	0.0535	0.0807	0.0527	0.0770	0.0533
2019	0.0557	0.0745	0.1236	0.0842	0.0561	0.0497	0.0530	0.0659	0.0433	0.0809	0.0543	0.0752	0.0524	0.0760	0.0553

To visualize the significance of the evaluation criteria, the weights are additionally displayed in the column chart shown in Fig. 1. It can be observed that the highest significance values in all the years given were assigned by the CRITIC method to criterion C_3, annual electricity generation from solar.

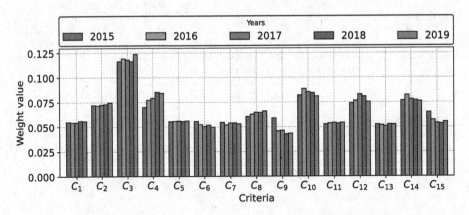

Fig. 1. CRITIC criteria weights determined for each investigated year.

In the next stage, the performance of countries was evaluated using the SPO-TIS method for each year. At this stage, a comparative analysis of the rankings of the SPOTIS method with another MCDA benchmarking method called TOP-SIS [5] was conducted. In order to objectively compare the rankings, the correlation coefficients of the r_w and r_s rankings were determined, which are provided in Table 4. It can be noticed that the correlation values are high, close to 1, which implies high convergence of the obtained rankings and confirms the reliability

Table 4. Correlation coefficients between SPOTIS and TOPSIS rankings for investigated years.

Year	2015	2016	2017	2018	2019
r_w	0.9656	0.9381	0.9569	0.9282	0.8917
r_s	0.9644	0.9448	0.9600	0.9408	0.9070

of SPOTIS results. The observed differences in the rankings provided by the compared MCDA methods are due to differences in their algorithms.

A comparison of the SPOTIS and TOPSIS rankings by year is illustrated graphically in the charts displayed in Fig. 2. It can be observed that Sweden (A_{27}) is the leader of both SPOTIS and TOPSIS rankings in all years analyzed. Thus, Sweden is expected to be the leader of the ranking aggregating the grades achieved in all the years analyzed. For the other countries, performing a reliable assessment that incorporates the dynamics of performance changes over time is no longer straightforward and intuitive. Instead, it requires the use of an appropriate methodology. It is justified by the fact that a noticeable variability in the annual rankings is observed for the rest of the countries. In order to aggregate this variability, the Temporal SWARA-SPOTIS method is proposed which allows multi-criteria, temporal evaluation of alternatives against multiple criteria considering multiple periods.

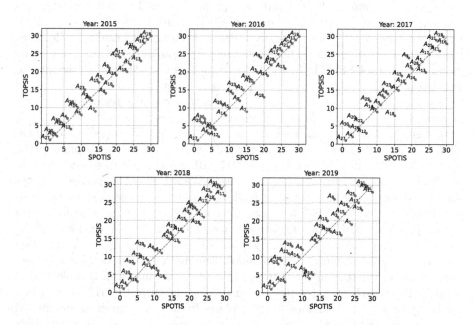

Fig. 2. Comparison of SPOTIS and TOPSIS rankings in investigated years 2015–2019.

Table 5 contains the results of the subsequent stages of the SWARA method applied to determine the significance of particular periods of time, i.e., the analyzed years. In this case, the most recent year is considered the most significant because it is the most interesting for decision-makers, while for the earlier years, the significance gradually decreases. Therefore, a strategy was applied in which each subsequent year is 50% more significant than the year preceding it. The advantage of the proposed method is that the decision-maker can arbitrarily model the relevance of each period by setting arbitrary values of comparative importance ratio c_p for each period of investigated time. For example, in Table 5, it can be noticed that 2015 is assigned a value of 0.5 (50%).

Table 5. SWARA weights assigned for particular years investigated.

Year	c_p	k_p	v_p	w_p
2019	-	1	1.0000	0.3839
2018	0.5	1.5	0.6667	0.2559
2017	0.5	1.5	0.4444	0.1706
2016	0.5	1.5	0.2963	0.1137
2015	0.5	1.5	0.1975	0.0758

It implies that 2016 is 50% more significant than 2015. For subsequent years, the procedure is analogous. Column w_p contains the final SWARA weights calculated for each period p. Table 6 includes SPOTIS utility function values calculated for each country in each analyzed period and generated rankings. Columns named "TSS" contain utility function values and rankings obtained using the Temporal SWARA-SPOTIS method aggregating results obtained in the investigated years with SWARA weights of particular years.

As expected, Sweden (A_{27}) is the best-scored country regarding the sustainable share and use of RES in the considered industries. Austria (A_{20}) took second place. Austria ranked second in 2015 and 2016, dropped to fourth in 2017, and ranked third in 2018 and 2019. Therefore, it may be surprising that despite the worsening performance in 2017–2019, Austria is in second place in the final evaluation. However, the Temporal SWARA-SPOTIS method employs the utility function values obtained in the individual years as performance values, which are more precise than the positions in the rankings. This feature of the proposed method allows for a more accurate and reliable reflection of the aggregate performance of the countries over the years under review. Third place was achieved by Denmark (A_4). Denmark demonstrated a noticeable improvement in the use of RES in the economy over the years analyzed. It ranked sixth in SPOTIS in 2015, then jumped to fourth place in 2016. In 2017, there was a further promotion of Denmark to third place. In 2018, Denmark again climbed to second place and remained there in 2019. Because most recent years are more relevant and have higher SWARA weight than earlier years, the promotions registered between 2017 and 2019 allowed Denmark to reach the third position in

Table 6. Results of classical SPOTIS and Temporal SWARA-SPOTIS for 2015–2019.

A_i	Utility function value						Rank					
	2015	2016	2017	2018	2019	TSS	2015	2016	2017	2018	2019	TSS
A_1	0.8452	0.8322	0.8373	0.8430	0.8343	0.8298	24	22	23	24	24	24
A_2	0.7576	0.7569	0.7801	0.7838	0.7740	0.6677	12	14	16	14	15	14
A_3	0.7830	0.7950	0.8102	0.8228	0.8151	0.7635	16	18	20	20	20	19
A_4	0.6547	0.6333	0.6277	0.6372	0.6352	0.3105	6	4	3	2	2	3
A_5	0.7384	0.7440	0.7534	0.7497	0.7383	0.5901	10	10	11	11	11	11
A_6	0.7645	0.7515	0.7547	0.7356	0.7251	0.5748	13	11	12	10	10	10
A_7	0.7672	0.7628	0.7428	0.7642	0.7398	0.6073	14	15	10	12	12	12
A_8	0.7932	0.7524	0.7614	0.7877	0.7701	0.6637	17	13	13	15	14	13
A_9	0.7952	0.8041	0.8093	0.8231	0.8144	0.7674	18	19	19	21	19	20
A_{10}	0.7969	0.7946	0.8092	0.8116	0.8055	0.7483	19	17	18	18	17	17
A_{11}	0.8978	0.9052	0.8978	0.9102	0.8996	0.9969	29	29	28	30	30	30
A_{12}	0.6774	0.6818	0.6811	0.7224	0.7181	0.4919	7	7	7	9	8	7
A_{13}	0.8629	0.8565	0.8579	0.8026	0.8158	0.8032	27	26	24	17	21	23
A_{14}	0.7047	0.7110	0.7176	0.7169	0.7228	0.5218	9	9	9	8	9	9
A_{15}	0.7714	0.7872	0.8021	0.8125	0.8192	0.7531	15	16	17	19	22	18
A_{16}	0.8911	0.9033	0.9012	0.9063	0.8914	0.9856	28	28	30	29	29	29
A_{17}	0.8398	0.8428	0.8603	0.8683	0.8452	0.8696	22	24	25	25	26	26
A_{18}	0.8442	0.8045	0.7730	0.7735	0.7639	0.6767	23	20	15	13	13	15
A_{19}	0.9057	0.9061	0.9004	0.8886	0.8495	0.9344	30	30	29	27	27	27
A_{20}	0.5891	0.6100	0.6299	0.6398	0.6437	0.3032	2	2	4	3	3	2
A_{21}	0.8509	0.8736	0.8878	0.8913	0.8800	0.9427	25	27	27	28	28	28
A_{22}	0.6401	0.6458	0.6619	0.6940	0.6961	0.4255	5	5	6	6	6	6
A_{23}	0.7516	0.7524	0.7720	0.8002	0.7935	0.6925	11	12	14	16	16	16
A_{24}	0.8023	0.8049	0.8147	0.8279	0.8196	0.7797	20	21	21	22	23	21
A_{25}	0.8165	0.8428	0.8680	0.8749	0.8406	0.8684	21	25	26	26	25	25
A_{26}	0.6161	0.6659	0.6543	0.6637	0.6546	0.3612	3	6	5	5	5	5
A_{27}	0.4957	0.4944	0.5048	0.5255	0.5214	0.0000	1	1	1	1	1	1
A_{28}	0.8563	0.8379	0.8366	0.8289	0.8110	0.8002	26	23	22	23	18	22
A_{29}	0.6974	0.6951	0.7093	0.7148	0.7137	0.5019	8	8	8	7	7	8
A_{30}	0.6362	0.6221	0.6091	0.6496	0.6447	0.3138	4	3	2	4	4	4

the final ranking despite the sixth place occupied in the earliest year analyzed, 2015. Norway (A_{30}) took fourth place in the final ranking. Norway in 2015 was assessed such that it was ranked fourth. In 2016, Norway moved up to the third place and in 2017 to second place. However, it was again ranked fourth in 2018 and 2019. The greater importance of most recent years caused that the better performance in 2016–2017 did not enable Norway to rank higher than fourth in the final ranking. Finland (A_{26}) received fifth place in the final ranking. This country was ranked third in 2015. Then in 2016, Finland dropped to sixth place. In contrast, Norway advanced to fifth place in the ranking in 2017. Therefore, this country retained fifth place in the remaining years analyzed.

Table 7 contains the values of the correlation coefficients r_w and r_s representing the convergence of the final aggregated rankings obtained with Temporal SWARA-SPOTIS with the SPOTIS rankings generated for the individual years analyzed. High values of both correlation coefficients close to 1 indicate high convergence of the compared rankings.

Table 7. Correlation of Temporal SWARA-SPOTIS with classical SPOTIS for 2015–2019.

Year	2015	2016	2017	2018	2019
r_w	0.9562	0.9835	0.9912	0.9885	0.9906
r_s	0.9448	0.9795	0.9907	0.9867	0.9884

The results confirm that the Temporal SWARA-SPOTIS ranking is more consistent with the most recent analyzed years, 2017–2019, than with the earlier years, 2015–2016. The obtained results are consistent with the assumption that the most recent years are more interesting for decision-makers and reflect appropriately the influence of the weights assigned to the following years by the SWARA method.

5   Discussion of Findings

Individual European countries show differences in the transition dynamics to renewable energy sources and the type of dominant RES. These differences influence the assessment results of the RES utilization by the analyzed countries. This research indicated Nordic countries such as Sweden, Denmark, Norway, and Finland as the best-rated countries regarding RES contribution to the overall economy. Besides, the second place in the final ranking was achieved by Austria. Sweden is the leader among European countries relating to energy production from renewable sources [15]. In an assessment of sustainable RES exploitation by selected European countries using a hybrid V-COMET method combining VIKOR and COMET [18], which is based on fuzzy numbers [33], the Nordic countries of Sweden, Iceland, Finland and Norway were among the best rated [38]. Swedish public institutions are strongly involved in supporting activities to promote RES and increase their share in the economy. Such efforts are partially being carried out as grassroots initiatives in other countries. However, Sweden's energy economy has relied mainly for a long time on a growing number of commercial hydropower plants, whose technologies have primarily been developed domestically [34]. The biophysical conditions found in Sweden support the use of Hydro as a primary renewable source of electricity. In addition, Sweden also uses biofuels and biomass to produce heat [22]. The popularity of RES in Sweden is reflected in obtained research results, which indicted this country as the leader in the rankings. The excellent performance of Sweden in terms of RES contribution to the economy is confirmed in other research works. For example, in the multi-criteria analysis of the readiness of selected countries for a sustainable energy transition performed in the study presented in this paper using the PROMETHEE II and AHP methods, Sweden also achieved the first place in the obtained ranking [29]. Furthermore, Sweden has been identified as a ranking leader in a benchmarking analysis, including a multi-criteria assessment of sustainable energy consumption focusing on RES using COMET, VIKOR, PROMETHEE II, and TOPSIS [2]. Denmark, which gained third place in the final ranking, is making an intensive transition to renewable energy sources due to forecasts of decreasing domestic self-sufficiency based on natural gas and oil. In Denmark, electricity is mainly generated from wind power, and heat is produced from biofuels and biomass. In comparison, the energy economy in the Netherlands is based on fossil fuels, mostly domestically available cheap natural gas and imported coal [22]. Therefore, the low RES popularity in the Dutch economy is reflected in the result rankings in which this country achieves low positions.

The results of this research study are comparable with another research study, which aimed at a multi-criteria evaluation based on Eurostat data using the AHP method and comparing European countries against sustainable development, including environmental and energy aspects [8]. The investigation considered indicators such as the share of RES in electricity generation, transport, heating and cooling, among others. The top four countries in this analysis are Sweden, Denmark, Finland, and Austria. The analysis of the results of studies focused on the multi-criteria assessment of European countries against sustainable use of RES conducted by other researchers in recent years confirms the observations and conclusions obtained in this research. Nordic countries such as Sweden, Denmark, Finland, and Norway have strong and stable leadership positions nowadays due to their established RES status. The accurate reflection of final aggregated results by Temporal SWARA-SPOTIS, observed as comparable results with other works of the last five years, confirms the reliability and usefulness of the temporal methodology proposed in this paper for the evaluated problem.

6   Conclusion

This paper demonstrated the application of the newly developed Temporal SWARA-SPOTIS method on the illustrative example of a multi-criteria problem involving evaluating the sustainable use of RES by European countries, considering the dynamics of performance variability over the observed time. For countries' assessment, a framework incorporating 15 indicators selected from the database available in Eurostat was developed. The application of the framework and the developed methodology made it possible to clearly indicate Sweden as the most sustainable country among the included European countries in the analysis covering the five examined years. Other Nordic countries such as Denmark, Norway, and Finland are also among the best-ranked countries. Austria is also a well-scored country. The proposed tool has a high potential of usefulness for information systems supporting multi-criteria sustainability assessment taking into account both multiple indicators and dimensions and the variability of results over time.

This paper has several limitations that can be addressed in future research works. Among them is the limited range of years analyzed, which could be expanded in further studies. The use of the temporal extension of one MCDA method, SPOTIS, is also a limitation, as it is an early attempt. It is the reason for the lack of Temporal SWARA-SPOTIS benchmarking with other temporal methods, which could be performed in the following research works.

The proven usefulness of the proposed tool in the temporal evaluation of sustainable development focused on RES exploitation suggests extending the conducted research to explore other MCDA methods and techniques for determining and considering the relevance of analyzed periods during the multi-criteria evaluation. An interesting direction for further research seems to be an approach adapting the PROMETHEE II method for multi-criteria temporal sustainability assessment. This method appears to be promising due to its ability to employ different preference functions and limited criteria compensation [6]. Further research focused on temporal multi-criteria sustainability assessment is also planned to include a study of the impact of other objective criteria weighting methods on the results. Investigating the utility of the proposed sustainability assessment approach based on other RES indicators may also be an interesting research direction.

Acknowledgment. This research was partially funded by National Science Centre, Poland 2022/45/N/HS4/03050

References

1. Andreopoulou, Z., Koliouska, C., Galariotis, E., Zopounidis, C.: Renewable energy sources: using PROMETHEE II for ranking websites to support market opportunities. Technol. Forecast. Soc. Chang. **131**, 31–37 (2018). https://doi.org/10.1016/j.rser.2017.05.190
2. Bączkiewicz, A., Kizielewicz, B.: Towards sustainable energy consumption evaluation in Europe for industrial sector based on MCDA methods. Procedia Comput. Sci. **192**, 1334–1346 (2021). https://doi.org/10.1016/j.procs.2021.08.137
3. Bączkiewicz, A., Kizielewicz, B., Shekhovtsov, A., Wątróbski, J., Sałabun, W.: Methodical aspects of MCDM based E-commerce recommender system. J. Theor. Appl. Electron. Commer. Res. **16**(6), 2192–2229 (2021). https://doi.org/10.3390/jtaer16060122
4. Bączkiewicz, A., Kizielewicz, B., Shekhovtsov, A., Yelmikheiev, M., Kozlov, V., Sałabun, W.: Comparative analysis of solar panels with determination of local sig-

nificance levels of criteria using the MCDM methods resistant to the rank reversal phenomenon. Energies **14**(18), 5727 (2021). https://doi.org/10.3390/en14185727

5. Chmielarz, W., Zborowski, M.: Towards sustainability in E-banking website assessment methods. Sustainability **12**(17), 7000 (2020). https://doi.org/10.3390/su12177000

6. Chmielarz, W., Zborowski, M.: On the assessment of e-banking websites supporting sustainable development goals. Energies **15**(1), 378 (2022). https://doi.org/10.3390/en15010378

7. Chmielarz, W., Zborowski, M., Fandrejewska, A., Atasever, M.: The contribution of socio-cultural aspects of smartphone applications to smart city creation. Poland-Turkey Comparison. Energies **14**(10), 2821 (2021). https://doi.org/10.3390/en14102821

8. Cucchiella, F., D'Adamo, I., Gastaldi, M., Koh, S.L., Rosa, P.: A comparison of environmental and energetic performance of European countries: a sustainability index. Renew. Sustain. Energy Rev. **78**, 401–413 (2017). https://doi.org/10.1016/j.rser.2017.04.077

9. Delponte, I., Schenone, C.: RES implementation in urban areas: an updated overview. Sustainability **12**(1), 382 (2020). https://doi.org/10.3390/su12010382

10. Dezert, J., Tchamova, A., Han, D., Tacnet, J.M.: The spotis rank reversal free method for multi-criteria decision-making support. In: 2020 IEEE 23rd International Conference on Information Fusion (FUSION), pp. 1–8. IEEE (2020). https://doi.org/10.23919/FUSION45008.2020.9190347

11. energyinpython: Towards the Temporal Multi-Criteria Assessment of Sustainable RES Exploitation in European Countries (2022). https://github.com/energyinpython/fedcsis-2022-RES

12. Eurostat: Energy from renewable sources (2022). https://ec.europa.eu/eurostat/web/energy/data/shares

13. Faizi, S., Sałabun, W., Rashid, T., Zafar, S., Wątróbski, J.: Intuitionistic fuzzy sets in multi-criteria group decision making problems using the characteristic objects method. Symmetry **12**(9), 1382 (2020). https://doi.org/10.3390/sym12091382

14. Frini, A., Benamor, S.: Making decisions in a sustainable development context: a state-of-the-art survey and proposal of a multi-period single synthesizing criterion approach. Comput. Econ. **52**(2), 341–385 (2017). https://doi.org/10.1007/s10614-017-9677-5

15. Gökgöz, F., Güvercin, M.T.: Energy security and renewable energy efficiency in EU. Renew. Sustain. Energy Rev. **96**, 226–239 (2018). https://doi.org/10.1016/j.rser.2018.07.046

16. Jahan, A., Mustapha, F., Sapuan, S., Ismail, M.Y., Bahraminasab, M.: A framework for weighting of criteria in ranking stage of material selection process. Int. J. Adv. Manuf. Technol. **58**(1–4), 411–420 (2012). https://doi.org/10.1007/s00170-011-3366-7

17. Jankowski, J., Kolomvatsos, K., Kazienko, P., Wątróbski, J.: Fuzzy modeling of user behaviors and virtual goods purchases in social networking platforms. J. Univ. Comput. Sci. **22**(3), 416–437 (2016). https://doi.org/10.3217/jucs-022-03-0416

18. Jankowski, J., Sałabun, W., Wątróbski, J.: Identification of a multi-criteria assessment model of relation between editorial and commercial content in web systems. In: Zgrzywa, A., Choroś, K., Siemiński, A. (eds.) Multimedia and Network Information Systems. AISC, vol. 506, pp. 295–305. Springer, Cham (2017). https://doi.org/10.1007/978-3-319-43982-2_26

19. Jankowski, J., Ziemba, P., Wątróbski, J., Kazienko, P.: Towards the tradeoff between online marketing resources exploitation and the user experience with the use of eye tracking. In: Nguyen, N.T., Trawiński, B., Fujita, H., Hong, T.-P. (eds.) ACIIDS 2016. LNCS (LNAI), vol. 9621, pp. 330–343. Springer, Heidelberg (2016). https://doi.org/10.1007/978-3-662-49381-6_32

20. Karabasevic, D., Stanujkic, D., Urosevic, S., Maksimovic, M.: Selection of candidates in the mining industry based on the application of the SWARA and the MULTIMOORA methods. Acta Montanistica Slovaca 20(2), 116–124 (2015)

21. Kizielewicz, B., Więckowski, J., Shekhovtsov, A., Wątróbski, J., Depczyński, R., Sałabun, W.: Study towards the time-based MCDA ranking analysis-a supplier selection case study. Facta Universitatis. Series: Mech. Eng. 19(3), 381–399 (2021). https://doi.org/10.22190/FUME210130048K

22. Kooij, H.J., Oteman, M., Veenman, S., Sperling, K., Magnusson, D., Palm, J., Hvelplund, F.: Between grassroots and treetops: Community power and institutional dependence in the renewable energy sector in Denmark, Sweden and the Netherlands. Energy Res. Soc. Sci. 37, 52–64 (2018). https://doi.org/10.1016/j.erss.2017.09.019

23. Kumar, A., Sah, B., Singh, A.R., Deng, Y., He, X., Kumar, P., Bansal, R.: A review of multi criteria decision making (MCDM) towards sustainable renewable energy development. Renew. Sustain. Energy Rev. 69, 596–609 (2017). https://doi.org/10.1016/j.rser.2016.11.191

24. Łatuszyńska, M., Nermend, K.: Energy decision making: problems, methods, and tools-an overview. Energies 15(15), 5545 (2022). https://doi.org/10.3390/en15155545

25. Lee, H.C., Chang, C.T.: Comparative analysis of MCDM methods for ranking renewable energy sources in Taiwan. Renew. Sustain. Energy Rev. 92, 883–896 (2018). https://doi.org/10.1016/j.rser.2018.05.007

26. Lombardi Netto, A., Salomon, V.A.P., Ortiz Barrios, M.A.: Multi-criteria analysis of green bonds: Hybrid multi-method applications. Sustainability 13(19), 10512 (2021). https://doi.org/10.3390/su131910512

27. Marinakis, V., Doukas, H., Xidonas, P., Zopounidis, C.: Multicriteria decision support in local energy planning: an evaluation of alternative scenarios for the Sustainable Energy Action Plan. Omega 69, 1–16 (2017). https://doi.org/10.1016/j.omega.2016.07.005

28. McIntosh, R.D., Becker, A.: Applying MCDA to weight indicators of seaport vulnerability to climate and extreme weather impacts for U.S. North Atlantic ports. Environ. Syst. Decisions 40(3), 356–370 (2020). https://doi.org/10.1007/s10669-020-09767-y

29. Neofytou, H., Nikas, A., Doukas, H.: Sustainable energy transition readiness: a multicriteria assessment index. Renew. Sustain. Energy Rev. 131, 109988 (2020). https://doi.org/10.1016/j.rser.2020.109988

30. Piwowarski, M., Borawski, M., Nermend, K.: The problem of non-typical objects in the multidimensional comparative analysis of the level of renewable energy development. Energies 14(18), 5803 (2021). https://doi.org/10.3390/en14185803

31. Piwowarski, M., Miłaszewicz, D., Łatuszyńska, M., Borawski, M., Nermend, K.: Application of the vector measure construction method and technique for order preference by similarity ideal solution for the analysis of the dynamics of changes in the poverty levels in the European union countries. Sustainability 10(8), 2858 (2018). https://doi.org/10.3390/su10082858

32. Sajjad, M., Sałabun, W., Faizi, S., Ismail, M., Wątróbski, J.: Statistical and analytical approach of multi-criteria group decision-making based on the correlation coefficient under intuitionistic 2-tuple fuzzy linguistic environment. Expert Syst. Appl. **193**, 116341 (2022). https://doi.org/10.1016/j.eswa.2021.116341

33. Sałabun, W., et al.: A fuzzy inference system for players evaluation in multi-player sports: the football study case. Symmetry **12**(12), 2029 (2020). https://doi.org/10.3390/sym12122029

34. Shabani, M., Dahlquist, E., Wallin, F., Yan, J.: Techno-economic comparison of optimal design of renewable-battery storage and renewable micro pumped hydro storage power supply systems: A case study in Sweden. Appl. Energy **279**, 115830 (2020). https://doi.org/10.1016/j.apenergy.2020.115830

35. Tuş, A., Aytaç Adalı, E.: The new combination with CRITIC and WASPAS methods for the time and attendance software selection problem. Opsearch **56**(2), 528–538 (2019). https://doi.org/10.1007/s12597-019-00371-6

36. Urli, B., Frini, A., Amor, S.B.: PROMETHEE-MP: a generalisation of PROMETHEE for multi-period evaluations under uncertainty. Int. J. Multicriteria Decision Making **8**(1), 13–37 (2019). https://doi.org/10.1504/IJMCDM.2019.098042

37. Wątróbski, J., Bączkiewicz, A., Król, R., Sałabun, W.: Green electricity generation assessment using the CODAS-COMET method. Ecol. Ind. **143**, 109391 (2022). https://doi.org/10.1016/j.ecolind.2022.109391

38. Wątróbski, J., Bączkiewicz, A., Sałabun, W.: New multi-criteria method for evaluation of sustainable RES management. Appl. Energy **324**, 119695 (2022). https://doi.org/10.1016/j.apenergy.2022.119695

39. Wątróbski, J., Bączkiewicz, A., Sałabun, W.: pyrepo-mcda-Reference objects based MCDA software package. SoftwareX **19**, 101107 (2022). https://doi.org/10.1016/j.softx.2022.101107

40. Wątróbski, J., Bączkiewicz, A., Ziemba, E., Sałabun, W.: Sustainable cities and communities assessment using the DARIA-TOPSIS method. Sustainable Cities and Society, p. 103926 (2022). https://doi.org/10.1016/j.scs.2022.103926

41. Wątróbski, J., Jankowski, J., Piotrowski, Z.: The selection of multicriteria method based on unstructured decision problem description. In: Hwang, D., Jung, J.J., Nguyen, N.-T. (eds.) ICCCI 2014. LNCS (LNAI), vol. 8733, pp. 454–465. Springer, Cham (2014). https://doi.org/10.1007/978-3-319-11289-3_46

42. Wątróbski, J., Jankowski, J., Ziemba, P., Karczmarczyk, A., Zioło, M.: Generalised framework for multi-criteria method selection. Omega **86**, 107–124 (2019). https://doi.org/10.1016/j.omega.2018.07.004

43. Ziemba, E.: The contribution of ICT adoption to sustainability: households' perspective. Inf. Technol. People **32**(3), 731–753 (2019). https://doi.org/10.1108/ITP-02-2018-0090

44. Ziemba, E.: The contribution of ICT adoption to the sustainable information society. J. Comput. Inf. Syst. **59**(2), 116–126 (2019). https://doi.org/10.1080/08874417.2017.1312635

45. Zolfani, S.H., Chatterjee, P.: Comparative evaluation of sustainable design based on Step-Wise Weight Assessment Ratio Analysis (SWARA) and Best Worst Method (BWM) methods: a perspective on household furnishing materials. Symmetry **11**(1), 74 (2019). https://doi.org/10.3390/sym11010074

A Sustainable Approach for Determining Compromise Ranking Based on Intuitonistic Fuzzy Score Functions

Bartosz Paradowski[1] , Bartłomiej Kizielewicz[1,2] , Jakub Więckowski[1,2] ,
and Wojciech Sałabun[1,2(✉)]

[1] Research Team on Intelligent Decision Support Systems, Department of Artificial
Intelligence and Applied Mathematics, Faculty of Computer Science and Information
Technology, West Pomeranian University of Technology, Szczecin, Poland
{bartosz-paradowski,bartlomiej-kizielewicz,jakub-wieckowski,
wojciech.salabun}@zut.edu.pl
[2] National Institute of Telecommunications, Szachowa 1, 04-894 Warsaw, Poland

Abstract. Many real-world decision-making problems require some
degree of uncertainty to be taken into account. For purpose of representing such problems, intuitionistic fuzzy sets are used, however, most
well-known multi-criteria decision-making methods operate in a crisp
environment. In this paper, we present an assessment of score functions
that are used to convert fuzzy numbers into crisp ones. Five score functions were selected to assess their usefulness and effectiveness. Those
functions were used to transform the theoretical fuzzy decision matrix
problems into a crisp environment for evaluating alternatives using the
Measurement Alternatives and Ranking according to COmpromise Solution (MARCOS) method. In addition, the compromise between score
functions is presented and compared with the other results. The research
showed that score functions are useful tools when dealing with problems
in an uncertain environment and might prove helpful for decision-makers.

Keywords: Score functions · Uncertain environment · MCDA ·
MARCOS · Intuitionistic fuzzy sets

1 Introduction

Multi-criteria decision-making problems consider problems that are represented
either by crisp values, or ones that consist of some type of uncertainty. There are
many studies devoted to providing a way of modeling uncertain data based on
classical arithmetic methods [1]. Most real-world problems are presented with
some kind of uncertainty, thus such an approach is crucial to model problems as
precisely as possible to reflect uncertain knowledge flexibly. Uncertainty modeling is often used in multi-criteria decision-making problems due to its high
reliability [15].

© The Author(s), under exclusive license to Springer Nature Switzerland AG 2023
E. Ziemba et al. (Eds.): FedCSIS-AIST 2022/ISM 2022, LNBIP 471, pp. 192–211, 2023.
https://doi.org/10.1007/978-3-031-29570-6_10

Throughout the years, numerous ways of representing uncertain knowledge emerged. Among the classical approaches are fuzzy sets (FS), based on the idea related to partial membership [10]. Over the years, fuzzy sets have seen many developments: Hesitant Fuzzy Sets (HFS) [24], Fermatean Fuzzy Sets (FFS) [22], or Intuitionistic Fuzzy Sets (IFS) [11]. Indeed, the main advantage of the generalization of fuzzy sets is a new approach to uncertainty modeling that considers new degrees of membership, which gives the expert the ability to adapt to the characteristics of the problem.

The Intuitionistic Fuzzy Sets are one of the most popular fuzzy approaches, as it introduces the possibility of determining the degree of membership and non-membership, which provides its usefulness in many areas e.g. sustainable supplier selection [18], medical diagnosis [9] or investment selection [31]. The wide use of Intuitionistic Fuzzy Sets has led to many studies which improved their usability and significance in multi-criteria decision-making environments.

Many multi-criteria decision-making methods were extended to enable problem-solving in an uncertain environment. However, most of the highly developed methods are designed to solve problems where the values are crisp [2]. This has given rise to a number of methods for converting fuzzy values to sharp values, and one approach is the use of the score functions which was originally proposed by Chen and Tan [6]. The consequence of the appearance of such a solution was a trend in which various score functions were proposed. This emerged a new problem, as their use within the same problem may be characterized by obtaining different results. It creates a research gap that needs to be filled and determines which score function to select so that the results are satisfactory.

In this study, five different score functions were chosen to carry out the analysis. The score functions provide a way to convert fuzzy numbers into crisp ones which then can be used with the Measurement Alternatives and Ranking according to COmpromise Solution (MARCOS) method to assess alternatives of the decision matrix. The decision problems were generated to ensure that solution would not depend on a specific problem. The theoretical problems were then assessed using the previously mentioned approach to provide rankings that can be compared with selected correlation coefficients. Additionally, the compromise solution of all score function preferences is proposed. The main purpose of this study is to emphasize the differences in utilizing different score functions regarding their influence on the final rankings of multi-criteria decision problems.

The rest of the paper is organized as follows. Section 2 presents a literature review providing a view of current trends in fuzzy problem-solving and the score functions used in them. In Sect. 3 the preliminaries of the IFS, the scores functions, the MARCOS method, and selected similarity coefficients are presented. In Sect. 4, the study case is shown, where the theoretical problem of the functioning of the different scores function is raised. Section 5 includes a description of the results obtained from the examined research. Finally, in Sect. 6, the summary is presented, and the conclusions are drawn.

2 Literature Review

The utility of score functions has been demonstrated in a number of researches that solve real-world problems that are based on intuitionistic fuzzy data.

G. Büyüközkan and F. Göçer [4] showed the usefulness of score functions in the problem of supplier selection, where five alternatives were considered. They proposed a new approach consisting of IF-AHP, IFAD, and score functions which they compared to IF-TOPSIS. C. Zhang et al. [32] presented a similar approach to solving MCDA problems, as they have as well utilized the MCDA method with score functions, but the method they chose was MULTIMOORA. In their work, they have created the assessment of the energy storage technologies, where fourteen alternatives described by eleven criteria were considered. A different approach was presented by Y. Chen [8] in his work, where for the evaluation of physical education teachers he proposed an evaluation solely based on intuitionistic fuzzy information. Jian Lin et al. [17] presented a new MCDA method based on a score function which they called Preference Attitude-Based. Moreover, they presented its usage in a real problem, which considered renewable energy source selection, where four different alternatives were considered. D. Tripathi et al. [25] presented an improved CoCoSo method that incorporated intuitionistic fuzzy parametric divergence measures and score function. The usage of this method was presented as a medical decision-maker support system where treatment options for patients were evaluated. S. Zeng et al. [30] and JH Park et al. [20], both presented their approach to modifying the VIKOR method that incorporated the score functions, however, S. Zeng et al. presented its usage in the subject of supply chain management, on the other hand, JH Park et al. problem at hand was evaluating university faculty. Moreover, the usage of score functions was adopted for interval-valued intuitionistic fuzzy problems. Their usage was presented for example by Jin Han Park [21] in his work where he proposed an extended TOPSIS method that incorporated the score function for IVIFNs, which usage was shown through the evaluation of five air-conditioning systems should be installed in a library. Additionally, Liangping Wu et al. [27] provided a way of using the score function with the VIKOR method for financing risk assessment of rural tourism projects under interval-valued intuitionistic fuzzy circumstances. Aside from the practical presentations of usage, the score functions utility is researched through many angles, which is presented in Table 1. The literature review shows how crucial the score functions are in the MCDM problems, but not enough analysis was carried out. This research tries to provide a comprehensive view of how the usage of different score functions alters the final results and advises the most favourable score function depending on the problem at hand.

Table 1. Applications of score functions in MCDA

Authors	Core principles used	Contribution
Jian Wu et al. [26]	Score and accuracy functions for IVIFNs	Functions for total order on the set of IVIFNs, a new method for IVIFN problems highly depending on decision maker's risk attitude
Muhammad Irfan Ali et al. [3]	Entropy, the uncertainty index, score functions	New graphical technique for ranking IFVs
Zeshui Xu [28]	Score function and accuracy function	A method for the comparison between two IFNs, aggregation operators based on score and accuracy functions
Harish Garg [13]	Generalized IVIF interactive weighted averaging operator, interval-valued IFS	A new generalized improved score function of IVIF sets
Shyi-Ming Chen et al. [5]	Score functions, nonlinear programming	A method using the nonlinear programming methodology and the proposed score function of IVIFNs
Zeshui Xu [29]	Score function, accuracy function, IF hybrid aggregation operator, IF weighted averaging operator	New IF multiple attribute group decision-making method
Hoang Nguyen [19]	Score function,	A generalized p-norm knowledge-based score function for the IVIF set
Feng Feng et al. [12]	Generalized IF soft sets, score function, accuracy function, IF weighted averaging operator	Provides a new perspective on generalized intuitionistic fuzzy soft sets
Deng-Feng Li [16]	Generalized ordered weighted averaging, score function, accuracy function	Extended generalized ordered weighted averaging (GOWA) to aggregate IF sets, presented a procedure of utilizing GOWA in multi-attribute decision-making problems
Harish Garg [14]	Score function, accuracy function, Pythagorean fuzzy sets	New generalized aggregation operators for Pythagorean fuzzy sets

3   Research Methodology

3.1   Intuitionistic Fuzzy Sets

Definition 1. *An Intuitionistic Fuzzy Set (IFS) A in a universe X is defined as an object of the following form:*

$$A = \{\langle x_j, \mu_j, \nu_j \rangle \mid x_j \in X\} \tag{1}$$

where $\mu : X \to [0,1]$ and $\nu : X \to [0,1]$ such that $0 \leqslant \mu_j + \nu_j \leqslant 1$ for all $x_j \in X$. The values of μ_j and ν_j represent the degrees of membership and non-membership of $x_j \in X$ in A respectively [7].

For every $A \in IFS(X)$ (the class of IFSs in the universe X), the value of

$$\pi_j = 1 - \mu_j - \nu_j \tag{2}$$

represents the degree of hesitation (or uncertainty) associated with the membership of element $x_j \in X$ in IFS A, where $0 \leqslant \pi_j \leqslant 1$.

3.2   IFS Score Functions

The purpose of the score function is to convert the uncertain data representation to a crisp value. Different approaches to performing such an action obtain diverse values as a final output. Selected score functions and the formulas for their calculations are presented below [7,9,15].

$$S_{\mathrm{I}}(X_{ij}) = \mu_{ij} - v_{ij} \tag{3}$$

$$S_{\mathrm{II}}(X_{ij}) = \mu_{ij} - v_{ij} \cdot \pi_{ij} \tag{4}$$

$$S_{\mathrm{III}}(X_{ij}) = \mu_{ij} - \left(\frac{v_{ij} + \pi_{ij}}{2}\right) \tag{5}$$

$$S_{\mathrm{IV}}(X_{ij}) = \left(\frac{\mu_{ij} + v_{ij}}{2}\right) - \pi_{ij} \tag{6}$$

$$S_{\mathrm{V}}(X_{ij}) = \gamma \cdot \mu_{ij} + (1 - \gamma) \cdot (1 - v_{ij}), \quad \gamma \in [0,1] \tag{7}$$

where $S_I(X_{ij}), S_{II}(X_{ij}), S_V(X_{ij}) \in [-1,1]$, $S_{III}(X_{ij}) \in [-0.5,1]$, and $S_{IV}(X_{ij}) \in [-1,0.5]$.

3.3   MARCOS Method

The Measurement Alternatives and Ranking according to COmpromise Solution (MARCOS) method was introduced by Željko Stević in 2020 [23] as a new multi-criteria decision-making method, which was presented in the study case of sustainable supplier selection in healthcare industries. This method provides a new approach to solving decision problems, as it considers an anti-ideal and an ideal solution at the initial steps of consideration of the problem. Moreover, it proposes a new way to determine utility functions and their further aggregation, while maintaining stability in the problems requiring a large set of alternatives and criteria.

Step 1. The initial step requires to define set of n criteria and m alternatives to create decision matrix.

Step 2. Next, the extended initial matrix X should be formed by defining ideal (AI) and anti-ideal (AAI) solution.

$$
X = \begin{matrix} AII \\ A_1 \\ A_2 \\ \dots \\ A_m \\ AI \end{matrix}
\begin{bmatrix}
x_{aa1} & x_{aa2} & \dots & x_{aan} \\
x_{11} & x_{12} & \cdots & x_{1n} \\
x_{21} & x_{22} & \dots & x_{2n} \\
\dots & \dots & \dots & \dots \\
x_{m1} & x_{22} & \cdots & x_{mn} \\
x_{ai1} & x_{ai2} & \cdots & x_{ain}
\end{bmatrix}
\tag{8}
$$

The anti-ideal solution (AAI) which is the worst alternative is defined by Eq. (9), whereas the ideal solution (AI) is the best alternative in the problem at hand defined by Eq. (10).

$$
AAI = \min_i x_{ij} \quad \text{if } j \in B \text{ and } \max_i x_{ij} \quad \text{if } j \in C
\tag{9}
$$

$$
AI = \max_i x_{ij} \quad \text{if } j \in B \text{ and } \min_i x_{ij} \quad \text{if } j \in C
\tag{10}
$$

where B is a benefit group of criteria and C is a group of cost criteria.

Step 3. After defining anti-ideal and ideal solutions, the extended initial matrix X needs to be normalized, by applying Eqs. (11) and (12) creating normalized matrix N.

$$
n_{ij} = \frac{x_{ai}}{x_{ij}} \quad \text{if } j \in C
\tag{11}
$$

$$
n_{ij} = \frac{x_{ij}}{x_{ai}} \quad \text{if } j \in B
\tag{12}
$$

Step 4. The weight for each criterion needs to be defined to present its importance in accordance with others. The weighted matrix V needs to be calculated by multiplying the normalized matrix N with the weight vector through Eq. (13).

$$
v_{ij} = n_{ij} \times w_j
\tag{13}
$$

Step 5. Next, the utility degree K of alternatives in relation to the anti-ideal and ideal solutions needs to be calculated by using Eqs. (14) and (15).

$$
K_i^- = \frac{\sum_{i=1}^n v_{ij}}{\sum_{i=1}^n v_{aai}}
\tag{14}
$$

$$K_i^+ = \frac{\sum_{i=1}^{n} v_{ij}}{\sum_{i=1}^{n} v_{ai}} \tag{15}$$

Step 6. The utility function f of alternatives, which is the compromise of the observed alternative in relation to the ideal and anti-ideal solution, needs to be determined. Its done using Eq. (16).

$$f(K_i) = \frac{K_i^+ + K_i^-}{1 + \frac{1-f(K_i^+)}{f(K_i^+)} + \frac{1-f(K_i^-)}{f(K_i^-)}} \tag{16}$$

where $f(K_i^-)$ represents the utility function in relation to the anti-ideal solution and $f(K_i^+)$ represents the utility function in relation to the ideal solution.

Utility functions in relation to the ideal and anti-ideal solution are determined by applying Eqs. (17) and (18).

$$f(K_i^-) = \frac{K_i^+}{K_i^+ + K_i^-} \tag{17}$$

$$f(K_i^+) = \frac{K_i^-}{K_i^+ + K_i^-} \tag{18}$$

Step 7. Finally, rank alternatives accordingly to the values of the utility functions. The higher the value the better an alternative is.

3.4   Rank Similarity Coefficients

In order to compare the performance of the score functions, it would be useful to compare the rankings obtained after evaluating the values calculated using these functions. For this purpose, one can use rank similarity coefficients, which are often used in the literature to compare the resulting rankings. In the case of our study, we decided to use the weighted Spearman's correlation coefficient, which allows comparing rankings considering alternatives rated the best as more significant, and the WS ranking similarity coefficient, which the main assumption that the positions of top of the rankings have a more significant influence on similarity. The formulas for the calculation of both coefficients are presented below in Eq. (19) for weighted Spearman's correlation and Eq. (20) for WS rank similarity coefficient.

$$r_w = 1 - \frac{6 \cdot \sum_{i=1}^{n} (x_i - y_i)^2 ((n - x_i + 1) + (n - y_i + 1))}{n \cdot (n^3 + n^2 - n - 1)} \tag{19}$$

$$WS = 1 - \sum_{i=1}^{n} \left(2^{-x_i} \frac{|x_i - y_i|}{\max\{|x_i - 1|, |x_i - n|\}} \right) \tag{20}$$

where x_i means position in the reference ranking, y_i is the position in the second ranking and n is a number of ranked elements.

4   Research Findings

With the increasing popularity of multi-criteria decision-making, the need has arisen to reflect real-world problems as accurately as possible. However, in many real-world problems, it is impossible to give crisp values, as uncertainties arise that can significantly alter the results. For the purposes of mapping expert knowledge as accurately as possible and providing sufficient flexibility, fuzzy sets have been proposed as one of the solutions. The intuitionistic fuzzy sets are a type of fuzzy set that represents decisiveness and indecisiveness for a given alternative. However, many multi-criteria decision-making methods have been developed that base their operation on crisp values, rendering them unsuitable for use with IFS problems.

In order to ensure that existing methods can be used for fuzzy problems, score functions were proposed to convert crisp to fuzzy values. However, as a number of score functions were developed, it presented a need of comparing those functions. For this purpose, we present two examples, one with a small decision matrix and the second with a big one. The matrices were generated to provide an objective view of the results, as the field of the problems is no concern in this matter. Moreover, the compromise ranking was calculated, by creating a matrix from the preferences acquired by score functions and executing the MARCOS method for such a decision matrix.

4.1   Small Example

The small example was generated for six alternatives and four criteria and is presented in Table 2. Such matrix dimensions should represent most of the problems considered, as small problems are the most prevailing in the literature. In the matrix, the first value indicates the value of decisiveness, while the second determines the degree of indecisiveness.

Table 2. Small decision matrix represented by intuitionistic fuzzy sets.

A_i	C_1	C_2	C_3	C_4
	(μ, ν)	(μ, ν)	(μ, ν)	(μ, ν)
A_1	(0.66588, 0.23451)	(0.01186, 0.58725)	(0.27335, 0.24798)	(0.19894, 0.13208)
A_2	(0.22461, 0.70848)	(0.17635, 0.79087)	(0.26652, 0.43553)	(0.73207, 0.01165)
A_3	(0.77158, 0.22185)	(0.31678, 0.08189)	(0.58012, 0.06394)	(0.43352, 0.41035)
A_4	(0.10396, 0.46207)	(0.41412, 0.58285)	(0.72563, 0.02145)	(0.70608, 0.16961)
A_5	(0.03777, 0.17833)	(0.21884, 0.66360)	(0.36338, 0.55215)	(0.02329, 0.40128)
A_6	(0.31007, 0.44148)	(0.55196, 0.19111)	(0.49831, 0.15947)	(0.04384, 0.94746)

4.2   Big Example

The second example taken into consideration is supposed to represent problems with a large number of alternatives. For this purpose, the matrix of twenty alternatives and six criteria was generated. Problems with such dimensionality are less frequently used in literature, however, in real-world problems, one often encounters even more alternatives and it is usually even more difficult for the decision-maker to make the right choice, which makes it an important case to check with every MCDA solution. The generated values for the decision matrix are presented in Table 3 for criteria one to three and in Table 4 for criteria four to six.

Table 3. Big decision matrix represented by intuitionistic fuzzy sets $C_1 - C_3$.

A_i	C_1 (μ, ν)	C_2 (μ, ν)	C_3 (μ, ν)
A_1	(0.03008, 0.59822)	(0.54799, 0.26195)	(0.44687, 0.28107)
A_2	(0.65028, 0.34754)	(0.39855, 0.52727)	(0.45998, 0.15288)
A_3	(0.65990, 0.15513)	(0.13322, 0.20364)	(0.01991, 0.45287)
A_4	(0.11286, 0.15714)	(0.38047, 0.01957)	(0.09701, 0.10392)
A_5	(0.06691, 0.23208)	(0.20909, 0.62088)	(0.44542, 0.47977)
A_6	(0.45541, 0.22584)	(0.01929, 0.87036)	(0.01559, 0.17132)
A_7	(0.20855, 0.46328)	(0.02354, 0.66232)	(0.11760, 0.37040)
A_8	(0.47737, 0.22873)	(0.28764, 0.29996)	(0.00493, 0.38813)
A_9	(0.04359, 0.47662)	(0.07547, 0.82165)	(0.50706, 0.36966)
A_{10}	(0.37778, 0.10292)	(0.26738, 0.41870)	(0.02580, 0.87791)
A_{11}	(0.06616, 0.27073)	(0.03201, 0.89392)	(0.38430, 0.52810)
A_{12}	(0.03170, 0.27506)	(0.90900, 0.04329)	(0.77808, 0.05569)
A_{13}	(0.04928, 0.16643)	(0.18588, 0.76387)	(0.12327, 0.65232)
A_{14}	(0.48724, 0.23737)	(0.06983, 0.47740)	(0.08177, 0.68484)
A_{15}	(0.18019, 0.71784)	(0.60128, 0.07074)	(0.27282, 0.10789)
A_{16}	(0.11729, 0.25536)	(0.60794, 0.35294)	(0.65381, 0.00884)
A_{17}	(0.29735, 0.04217)	(0.23092,0.01618)	(0.00990, 0.98991)
A_{18}	(0.07894, 0.72784)	(0.27682, 0.34924)	(0.52028, 0.19206)
A_{19}	(0.14809, 0.76951)	(0.61404, 0.34116)	(0.74713, 0.06286)
A_{20}	(0.64628, 0.35096)	(0.15257, 0.26666)	(0.79898, 0.02703)

5   Discussion of Findings

5.1   Small Example

The crisp values of criteria for each alternative calculated by the score function are presented by corresponding Tables. Table 5 presents the values for the S_I score function. This function operates in the range $[-1, 1]$ and the spread of its values is around 1.624, which shows that the range is used effectively, and values should differ greatly from each other.

Table 6 presents values calculated using S_{II} score function. This function is defined as the degree of membership minus the product of the non-membership

Table 4. Big decision matrix represented by intuitionistic fuzzy sets $C_4 - C_6$.

A_i	C_4 (μ, ν)	C_5 (μ, ν)	C_6 (μ, ν)
A_1	(0.17807, 0.62603)	(0.79718, 0.09979)	(0.11472, 0.53089)
A_2	(0.43069, 0.17812)	(0.42217, 0.28637)	(0.41295, 0.06847)
A_3	(0.06626, 0.15496)	(0.48144, 0.15189)	(0.22848, 0.41295)
A_4	(0.47157, 0.37453)	(0.46475, 0.25735)	(0.15571, 0.26099)
A_5	(0.35187, 0.15178)	(0.12133, 0.53977)	(0.11654, 0.71676)
A_6	(0.03106, 0.22659)	(0.02487, 0.46356)	(0.56558, 0.04465)
A_7	(0.15746, 0.28173)	(0.42951, 0.00288)	(0.25495, 0.53578)
A_8	(0.18569, 0.48341)	(0.49683, 0.10407)	(0.31878, 0.15729)
A_9	(0.14470, 0.10471)	(0.35489, 0.12449)	(0.71246, 0.21683)
A_{10}	(0.04063, 0.16260)	(0.96672, 0.00880)	(0.83796, 0.11231)
A_{11}	(0.09013, 0.34629)	(0.37471, 0.01166)	(0.43074, 0.50213)
A_{12}	(0.48861, 0.43642)	(0.42810, 0.51547)	(0.15026, 0.38831)
A_{13}	(0.23309, 0.30895)	(0.15394, 0.57738)	(0.30725, 0.53843)
A_{14}	(0.46602, 0.07656)	(0.29870, 0.10660)	(0.06250, 0.16147)
A_{15}	(0.30307, 0.23982)	(0.03609, 0.42349)	(0.25163, 0.41869)
A_{16}	(0.47752, 0.51659)	(0.49845, 0.41165)	(0.04280, 0.02324)
A_{17}	(0.64467, 0.05589)	(0.07594, 0.92166)	(0.17589, 0.22486)
A_{18}	(0.49845, 0.48739)	(0.42027, 0.02709)	(0.37743, 0.61117)
A_{19}	(0.03727, 0.38806)	(0.04631, 0.71954)	(0.34496, 0.03066)
A_{20}	(0.53209, 0.08420)	(0.20154, 0.59238)	(0.45175, 0.53248)

Table 5. Crisp small decision matrix calculated with S_I score function.

A_i	C_1	C_2	C_3	C_4
A_1	0.4313	−0.5753	0.0253	0.0668
A_2	−0.4838	−0.6145	−0.1690	0.7204
A_3	0.5497	0.2348	0.5161	0.0231
A_4	−0.3581	−0.1687	0.7041	0.5364
A_5	−0.1405	−0.4447	−0.1887	−0.3779
A_6	−0.1314	0.3608	0.3388	−0.9036

and hesitation degrees. This function operates in the same range as the S_I functions, which is $[-1, 1]$. However, in its case, the spread of the values is around 0.9937 which is significantly lower than the one for the S_I function. Which might be crucial in terms of highlighting the differences between alternatives.

Table 6. Crisp small decision matrix calculated with S_{II} score function.

A_i	C_1	C_2	C_3	C_4
A_1	0.6425	−0.2235	0.1546	0.1105
A_2	0.1772	0.1504	0.1367	0.7290
A_3	0.7701	0.2675	0.5573	0.3694
A_4	−0.0965	0.4123	0.7202	0.6849
A_5	−0.1020	0.1408	0.3167	−0.2076
A_6	0.2003	0.5028	0.4437	0.0356

The values acquired by execution of S_{III} function are presented in Table 7. This function subtracts the arithmetic mean of the non-membership and hesitation degrees and operates in the range of $[−0.5, 1]$. Considering this and the fact that the spread of the values is around 1.1396 it presents high differentiation of the individual IFS values from the initial decision matrix.

Table 7. Crisp small decision matrix calculated with S_{III} score function.

A_i	C_1	C_2	C_3	C_4
A_1	0.4988	−0.4822	−0.0899	−0.2015
A_2	−0.1630	−0.2354	−0.1002	0.5981
A_3	0.6573	−0.0248	0.3701	0.1502
A_4	−0.3440	0.1211	0.5884	0.5591
A_5	−0.4433	−0.1717	0.0450	−0.4650
A_6	−0.0349	0.3279	0.2474	−0.4342

Score function S_{IV} operates in a similar range as the S_{III} function, but the exact values are different, namely, the range of this function is $[−1, 0.5]$. This function is defined as the arithmetic mean of the membership and non-membership degrees minus the hesitation degree and the values calculated using it, are presented in Table 8. The spread of calculated values is around 1.1713, which suggests that this function is used to a similar extent as the S_{III} function, making visible differences between original IFS values.

In Table 9, the values calculated using the function S_V are presented. This function operates in exactly the same range as the S_I and S_{II} functions, however, the spread of the values is the smallest, being around 0.812. This function differentiates the original values the least and even though it may not be suitable for all decision-makers, this function may prove to be more suitable for use with decision-making methods.

Each of the matrices acquired with the usage of score functions was used to execute the MARCOS method to calculate the preference of considered alternatives. The preferences for specific score functions are shown in Table 10. Those

Table 8. Crisp small decision matrix calculated with S_{IV} score function.

A_i	C_1	C_2	C_3	C_4
A_1	0.3505	−0.1013	−0.2180	−0.5034
A_2	0.3996	0.4508	0.0530	0.1155
A_3	0.4901	−0.4019	−0.0339	0.2658
A_4	−0.1509	0.4954	0.1206	0.3135
A_5	−0.6758	0.3236	0.3733	−0.3631
A_6	0.1273	0.1146	−0.0133	0.4869

Table 9. Crisp small decision matrix calculated with S_V score function.

A_i	C_1	C_2	C_3	C_4
A_1	0.7156	0.2123	0.5126	0.5334
A_2	0.2580	0.1927	0.4154	0.8602
A_3	0.7748	0.6174	0.7580	0.5115
A_4	0.3209	0.4156	0.8520	0.7682
A_5	0.4297	0.2776	0.4056	0.3110
A_6	0.4342	0.6804	0.6694	0.0481

results provide us with a better view of how those functions differ in terms of the final results of conducting a multi-criteria decision analysis. Functions S_I and S_{IV} provide values, that might be hard to distinguish by the decision maker as most of them are on the second decimal place and the spread of the values is 0.0301 and 0.0403 respectively. The function S_{III} is somewhat in the middle presenting relatively easy-to-distinguish differences between preferences with a spread of 0.2547. While functions S_{II} and S_V allowed to obtain values that are easy to distinguish and their spread is 0.6069 and 0.3739 respectively.

Table 10. Preferences for small decision matrix computed with MARCOS method for S_I-S_V score functions.

A_i	S_{I}	S_{II}	S_{III}	S_{IV}	S_{V}	S_{comp}
A_1	0.0044	0.1828	−0.0826	−0.0139	0.5774	0.0158
A_2	0.0117	0.4157	−0.0094	0.0264	0.4943	0.4667
A_3	−0.0155	0.6801	0.1241	0.0081	0.7969	0.3547
A_4	−0.0040	0.6369	0.1225	0.0208	0.6856	0.5207
A_5	0.0146	0.0732	−0.1306	−0.0059	0.4230	0.0571
A_6	0.0001	0.4655	0.0441	0.0183	0.5644	0.3861

In order to better reflect the differences in the obtained rankings, two similarity coefficients were used. The first one, Weighted Spearman's correlation coefficient is shown on the heatmap in Fig. 1. In this specific example, we can see that rankings provided by the function S_{II} and S_{III} are identical. Considering this, the score function S_{II} might be preferred by decision-makers as it provided more distinctive values of preference. Those two rankings are highly similar to the one provided by the function S_V which was the second function with the highest spread in terms of preference values. However, the compromise ranking showed the highest similarity with the one acquired using the function S_{IV}. This is an interesting case and should be taken into account when choosing the score function, because even though the score function S_{IV} provided values with low spread, the consensus of all score functions is the closest to provided by this exact function.

The second coefficient, namely the WS coefficient is presented in Fig. 1. In the case of this coefficient, the situation is very similar, which only confirms the previous conclusions. The use of this coefficient is important not only to confirm but also to see how the podium changes, as this coefficient is asymmetric. As can be seen from the presented heatmap, it is not very significant in the case under consideration.

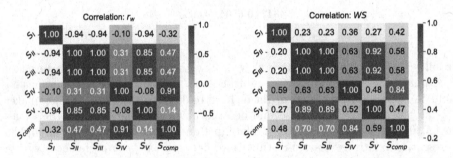

Fig. 1. Weighted Spearman's correlation and WS coefficient of rankings for small decision matrix.

5.2   Big Example

Table 11 presents values calculated using S_I function. Similarly to the small problem in this case the function managed to utilize almost the whole range considering that it operates in the range $[-1, 1]$, and provided values which spread is around 1.9379 (Table 11).

The second function, namely the S_{II} function yielded values presented in Table 12. Their spread is about 1.1971, which is higher than in the case of the small example, but there may be a tendency for more alternatives to result in more spread-out values.

The values acquired using the function S_{III} are presented in Table 13. This function operates in the range of $[-0.5, 1]$ and its spread is around 1.4427, which

Table 11. Crisp big decision matrix calculated with S_I score function.

A_i	C_1	C_2	C_3	C_4	C_5	C_6
A_1	−0.5681	0.2860	0.1658	−0.4480	0.6974	−0.4162
A_2	0.3027	−0.1287	0.3071	0.2526	0.1358	0.3445
A_3	0.5048	−0.0704	−0.4330	−0.0887	0.3296	−0.1845
A_4	−0.0443	0.3609	−0.0069	0.0970	0.2074	−0.1053
A_5	−0.1652	−0.4118	−0.0343	0.2001	−0.4184	−0.6002
A_6	0.2296	−0.8511	−0.1557	−0.1955	−0.4387	0.5209
A_7	−0.2547	−0.6388	−0.2528	−0.1243	0.4266	−0.2808
A_8	0.2486	−0.0123	−0.3832	−0.2977	0.3928	0.1615
A_9	−0.4330	−0.7462	0.1374	0.0400	0.2304	0.4956
A_{10}	0.2749	−0.1513	−0.8521	−0.1220	0.9579	0.7257
A_{11}	−0.2046	−0.8619	−0.1438	−0.2562	0.3630	−0.0714
A_{12}	−0.2434	0.8657	0.7224	0.0522	−0.0874	−0.2381
A_{13}	−0.1172	−0.5780	−0.5291	−0.0759	−0.4234	−0.2312
A_{14}	0.2499	−0.4076	−0.6031	0.3895	0.1921	−0.0990
A_{15}	−0.5377	0.5305	0.1649	0.0633	−0.3874	−0.1671
A_{16}	−0.1381	0.2550	0.6450	−0.0391	0.0868	0.0196
A_{17}	0.2552	0.2147	−0.9800	0.5888	−0.8457	−0.0490
A_{18}	−0.6489	−0.0724	0.3282	0.0111	0.3932	−0.2337
A_{19}	−0.6214	0.2729	0.6843	−0.3508	−0.6732	0.3143
A_{20}	0.2953	−0.1141	0.7720	0.4479	−0.3908	−0.0807

Table 12. Crisp big decision matrix calculated with S_{II} score function.

A_i	C_1	C_2	C_3	C_4	C_5	C_6
A_1	−0.1923	0.4982	0.3704	0.0554	0.7869	−0.0734
A_2	0.6495	0.3594	0.4008	0.3610	0.3387	0.3774
A_3	0.6312	−0.0018	−0.2189	−0.0544	0.4257	0.0804
A_4	−0.0019	0.3687	0.0140	0.4139	0.3932	0.0035
A_5	−0.0958	0.1035	0.4095	0.2765	−0.0616	−0.0029
A_6	0.3834	−0.0768	−0.1237	−0.1371	−0.2123	0.5482
A_7	0.0565	−0.1845	−0.0720	−0.0005	0.4279	0.1428
A_8	0.4101	0.1639	−0.2306	0.0257	0.4553	0.2364
A_9	−0.1851	−0.0091	0.4615	0.0661	0.2901	0.6971
A_{10}	0.3243	0.1359	−0.0587	−0.0889	0.9665	0.8324
A_{11}	−0.1134	−0.0342	0.3380	−0.1050	0.3676	0.3970
A_{12}	−0.1590	0.9069	0.7688	0.4559	0.3990	−0.0289
A_{13}	−0.0813	0.1475	−0.0231	0.0916	−0.0012	0.2242
A_{14}	0.4219	−0.1463	−0.0781	0.4310	0.2353	−0.0628
A_{15}	0.1070	0.5781	0.2060	0.1934	−0.1928	0.1136
A_{16}	−0.0429	0.5941	0.6508	0.4745	0.4614	0.0211
A_{17}	0.2695	0.2187	0.0097	0.6279	0.0737	0.0411
A_{18}	−0.0617	0.1462	0.4650	0.4916	0.4053	0.3705
A_{19}	0.0847	0.5988	0.7352	−0.1857	−0.1222	0.3258
A_{20}	0.6453	−0.0023	0.7943	0.4998	0.0795	0.4434

Table 13. Crisp big decision matrix calculated with S_{III} score function.

A_i	C_1	C_2	C_3	C_4	C_5	C_6
A_1	−0.4549	0.3220	0.1703	−0.2329	0.6958	−0.3279
A_2	0.4754	0.0978	0.1900	0.1460	0.1333	0.1194
A_3	0.4899	−0.3002	−0.4701	−0.4006	0.2222	−0.1573
A_4	−0.3307	0.0707	−0.3545	0.2074	0.1971	−0.2664
A_5	−0.3996	−0.1864	0.1681	0.0278	−0.3180	−0.3252
A_6	0.1831	−0.4711	−0.4766	−0.4534	−0.4627	0.3484
A_7	−0.1872	−0.4647	−0.3236	−0.2638	0.1443	−0.1176
A_8	0.2160	−0.0685	−0.4926	−0.2215	0.2452	−0.0218
A_9	−0.4346	−0.3868	0.2606	−0.2830	0.0323	0.5687
A_{10}	0.0667	−0.0989	−0.4613	−0.4390	0.9501	0.7569
A_{11}	−0.4008	−0.4520	0.0765	−0.3648	0.0621	0.1461
A_{12}	−0.4524	0.8635	0.6671	0.2329	0.1421	−0.2746
A_{13}	−0.4261	−0.2212	−0.3151	−0.1504	−0.2691	−0.0391
A_{14}	0.2309	−0.3953	−0.3773	0.1990	−0.0519	−0.4062
A_{15}	−0.2297	0.4019	−0.0908	−0.0454	−0.4459	−0.1226
A_{16}	−0.3241	0.4119	0.4807	0.2163	0.2477	−0.4358
A_{17}	−0.0540	−0.1536	−0.4851	0.4670	−0.3861	−0.2362
A_{18}	−0.3816	−0.0848	0.2804	0.2477	0.1304	0.0661
A_{19}	−0.2779	0.4211	0.6207	−0.4441	−0.4305	0.0174
A_{20}	0.4694	−0.2711	0.6985	0.2981	−0.1977	0.1776

shows that it yielded values almost across the whole range similar to function S_I.

The function S_{IV} similar to function S_{III} used up almost the whole range of values, as its spread is 1.4 and presented values are easily distinguishable from each other. Once again the spread is even higher than in the small example, which is preferable considering that such differences should be more prominent to the decision maker making it suitable for problems where a high number of alternatives is considered.

The last function, namely function S_V yielded values presented in Table 15. This function operates in the same range as functions S_I and S_{II}, however, the spread of its values which is around 0.9689 is the smallest out of all presented functions. The same characteristics are present as in the small problem, where function S_V provides the smallest spread of values, which might be less preferable by a decision maker, as the perceived differences are not so apparent. However, in some of the decision-making methods, such an approach might be preferable.

Each of the score functions provided matrices of crisp values, which then were used in the MARCOS method. The calculated preferences of considered alternatives are presented in Table 16. Similar to the small problem, using score function S_I the calculated preferences are hard to distinguish as almost all values have zeros on the first two decimal places. This function provided preferences with a spread of 0.0026, which might be perceived by decision-makers that this function does not differentiate the values enough. Functions S_{III}, S_{IV} and S_V

Table 14. Crisp big decision matrix calculated with S_{IV} score function.

A_i	C_1	C_2	C_3	C_4	C_5	C_6
A_1	−0.0576	0.2149	0.0919	0.2061	0.3455	−0.0316
A_2	0.4967	0.3887	−0.0807	−0.0868	0.0628	−0.2779
A_3	0.2226	−0.4947	−0.2908	−0.6682	−0.0500	−0.0378
A_4	−0.5950	−0.3999	−0.6986	0.2691	0.0831	−0.3749
A_5	−0.5515	0.2450	0.3878	−0.2445	−0.0083	0.2500
A_6	0.0219	0.3345	−0.7196	−0.6135	−0.2674	−0.0847
A_7	0.0077	0.0288	−0.2680	−0.3412	−0.3514	0.1861
A_8	0.0591	−0.1186	−0.4104	0.0036	−0.0987	−0.2859
A_9	−0.2197	0.3457	0.3151	−0.6259	−0.2809	0.3939
A_{10}	−0.2789	0.0291	0.3556	−0.6951	0.4633	0.4254
A_{11}	−0.4947	0.3889	0.3686	−0.3454	−0.4204	0.3993
A_{12}	−0.5398	0.4284	0.2506	0.3875	0.4153	−0.1922
A_{13}	−0.6764	0.4246	0.1634	−0.1869	0.0970	0.2685
A_{14}	0.0869	−0.1792	0.1499	−0.1861	−0.3920	−0.6640
A_{15}	0.3470	0.0080	−0.4289	−0.1857	−0.3106	0.0055
A_{16}	−0.4410	0.4413	−0.0060	0.4912	0.3651	−0.9009
A_{17}	−0.4907	−0.6294	0.4997	0.0508	0.4964	−0.3989
A_{18}	0.2102	−0.0609	0.0685	0.4788	−0.3290	0.4829
A_{19}	0.3764	0.4328	0.2150	−0.3620	0.1488	−0.4366
A_{20}	0.4959	−0.3712	0.2390	−0.0756	0.1909	0.4764

Table 15. Crisp big decision matrix calculated with S_V score function.

A_i	C_1	C_2	C_3	C_4	C_5	C_6
A_1	0.2159	0.6430	0.5829	0.2760	0.8487	0.2919
A_2	0.6514	0.4356	0.6535	0.6263	0.5679	0.6722
A_3	0.7524	0.4648	0.2835	0.4557	0.6648	0.4078
A_4	0.4779	0.6804	0.4965	0.5485	0.6037	0.4474
A_5	0.4174	0.2941	0.4828	0.6000	0.2908	0.1999
A_6	0.6148	0.0745	0.4221	0.4022	0.2807	0.7605
A_7	0.3726	0.1806	0.3736	0.4379	0.7133	0.3596
A_8	0.6243	0.4938	0.3084	0.3511	0.6964	0.5807
A_9	0.2835	0.1269	0.5687	0.5200	0.6152	0.7478
A_{10}	0.6374	0.4243	0.0739	0.4390	0.9790	0.8628
A_{11}	0.3977	0.0690	0.4281	0.3719	0.6815	0.4643
A_{12}	0.3783	0.9329	0.8612	0.5261	0.4563	0.3810
A_{13}	0.4414	0.2110	0.2355	0.4621	0.2883	0.3844
A_{14}	0.6249	0.2962	0.1985	0.6947	0.5960	0.4505
A_{15}	0.2312	0.7653	0.5825	0.5316	0.3063	0.4165
A_{16}	0.4310	0.6275	0.8225	0.4805	0.5434	0.5098
A_{17}	0.6276	0.6074	0.0100	0.7944	0.0771	0.4755
A_{18}	0.1755	0.4638	0.6641	0.5055	0.6966	0.3831
A_{19}	0.1893	0.6364	0.8421	0.3246	0.1634	0.6572
A_{20}	0.6477	0.4430	0.8860	0.7239	0.3046	0.4596

provide preferences whose spread is respectively 0.2851, 0.2291 and 0.2961. The function S_{II} once again provided the highest spread of preference values, as its spread is 0.4665, which might be highly preferable by decision-makers.

Table 16. Preferences for big decision matrix computed with MARCOS method for S_I-S_V score functions.

A_i	S_I	S_{II}	S_{III}	S_{IV}	S_V	S_{comp}
A_1	0.000706	0.238862	−0.032103	−0.067912	0.519326	0.177506
A_2	−0.001127	0.510740	0.123427	−0.046274	0.687340	0.305169
A_3	−0.000177	0.178261	−0.053505	0.118224	0.577427	0.257636
A_4	−0.000331	0.232269	−0.050289	0.150741	0.611184	0.307373
A_5	0.001054	0.133209	−0.093876	−0.009465	0.439827	0.156982
A_6	0.000477	0.088837	−0.116222	0.110048	0.496652	0.200024
A_7	0.001024	0.063267	−0.122511	0.062309	0.457438	0.183669
A_8	−0.000065	0.205221	−0.036939	0.074221	0.575831	0.248356
A_9	0.000327	0.238104	−0.049121	0.002237	0.538470	0.198030
A_{10}	−0.000630	0.378988	0.026421	−0.026016	0.641746	0.215489
A_{11}	0.001036	0.140678	−0.110144	0.004242	0.454364	0.157308
A_{12}	−0.000668	0.440281	0.082662	−0.068258	0.659115	0.254490
A_{13}	0.001472	0.065774	−0.140213	−0.012616	0.391144	0.112410
A_{14}	0.000019	0.193764	−0.043427	0.104703	0.550408	0.275579
A_{15}	0.000455	0.203464	−0.054095	0.047976	0.529571	0.246673
A_{16}	−0.000540	0.415292	0.040908	0.001269	0.639517	0.286787
A_{17}	0.000277	0.279380	−0.043999	0.048080	0.509463	0.257759
A_{18}	0.000498	0.358002	0.017530	−0.073369	0.533194	0.249278
A_{19}	0.000532	0.262462	−0.035903	−0.035001	0.524955	0.199734
A_{20}	−0.001008	0.529739	0.144936	−0.078379	0.666613	0.308986

Figure 2 presents a heatmap of the values of correlation calculated using Weighted Spearman's correlation coefficient for resulting rankings. Once again rankings acquired using functions S_{II} and S_{III} present high similarity equal to 0.96. Additionally, those two functions are highly similar to rankings provided by the function S_V. The compromise ranking shows the highest similarity of 0.78 with rankings yielded using the function S_{IV}, but it is worth mentioning that functions S_{II} and S_{III} have significant similarity as well. Contrary to the small example, the function S_{IV} did not provide a similar ranking to the compromise one.

WS similarity coefficient presented in Fig. 2 allows us to draw similar conclusions as in the case of Weighted Spearman's correlation coefficient. However, this coefficient shows a higher similarity of compromise ranking with rankings provided by functions S_{II} and S_{III}, which means that more important alternatives, namely the one closer to the podium are more alike than the end of the ranking. Additionally, the similarity of ranking of the function S_{IV} shows asymmetrical similarity to compromise ranking.

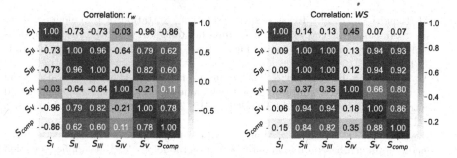

Fig. 2. Weighted Spearman's correlation and WS coefficient of rankings for big decision matrix.

6 Conclusion

The multitude of decision-making problems in the real world requires a constant search for new solutions in this area. Often the problems considered are problems in which there is a degree of uncertainty that renders a large proportion of the already-known solutions useless and unusable. This creates a great need to find ways of defuzzification of problems, so as not to be limited to methods that only solve a specific type of problem.

In this study, defuzzification of the intuitionistic fuzzy sets was taken into consideration. For this purpose, five different score functions were compared in terms of what values they return and ultimately how this affects the ranking obtained using the MARCOS method. From the results obtained, it can be concluded that the S_I function uses most of the range in which it operates, and yet the preference values that are obtained using this function differ from each other at the third decimal place, making the values unreadable to the decision-maker. The function S_{III} shows similar characteristics to the S_I function. On the other hand, functions S_{II}, S_{III} and S_V provide highly distinguishable preference values and moreover, the rankings acquired by using those functions are highly similar to the compromise ranking. Additionally, the decision maker could calculate the problem using all of the score functions and conduct additional MARCOS method assessment as the ranking yielded by such compromise showed to be a viable option.

In future studies, practical examples might be presented to encourage the use of score functions in real-world problems and present their reliability in practical settings. Moreover, the technique for compromise of score functions should be further studied, as it might prove to be even more reliable in decision-making problems than any of the considered score functions on its own.

References

1. Aggarwal, C.C., Philip, S.Y.: A survey of uncertain data algorithms and applications. IEEE Trans. Knowl. Data Eng. **21**(5), 609–623 (2008). https://doi.org/10.1109/TKDE.2008.190

2. Al-Humairi, S., et al.: Towards sustainable transportation: a pavement strategy selection based on the extension of dual-hesitant fuzzy multi-criteria decision-making methods. IEEE Trans. Fuzzy Syst. (2022). https://doi.org/10.1109/TFUZZ.2022.3168050

3. Ali, M.I., Feng, F., Mahmood, T., Mahmood, I., Faizan, H.: A graphical method for ranking atanassov's intuitionistic fuzzy values using the uncertainty index and entropy. Int. J. Intell. Syst. 34(10), 2692–2712 (2019). https://doi.org/10.1002/int.22174

4. Büyüközkan, G., Göçer, F.: Application of a new combined intuitionistic fuzzy mcdm approach based on axiomatic design methodology for the supplier selection problem. Appl. Soft Comput. 52, 1222–1238 (2017). https://doi.org/10.1016/j.asoc.2016.08.051

5. Chen, S.M., Deng, H.L.: Multiattribute decision making based on nonlinear programming methodology and novel score function of interval-valued intuitionistic fuzzy values. Inf. Sci. 607, 1348–1371 (2022). https://doi.org/10.1016/j.ins.2022.06.004

6. Chen, S.M., Tan, J.M.: Handling multicriteria fuzzy decision-making problems based on vague set theory. Fuzzy Sets Syst. 67(2), 163–172 (1994). https://doi.org/10.1016/0165-0114(94)90084-1

7. Chen, T.Y.: A comparative analysis of score functions for multiple criteria decision making in intuitionistic fuzzy settings. Inf. Sci. 181(17), 3652–3676 (2011). https://doi.org/10.1016/j.ins.2011.04.030

8. Chen, Y.: An approach to evaluating the quality of public physical education class in universal institutions of higher learning with intuitionistic fuzzy information. International Information Institute (Tokyo). Information 15(10), 3917 (2012)

9. De, S.K., Biswas, R., Roy, A.R.: An application of intuitionistic fuzzy sets in medical diagnosis. Fuzzy Sets Syst. 117(2), 209–213 (2001). https://doi.org/10.1016/S0165-0114(98)00235-8

10. Dubois, D., Prade, H.: Membership functions. In: Lesot, M.-J., Marsala, C. (eds.) Fuzzy Approaches for Soft Computing and Approximate Reasoning: Theories and Applications. SFSC, vol. 394, pp. 5–20. Springer, Cham (2021). https://doi.org/10.1007/978-3-030-54341-9_2

11. Ejegwa, P., Akowe, S., Otene, P., Ikyule, J.: An overview on intuitionistic fuzzy sets. Int. J. Sci. Technol. Res. 3(3), 142–145 (2014)

12. Feng, F., Fujita, H., Ali, M.I., Yager, R.R., Liu, X.: Another view on generalized intuitionistic fuzzy soft sets and related multiattribute decision making methods. IEEE Trans. Fuzzy Syst. 27(3), 474–488 (2018)

13. Garg, H.: A new generalized improved score function of interval-valued intuitionistic fuzzy sets and applications in expert systems. Appl. Soft Comput. 38, 988–999 (2016). https://doi.org/10.1016/j.asoc.2015.10.040

14. Garg, H.: A new generalized pythagorean fuzzy information aggregation using einstein operations and its application to decision making. Int. J. Intell. Syst. 31(9), 886–920 (2016). https://doi.org/10.1002/int.21809

15. Kharal, A.: Homeopathic drug selection using intuitionistic fuzzy sets. Homeopathy 98(1), 35–39 (2009). https://doi.org/10.1016/j.homp.2008.10.003

16. Li, D.F.: Multiattribute decision making method based on generalized owa operators with intuitionistic fuzzy sets. Expert Syst. Appl. 37(12), 8673–8678 (2010). https://doi.org/10.1016/j.eswa.2010.06.062

17. Lin, J., Meng, F., Chen, R., Zhang, Q.: Preference attitude-based method for ranking intuitionistic fuzzy numbers and its application in renewable energy selection. Complexity 2018 (2018). https://doi.org/10.1155/2018/6251384

18. Memari, A., Dargi, A., Jokar, M.R.A., Ahmad, R., Rahim, A.R.A.: Sustainable supplier selection: a multi-criteria intuitionistic fuzzy topsis method. J. Manuf. Syst. **50**, 9–24 (2019). https://doi.org/10.1016/j.jmsy.2018.11.002
19. Nguyen, H.: A generalized p-norm knowledge-based score function for an interval-valued intuitionistic fuzzy set in decision making. IEEE Trans. Fuzzy Syst. **28**(3), 409–423 (2019). https://doi.org/10.1109/TFUZZ.2018.2860967
20. Park, J.H., Cho, H.J., Kwun, Y.C.: Extension of the vikor method to dynamic intuitionistic fuzzy multiple attribute decision making. Comput. Math. Appl. **65**(4), 731–744 (2013). https://doi.org/10.1016/j.camwa.2012.12.008
21. Park, J.H., Park, I.Y., Kwun, Y.C., Tan, X.: Extension of the topsis method for decision making problems under interval-valued intuitionistic fuzzy environment. Appl. Math. Model. **35**(5), 2544–2556 (2011). https://doi.org/10.1016/j.apm.2010.11.025
22. Senapati, T., Yager, R.R.: Fermatean fuzzy sets. J. Ambient. Intell. Humaniz. Comput. **11**(2), 663–674 (2019). https://doi.org/10.1007/s12652-019-01377-0
23. Stević, Ž, Pamučar, D., Puška, A., Chatterjee, P.: Sustainable supplier selection in healthcare industries using a new mcdm method: Measurement of alternatives and ranking according to compromise solution (marcos). Comput. Ind. Eng. **140**, 106231 (2020). https://doi.org/10.1016/j.cie.2019.106231
24. Torra, V.: Hesitant fuzzy sets. Int. J. Intell. Syst. **25**(6), 529–539 (2010). https://doi.org/10.1002/int.20418
25. Tripathi, D.K., Nigam, S.K., Rani, P., Shah, A.R.: New intuitionistic fuzzy parametric divergence measures and score function-based cocoso method for decision-making problems. Decision Making: Applications in Management and Engineering (2022). https://doi.org/10.31181/dmame0318102022t
26. Wu, J., Chiclana, F.: A risk attitudinal ranking method for interval-valued intuitionistic fuzzy numbers based on novel attitudinal expected score and accuracy functions. Appl. Soft Comput. **22**, 272–286 (2014)
27. Wu, L., Gao, H., Wei, C.: Vikor method for financing risk assessment of rural tourism projects under interval-valued intuitionistic fuzzy environment. Journal of Intelligent & Fuzzy Systems **37**(2), 2001–2008 (2019). https://doi.org/10.1016/j.asoc.2014.05.005
28. Xu, Z.: Intuitionistic fuzzy aggregation operators. IEEE Trans. Fuzzy Syst. **15**(6), 1179–1187 (2007). https://doi.org/10.1109/TFUZZ.2006.890678
29. Xu, Z.: A deviation-based approach to intuitionistic fuzzy multiple attribute group decision making. Group Decis. Negot. **19**(1), 57–76 (2010). https://doi.org/10.1007/s10726-009-9164-z
30. Zeng, S., Chen, S.M., Kuo, L.W.: Multiattribute decision making based on novel score function of intuitionistic fuzzy values and modified vikor method. Inf. Sci. **488**, 76–92 (2019). https://doi.org/10.1016/j.ins.2019.03.018
31. Zeng, S., Xiao, Y.: Topsis method for intuitionistic fuzzy multiple-criteria decision making and its application to investment selection. Kybernetes (2016). https://doi.org/10.1108/K-04-2015-0093
32. Zhang, C., Chen, C., Streimikiene, D., Balezentis, T.: Intuitionistic fuzzy multimoora approach for multi-criteria assessment of the energy storage technologies. Appl. Soft Comput. **79**, 410–423 (2019). https://doi.org/10.1016/j.asoc.2019.04.008

Missing Types Prediction in Linked Data Using Deep Neural Network with Attention Mechanism: Case Study on DBpedia and UniProt Datasets

Oussama Hamel(✉) and Messaouda Fareh

LRDSI Laboratory, Faculty of Sciences, University Blida 1, B.P 270,
Route de Soumaa, Blida, Algeria
oussamahamel09@gmail.com

Abstract. The publication and use of linked data in various fields has become commonplace. However, data published under the linked data principles suffer from issues such as uncertainty, incompleteness, imprecision, etc. We distinguish the problem of missing types for RDF entities among the causes of data incompleteness. In this paper, we propose a deep learning approach for detecting missing types. Our approach consists of using an encoder-decoder model with an attention mechanism, in which we use embedding layers to improve data representation and GRU cells to increase efficiency when processing the different sequences in input and output. The main goal of this work is to improve the quality of the literature results and to take into account the various triples in order to detect the correct type for each entity. This allows us to detect the types of entities and thus deduce other connections with other entities. As a result, we will be able to address a portion of the problem of incompleteness, allowing the various applications that use this data to produce more relevant results. This work only considers types. The other semantic links between entities are not considered. We conducted a case study on the UniProt dataset to evaluate the quality of our approach, which is a large database of protein sequences and annotations. We used our model to generate the missing types in two datasets: DBpedia and UniProt. The effectiveness of our approach has been demonstrated by the evaluation results.

Keywords: Types prediction · RDF · Linked Data · Deep Learning · Attenion Mechanism

1 Introduction

The popularity of the Linked Open Data (LOD) cloud has grown in recent years. As a result of the LOD's success, many semantic datasets related to various domains are freely available on the Web in machine-readable format (primarily RDF (Resource Description Framework)).

With the advent of the semantic web and Linked Data, several issues concerning data uncertainty have emerged, such as imprecision, incompleteness, etc.

© The Author(s), under exclusive license to Springer Nature Switzerland AG 2023
E. Ziemba et al. (Eds.): FedCSIS-AIST 2022/ISM 2022, LNBIP 471, pp. 212–231, 2023.
https://doi.org/10.1007/978-3-031-29570-6_11

The principal reason of these issues is the method of creating datasets. These were constructed from incomplete data, heterogeneous formats, semi-structured data, etc. The anomalies cited above pose problems when using so-called uncertain data in reasoning, decision-making, the generation of new knowledge, etc.

According to [21], few approaches use links among datasets, so they can't able to exploit the endless possibilities with the full knowledge of the Semantic Web.

The approaches that exploit data from only one dataset, they stay below what is possible with Linked Data. The reason of this limitations and difficulties of links discovery in Linked Data applications are:

- The datasets are produced, kept or managed by different organizations in different schemas, models, locations, systems and licenses. There is not any "centralized control system," therefore, each publisher decides how to produce, manage and publish a dataset based on its needs and choices;
- The development of several applications which are independent of schema.
- The same real-world entities or relationships are referred with different URIs and names and in different languages, while languages have synonyms and homonyms that make harder that automatic links detection.
- The datasets usually contain complementary information, e.g., consider two datasets about the same domain each modeling a different aspect of the domain. The commonalities between these datasets can be very few and this does not aid automated linking and integration.
- The datasets can contain data that are erroneous, incomplete, out-of-date or conflicting.
- In addition, scalability challenges lie in developing solutions that could exploit the whole LOD as background knowledge by following links autonomously.

To improve the quality of RDF data, we choose to treat incompleteness, more specifically type incompleteness. Indeed, predicting missing types for dataset subjects will provide us with a more complete dataset.

Therefore, the results provided by applications using these datasets will become better. Our solution uses the predicates and objects belonging to the subject to predict its type. With the use of the encoder-decoder model, we will guarantee to extract the semantic relations between predicates and objects. This will improve the accuracy of subject type prediction. The attention mechanism was used to assign high weights to inputs with high importance. In this study, we will work on the DBpedia dataset, applying an approach based on deep learning.

Deep learning techniques have been recently used in many research axes to resolve different types of problems, Artificial intelligence systems use deep learning to solve computational tasks and complex problems quickly [10]. These techniques are very appropriate for dealing with large datasets. They have the ability to analyse and interpret Linked Data, that require efficient and effective tools. So, deep learning techniques are considered to be the most reliable solution that deal with the context of Linked Data, presented by RDF model.

Several approaches to dealing with this problem have been proposed in the literature. The method presented in [1] detects types by utilizing class characteristics. The approach proposed in [18] is to use Twitter data as features of the training data entities. The method proposed in [5] employs both word embedding and network embedding. Another method described in [16] based on machine learning with a binary classifier. The authors of [25] address this issue by employing a text classifier. The authors in [19] propose a statistical heuristic method based on link type prediction. The authors of [13] propose an SVM hierarchical supervised classification approach for DBpedia based on the content of Wikipedia articles. In [4], the authors propose a multi-label classification algorithm based on word embedding to capture the semantic aspect of entities and relationships.

The main limitations of these approaches are cited in the following points:

- The majority of works ignore the semantic relationships between the various components of the triples.
- Related works do not address the extraction of semantic relationships between different types and resources.
- No weights are given to triples during the type detection task based on their importance.
- The use of word embedding and statistical heuristics to predict types does not allow for the extraction of more significant features from the inputs as well as the possible semantic relationships between triples. The SVM algorithm is not suitable for large datasets with a large number of features.

In this paper, we have proposed an encoder-decoder network for multi-labeling. This neural network incorporates a attention mechanism to model the links between data. Our approach aims to predict missing types for RDF entities using data from their triples [11].

Our model was tested on subsets of two different DBpedia and UniProt datasets. The DBpedia project, which is a collaborative effort to extract structured information from Wikipedia and make it available on the Web. UnProt is a massive database of protein sequences and annotations.

Deep learning techniques will allow us to uncover hidden relationships between dataset triples. Furthermore, it gives us the ability to manipulate massive amounts of data. We chose the encoder-decoder model to handle long sequences. We add an attention mechanism that gives high weights to the most important data to improve the quality of the type's detection process.

The following are the primary goals and contributions of this work:

- An embedding model that takes advantage of the semantic relationships between RDF triples.
- A multi-label classification model based on neural networks for predicting entities types.

- The use of the attention mechanism to improve the quality of extraction of the relationships between entities, using the concepts of self-attention and global attention.
- The sequence-to-sequence model is used to process long sequences. Where the inputs and outputs are long sequences.
- Numerical representation (RDF2Vec) of resources and predicates in the DB-pedia dataset.

The remainder of this paper is organized as follows: in Sect. 2, we define some Linked Data concepts and explore the various related works that deal with the type detection problem. Section 3 shows in detail our proposed approach. Section 4 describes the experimental setup and reports the results, followed by a discussion of the results in Sect. 5. Finally, Sect. 6 shows the set of perspectives as well as the conclusion of our work.

2   Literature Review

2.1   Theoretical Background

In this section, we introduce the main principles of Linked Data, we briefly recall some necessary background knowledge including principles of Linked Data, uncertainty, incompleteness, and links detection. We will also look at some areas where linked data can be used to demonstrate its utility.

Semantic Web and Linked Data: The semantic web, also known as Web 3.0, is a developed version of the current web in which a semantic layer is added to give meaning to various data in order to make data machine-readable [3].

"Linked Data refers to a method of publishing structured data, so that it can be interlinked and become more useful through semantic queries, founded on HTTP, RDF and URIs" [6]. Linked Data is a design principle that presents links between RDF-formatted data published on the web rather than links between documents. This enables machines to explore the web and find other data using the links concept [2].

The various objects in this version of the web are identified by URIs (Uniform Resource Identifier).

Uncertainty Reasoning in Linked Data: With the emergence of the semantic web, there is an ever-increasing need for approaches to representation and reasoning under uncertainty. Several approaches have been proposed for reasoning under uncertainty. These are generally based on probability theory, possibility theory and fuzzy logic [9,15,20].

Data uncertainty represents the degree of reliability, inaccuracy and imprecision of the data. According to the W3C, uncertainty is either aleatory or epistemic [15].

- Aleatory: characterized by lack of information, incompleteness information, etc. from the world.
- Epistemic: it describes the non-systematic nature of the data (variability, irreducibility) and the natural variability of a system.

Links Dtection in Linked Data: Due that there is an overwhelming quantity of heterogeneous data on the web. Integration of data silos provided by the Linked Open Data community can provide information to curate this data and boost the Semantic Web field to its true potential. Nevertheless, even the largest graphs, for example DBpedia, suffer from incompleteness [22]. Linked Data within the enterprise can be plagued with issues of data incompleteness, inconsistency and noise.

Incompleteness in the context of Linked Data can take the form of missing information, incomplete triples, missing links between different resources, etc. To efficiently build the Web of data, there must be solutions capable of linking data between different datasets of web of data, to detect missing links between data.

The link detection task for Linked Data is seen as a solution for the datasets incompleteness. This task enables us to discover new triples and improves the quality of data delivered to applications and systems using datasets built on Linked Data concepts.

Applications of Linked Data: The Semantic Web and linked data can have a significant impact on a wide range of applications. Here are a few examples:

- Protein Dataset: The UniProt knowledge base is a large repository of various protein information with extensive annotations. Several biological ontologies are used to enrich each entry's annotation. Uncertainty handling approaches can be applied to this protein dataset to deal with various types of uncertainty.
- Medical field: medical and personal patient data is commonly stored in multiple incompatible systems [23]. This representation may cause issues when integrating the data (incompleteness, errors, etc.), resulting in inaccurate or completely false diagnoses. The use of linked data to represent medical data is viewed as a solution for easing data integration. The incompleteness problem can be solved by using type detection in linked data.
- E-commerce: based on the semantic web, agents collect product data from multiple stores in order to provide the best deals to customers. They can also perform auctions, negotiations, and contract drafting automatically (or semi-automatically).

2.2 Related Work

In this part, we will explore a number of related works that deal with type prediction in RDF datasets.

A statistical heuristic link based type prediction mechanism, has been proposed in [19], this work was evaluated on DBpedia.

In [13], the authors propose a supervised hierarchical SVM classification approach for DBpedia by exploiting the contents of Wikipedia articles.

In [4], the authors propose a multi-label classification algorithm based on word embedding such as Word2Vec, FastText and GloVe in order to capture the semantic aspect between entities and relations.

Another approach named Class Assignment Detector proposed by [1] to detect correct and incorrect classes assignments for entities in RDF data by analyzing class characteristics.

The authors in [18] solved the type prediction problem by using the Twitter profiles of RDF entities. The data extracted from these profiles were used as features in training data in order to facilitate the prediction task.

Another approach proposed in [5] uses word embedding and network embedding to predict the infobox types for Wikipedia articles. This information is useful for the type generation procedure for RDF entities.

In the work done in [16], the authors propose a binary classifier using structural data and based on machine learning techniques to predict the types of RDF entities.

The work carried out in [25] consists in proposing an approach which deals with types prediction by text classification. Two classifiers have been proposed to achieve this task.

The authors show in this paper that the incompleteness of data in datasets like UniProt can erect insurmountable barriers for researchers attempting to decipher the mechanisms underlying live system operation. In the work of [14], the authors describe an approach that can provide an efficient means for quality control of protein databases [17].

Analysis: After studying the different approaches proposed in the literature for type detection in Linked Data, we can deduce that:

- The majority of works do not take into account the semantic relations between the different components of the triples.
- Use of different techniques for links detection in related works, we cite: supervised hierarchical SVM classification, statistical heuristic, machine learning techniques, text classification and word embedding.
  - The SVM algorithm is not appropriate for large datasets and for high number of features.
  - The extraction of features by the programmer is the major disadvantage of machine learning algorithms. As a result, the data quality suffers. On the other hand, this task is performed automatically by neural networks. Deep learning allows for the extraction of more and significant features and thus produces better results.
  - Using word embedding and statistical heuristics to predict types does not allow for the extraction of more significant features from the inputs and the possible semantic relations between triples. This has a negative impact on the results quality.

- The results obtained can be improved by proposing other solutions.
- Several works test their proposed methods on a subset of DBpedia data, but the tested part is not specified in the research works.
- The extraction of semantic relationships between different types (classes) and resources is not addressed in related works.
- The proposed methods do not assign weights to triples based on their importance during the type detection task.

In order to achieve this goal, we propose our approach based on deep learning in order to explore semantic relationships between the different components of RDF triples. We base our choice on deep learning models' ability to learn from large amounts of data. We added the attention mechanism to give a weighting to inputs according to their importance.

3   Research Methodology

Before delving into our approach and giving more details, we first start by showing where the missing types problem lies in the ontology proposed by the World Wide Web Consortium (W3C)[1] organization, for modeling uncertain knowledge in the semantic web. This context is presented in Fig. 1. We use deep learning techniques for incompleteness processing.

Detecting links in Linked Data is a solution to identify classes of resources and therefore find new links between data and minimize incompleteness.

The automatic detection of missing types will improve data quality and provide reliable answers to queries launched by the various applications that use Linked Data.

Our solution allows predicting types for resources belonging to RDF datasets based on predicates and object values. It is a model built using deep learning techniques [11]. Google Colaboratory[2] was used for the training phase using the DBpedia and UniProt datasest.

3.1   Modeling Problem

Our solution consists in treating the link detection problem as a multi-label classification problem.

Multi-label Classification is the task of assigning data points to a set of classes or categories which are not mutually exclusive, meaning that a point can belong simultaneously to different classes. In multi-label classification, the examples are associated with a set of labels Y from a set of disjoint labels L, $Y \subseteq L$.

The inputs of our model represent the predicates $(P1, P2, ..., Pn)$ and objects $(O1, O2, ..., On)$ belonging to a subject S. These inputs are used to predict the output which represents the types of the subject S.

---

[1] https://www.w3.org/.
[2] https://colab.research.google.com/.

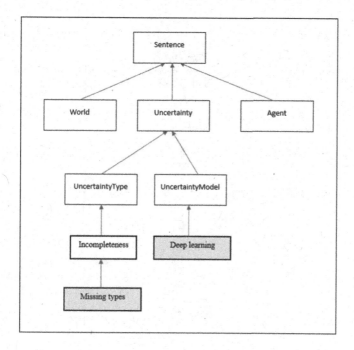

Fig. 1. Types detection in uncertainty ontology

3.2   Construction Steps

The different steps of our model construction are mentioned in Fig. 2.

Our Datasets: In order to train our model, we will use the DBpedia[3] and UniProt[4] datasets. The latter is built according to the Linked Data principles.

Each of our datasets is composed of a set of triples (Subject, predicate, object), where the predicate represents the link between the subject and the object.

Our goal is to predict missing types $(T1, T2, \ldots, Tn)$ for subjects Si based on their predicates $(P1, P2, \ldots, Pn)$ and objects $(S1, S2, \ldots, Sn)$ belonging to our dataset. i.e., for a given subject Si, we use all its predicates and objects as inputs to predict its different classes or types. As a result, by inferring new triples, we can have a more complete dataset. (Si, Pi, Oi).

The first step of our approach is dataset reading, choosing the triples concerned by the different learning phases, as well as transforming the format of these triples into a numerical format.

Once our dataset is ready, we proceed to the pre-processing step, which consists of transforming the format of the triples into a format suitable for deep learning models (numerical representation).

---

[3] http://gaia.infor.uva.es/hdt/dbpedia2016-10/dbpedia2016-10.hdt.
[4] https://www.uniprot.org/help/downloads.

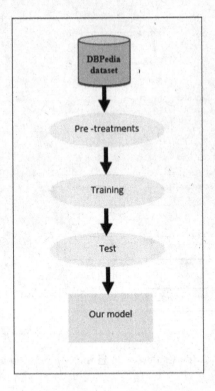

Fig. 2. Steps of our approach to type detection for Linked Data

Finally, we limit the number of predicates and objects belonging to each subject (inputs) , with the possible types as outputs.

In what follows, we will go over the number of subjects, predicates, and types that were used during the training of our model in precise detail. UniProtKB/TrEMBL has 229580745 sequence entries with a total of 80779997943 amino acids. As shown in Table 1, we extracted 80 unique types, 6392 unique predicates, and 38786 unique subjects from the UniProt dataset. Table 2 displays a collection of triples from the UniProt dataset.

Pre-treatments: Data preprocessing is an important or even crucial step for Machine Learning and Deep Learning. Data quality can directly affect the model learnability.

This step consists of transforming data into a more suitable format that can be used by the model. In this step we transformed each subject, object and predicate into numerical format. The numerical representation of inputs and outputs consists of giving numbers for each subject, predicate and object. Figure 3 shows an example of this transformation.

Table 1. The number of records for each step

Dataset	UniProt
Number of types	80
Number of predicates	6392
Number of subjects	38786

Table 2. Triples from UniProt dataset

Subject	Predicate	Object
http://purl.uniprot.org/ pfam/PF01512	http://www.w3.org/1999/ 02/22-rdf-syntax-ns#type	http://purl.uniprot.org/ core/Resource
http://purl.uniprot.org/ uniprot/A7H914	http://purl.uniprot.org/ core/classifiedWith	http://purl.uniprot.org/ keywords/1185
http://purl.uniprot.org/ uniprot/Q30TC5	http://www.w3.org/2000/ 01/rdf-schema#seeAlso	http://purl.uniprot.org/ hamap/MF_00315
http://purl.uniprot.org/ uniprot/Q1D8S3	http://purl.uniprot.org/ core/classifiedWith	http://purl.obolibrary.org/ obo/GO_0005886
http://purl.uniprot.org/ position/ 2285582822324286tt1	http://www.w3.org/1999/ 02/22-rdf-syntax-ns#type	http://biohackathon.org/ resource/faldo#Position

3.3 Our Model Proposal: Encoder-Decoder with Attention Mechanism for Missing Types Prediction

Our model is an encoder-decoder with attention mechanism which is a neural network design pattern that aids in the generation of an output sequence for every input sequence [11].

As shown in Fig. 4, the architecture is composed of two parts, encoder and decoder. Each part uses deep neural networks, more precisely gated recurrent units (GRU) in order to handle the sequence inputs of variable length.

The attention mechanism is a technique used in neural networks to focus on certain factors that can influence the model quality. The major contribution of this mechanism is to improve the sequence-to-sequence models performance. The details are mentioned in Sect. 3.3.

Our model uses as input the different predicates and objects belonging to the subject, and the types of the latter as output. We propose an embedding layer for each of the two components of our model (encoder and decoder).

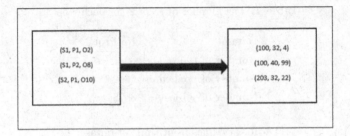

Fig. 3. An example of the preprocessing process

Encoder-Decoder: The encoder-decoder architecture is used to generate output sequences from input sequences. In our model, we used GRU cells to build each component.

Our encoder is composed of two distinct modules: the Embedding layer, and the generated vector containing the information relating to inputs. This vector is used as the first hidden state of the decoder, in order to guide the decoder in its predictions. In what follows, we will detail how it works.

For our decoder, we distinguish two layers, a GRU layer and a SoftMax layer.

The GRU layer works the same way as the encoder layer with one exception based on Input/Output:

- The decoder takes as initial input the last hidden state generated by the encoder. This hidden state contains the essential information contained in each element of the input sentence.
- Just like the encoder, the decoder has an Embedding layer that generates the Embedding vectors from the numerical representation of each subject.
- To generate a type Ti at a time step TSi, the decoder takes as input: the hidden state, the output generated at the previous time step $TSi - 1$, as well as the Embedding vector.

The SoftMax layer predicts a probability distribution over the possible types, and choose the type with the highest probability.

Embedding Layer: The embedding layer allow a reduced representation of inputs while keeping the semantic links between the subject's components. This layer enables the more features extraction from data.

Gated Recurrent Units: Gated recurrent neural networks GRU present a solution to the vanishing gradient problem. They have two gates, one for reset and another for update. They also use a hidden state mechanism, unlike LSTM which use a cell state and 3 gates. We will be able to process long sequences as a result of this.

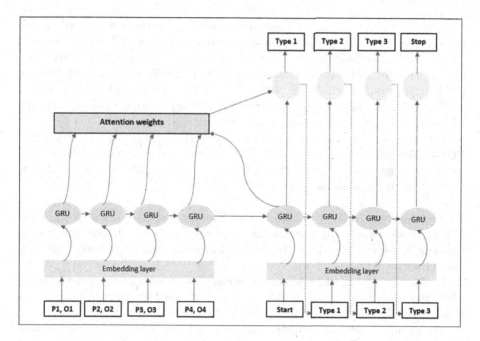

Fig. 4. Architecture of our encoder-decoder model with attention mechanism

Attention Mechanism: The attention mechanism manages and quantifies the interdependence within input elements (Self-Attention) and between inputs and outputs (General Attention). This mechanism was introduced to solve one of the problems of sequence-to-sequence models, namely their inability to provide good results when dealing with long sequences. This problem lies at the decoder level where only the last hidden state generated by the encoder is used as a context vector. An attention weight is generated for each input, giving high weights to the most important inputs in the type prediction phase. These values will be used by the decoder for the type prediction based on the results obtained from the SoftMax layer.

4   Research Findings

4.1   Experiments

To evaluate the performance of our method, we use a subset of DBpedia and UniProt in our experimentation.

Datasets

DBpedia Dataset. The DBpedia project is a community effort to extract structured information from Wikipedia and to make this information accessible on the Web.

DBpedia is a crowd-sourced community effort to extract structured, multilingual knowledge from the information created in various Wikimedia projects. The DBpedia knowledge bases are extracted from 125 Wikipedia editions. Altogether the DBpedia (2016-10) release consists of 13.1 billion pieces of information (RDF triples) out of which 1.7 billion were extracted from the English edition of Wikipedia, 6.6 billion were extracted from other language editions and 4.8 billion from Wikipedia Commons and Wikidata [12].

In this work, and due to technical constraints (RAM capacity), we used 15292 RDF triples for the different phases. These triples were divided as follows: 60% for the training phase, 20% for the validation phase and 20% for the test phase. the different details are mentioned in the Table 3.

UniProt Dataset. UniProt (The Universal Protein Resource) is a large database of protein sequences and annotations. UniProt databases include UniProtKB (the UniProt Knowledgebase), UniRef (UniProt Reference Clusters), and UniParc (UniProt Archive).

UniProt is a joint effort of the European Bioinformatics Institute (EMBL-EBI), the Swiss Institute of Bioinformatics (SIB), and the Protein Information Resource (PIR).

The members of these institutes work on a variety of tasks, including database maintenance and organization, software development, and support.Swiss-Prot and TrEMBL (Translated EMBL Nucleotide Sequence Data Library) was created by EMBL-EBI and SIB, while PIR-PSD (the Protein Sequence Database) was created by PIR. These two data sets coexisted with varying levels of protein sequence coverage and annotation priority.

To train our type detection model, we extracted the subset "eukaryota opisthokont choanoflagellates" from the UniProt dataset. Our dataset was split into three parts: x triples for training, y triples for validation, and z triples for testing. Table 1 depicts the partitioning of dataset by phase.

Hyper Parameters: For both models, we used the ADAM function as an optimizer and the 'Sparse Categorical Cross Entropy' function as a cost function. Table 4 shows the values of the various hyper parameters.

We trained our models in 70 and 78 epochs on the DBpedia and Uniprot datasets, respectively.

Table 3. The number of records for each step

Dataset	DBpedia	UniProt
Training (60%)	9174	25856
Validation (20%)	3059	6465
Test (20%)	3059	6465
Total (100%)	15292	38786

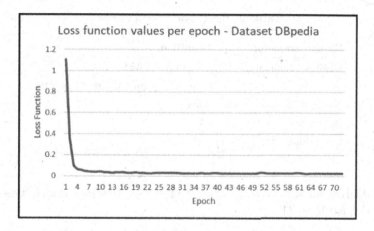

Fig. 5. Loss function values per epoch - Dataset DBpedia

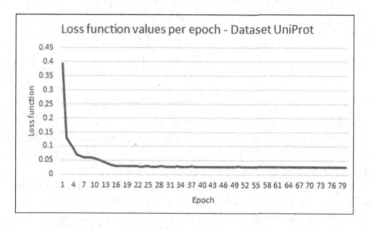

Fig. 6. Loss function values per epoch - Dataset UniProt

The Sparse Categorical Cross Entropy cost function was used to evaluate the training step. Figures 5 and 6 show the evolution of the cost function value per epoch for the two datasets, DBpedia and UniProt, respectively.

The best value for the DBpedia dataset was 0.0217. The minimum value of the cost function for UniProt was 0.0263.

4.2   Results

To evaluate our method for type prediction in Linked Data, we use the standard evaluation measures: precision, recall and F-measure. In multi label classification, these criteria are defined in the following.

The metrics evaluate the multi-label classification system's performance, on each test example separately by comparing the predicted labels with the gold

Table 4. Hyper parameters values

Hyper parameter	Definition
Optimization function	Function ADAM
Loss function	Sparse Categorical Cross Entropy
Number of GRU Nodes	1024
Batch Size	64
Embedding size	256

standard labels for each test example. We focus on 3 major example-based metrics, as defined in [8,24]:

$$Precision = \frac{1}{p}\sum_{i=1}^{p}\left(\frac{TP}{TP+FP}\right) \tag{1}$$

$$Recall = \frac{1}{p}\sum_{i=1}^{p}\left(\frac{TP}{TP+FN}\right) \tag{2}$$

$$F-measure = \frac{2.Precision.Recall}{Precision+Recall} \tag{3}$$

where p is the number of instances in the test set. The true positives (TP) is defined as the labels that are identical to the gold standard labels, false positives (FP) as labels that are not true positives, and false negatives (FN) as the gold standard labels that were missed in the prediction results.

The mean reciprocal rank, Hits@k, recall, precision, and f-measure metrics were used to evaluate our model trained on the UniProt dataset.

The inverse of the rank at which the first relevant document was found is computed by the reciprocal ranking (RR) information retrieval metric. The measure is known as the mean reciprocal rank (MRR) when averaged across queries [7]. The MRR metric formula is shown in Eq. 4. Where Q is the number of queries and $rank_i$ is the position of the relevant document.

$$MRR = \frac{1}{Q}\sum_{i=1}^{Q}\frac{1}{rank_i} \tag{4}$$

Hits@k calculates the proportion of true entities that appear in the first k entities of the sorted rank.

Table 5 illustrates the different results in two cases: Encoder-decoder model with Attention Mechanism (AM), witch represents our solution, and Encoder-decoder model without attention mechanism.

Histogram in Fig. 7 outline the evaluation results using the standard evaluation measures defined in Table 5.

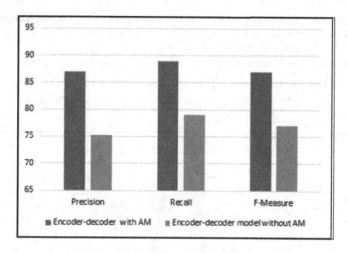

Fig. 7. Histogram of evaluation results

Table 5. Results of type predictions with our model and a simple encoder-decoder model

Model	Precision	Recall	F-Measure
Encoder-decoder with Attention mechanism	86.92	89.00	87.95
Encoder-decoder without Attention mechanism	75.16	79.02	77.04

During the training phase, we obtained a cost function value of 0.0217 for our model with attention mechanism and 0.0937 for the model without attention mechanism.

After calculating the recall, precision, and F-measure values, we discovered that our model outperformed the encoder-decoder model without an attention mechanism. On the DBPedia dataset, our model with the attention mechanism obtained the 89.00%, 86.92%, and 87.95% values for the recall, precision, and f-measure metrics, respectively. These values clearly outperform those obtained by the model without the attention mechanism.

On the UniProt dataset, we also evaluated our trained model by calculating the three metrics recall, precision, and f-measure, as well as the MRR and Hits@K metrics. To calculate the Hits@1, Hits@3, and Hits@10 metrics, we used the beam search algorithm to generate multiple output sequences.

This algorithm employs a beam search, in which decoding the most likely output sequence implies a search through all possible output sequences in order of probability. Depending on the size of the beam, several output sequences are generated.

After calculating the various metrics, we obtained 76.47%, 77.51%, and 73.00% as recall, precision, and f-measure values. We also obtained the 75.53%, 73.98%, 76.81% and 77.51% values for the MRR, Hits@1, Hits@3, and Hits@10 metrics. Table 6 and Fig. 8 depict the various outcomes. The promising results

Table 6. Evaluation results of our Encoder-decoder with attention mechanism for type prediction on UniProt dataset

Encoder-decoder model with Attention mechanism - UniProt						
MRR	Hits@1	Hits@3	Hits@10	Precision	Recall	F-Measure
75.53	73.98	76.81	77.51	76.47	71.68	73.00

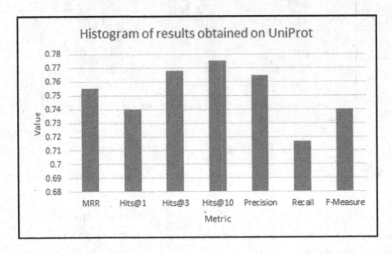

Fig. 8. Histogram of results obtained on UniProt

obtained on this dataset demonstrate the effectiveness of our model. We conclude that our model can produce good results even if the dataset is changed.

5   Discussion of Findings

According to the presented results in Table 5 and Fig. 7, we note that our modeling presents a good values for used evaluation metrics, comparing with encoder-decoder model without attention mechanism, witch is presented by 86.92% as precision value, 89.00% as Recall value and 87.95% as F-Measure value.

The results clearly demonstrated the significance of employing the attention mechanism. It enables the assignment of weights to inputs based on their importance. This increases the accuracy of output prediction. GRU cells positively influenced the results quality by making the features extraction task from inputs more efficient.

The results for the encoder-decoder model without an attention mechanism are less impressive because no attention value is assigned to the inputs to guide the type prediction process.

These results can be improved by running the model training phase on more powerful machines and by using larger datasets.

The use of triples for each entity to predict its type clearly influenced the quality of the obtained results. We believe that the structure and data associated with each entity provide a better understanding of the type of entity in question.

We approached the type incompleteness problem as a sequence-to-sequence problem, with predicates and objects serving as input sequences and types serving as output sequences. We were able to avoid the vanishing problem by using GRU cells.

We noticed that using the attention mechanism directs the detection of types by using the triples with the highest weights. This mechanism allows us to detect relationships between input elements (self-attention). On the other hand, it allows for the detection of relationships between input and output elements (global-attention). The triple set was used to represent the entities. These allow our model to understand and extract the different relationships between the entity and the dataset elements. As a result, we were able to extract all the semantic relationships and objects needed to represent each entity. This representation allowed us to consider both the structure and the semantics of the data. These results can be improved by utilizing the textual descriptions of the entities, as well as training our model on larger datasets and on more powerful machines.

Our solutions can be used in a variety of applications that use RDF datasets. Our model can help e-commerce applications that use these types of datasets detect missing types of data that are typically collected from multiple sources (stores). This will enable the detected types to be used to generate additional relationships with other entities. Applications in the medical field can also use our model to generate missing types, and therefore improve the quality of their diagnostics. We tested our model on the UniProt dataset to demonstrate its efficacy. The latter is regarded as the most significant and comprehensive protein dataset. The results have already been mentioned above.

The main limitations of this work are:

- This work only considers types. The other semantic links between entities are not considered.
- In order to be used in industry, our model must be trained and validated on larger datasets.
- Our model does not take advantage of entities' textual properties.

6   Conclusion

The semantic web community has been researching links detection and enrichment of Linked Data for last years. The volume of the available Linked Data on the web has been increasing considerably, along with the existence of erroneous, incomplete RDF data, kept this area active.

Links detection is a new research area of the Semantic Web which studies the problem of finding semantically related entities lying in different knowledge bases.

One of the most important challenges in Linked Data cloud is predicting the missing links between the entities, which is necessary to facilitate the interconnectivity of datasets in the LOD cloud, in order to enhance and enrich the information that is known about them. Moreover, in the LOD cloud, information about the same entities is available in multiple datasets in different forms.

Links detection aims to deal with the issue of missing data. The completeness of the data simplifies decision-making and task performance in any field of application, including medical diagnostics, e-commerce and ecological prediction.

In this paper, we have proposed a promising new approach dealing with the type detection problem in Linked Data. We have treated this problem as a multi-label classification task using an encoder-decoder model with attention mechanism, and we have obtained very good results. Our model was trained and tested using two large datasets: DBpedia and UniProt. The results demonstrated that our missing type generator was of high quality. The selection of the various components of our approach resulted in promising results. However, in the future, we want to validate our approach by testing it on different datasets and comparing it with the results of related works. We intend to propose a method for dealing with all possible semantic links. We also want to use NLP techniques on textual objects and to train our model on large datasets.

References

1. Barati, M., Bai, Q., Liu, Q.: An entropy-based class assignment detection approach for RDF data. In: Geng, X., Kang, B.-H. (eds.) PRICAI 2018. LNCS (LNAI), vol. 11013, pp. 412–420. Springer, Cham (2018). https://doi.org/10.1007/978-3-319-97310-4_47

2. Berners-Lee, T.: Linked data - design issues. https://www.w3.org/DesignIssues/LinkedData.html (2006). Accessed 09 May 2022

3. Berners-Lee, T., Hendler, J., Lassila, O.: The semantic web. Scientific Am. **284**(5), 34–43 (2001). https://www.sciam.com/article.cfm?articleID=00048144-10D2-1C70-84A9809EC588EF21

4. Biswas, R., Sofronova, R., Alam, M., Sack, H.: Entity type prediction in knowledge graphs using embeddings. arXiv preprint arXiv:2004.13702 (2020)

5. Biswas, R., Türker, R., Moghaddam, F.B., Koutraki, M., Sack, H.: Wikipedia infobox type prediction using embeddings. In: DL4KGS@ ESWC, pp. 46–55 (2018)

6. Bizer, C., Heath, T., Berners-Lee, T.: Linked data: the story so far. In: Sheth, A. (ed.) Semantic Services, Interoperability and Web Applications: Emerging Concepts, pp. 205–227. IGI Global (2011). https://doi.org/10.4018/978-1-60960-593-3.ch008

7. Craswell, N.: Mean reciprocal rank. In: Liu, L., Özsu, M.T. (eds.) Encyclopedia of Database Systems, p. 1703. Springer, Boston (2009). https://doi.org/10.1007/978-0-387-39940-9_488

8. Du, J., Chen, Q., Peng, Y., Xiang, Y., Tao, C., Lu, Z.: ML-Net: multi-label classification of biomedical texts with deep neural networks. J. Am. Med. Inform. Assoc. **26**(11), 1279–1285 (2019). https://doi.org/10.1093/jamia/ocz085

9. Fareh, M.: Modeling incomplete knowledge of semantic web using Bayesian networks. Appl. Artif. Intell. **33**(11), 1022–1034 (2019)

10. Fiorini, R.A.: Computational intelligence from autonomous system to super-smart society and beyond. Int. J. Softw. Sci. Comput. Intell. (IJSSCI) **12**(3), 1–13 (2020). https://doi.org/10.4018/IJSSCI.2020070101

11. Hamel, O., Fareh, M.: Encoder-decoder neural network with attention mechanism for types detection in linked data. In: 2022 17th Conference on Computer Science and Intelligence Systems (FedCSIS), pp. 733–739. IEEE (2022)

12. Jin, H., Li, C., Zhang, J., Hou, L., Li, J., Zhang, P.: Xlore2: large-scale cross-lingual knowledge graph construction and application. Data Intell. **1**(1), 77–98 (2019). https://doi.org/10.1162/dint_a_00003

13. Kliegr, T., Zamazal, O.: LHD 2.0: a text mining approach to typing entities in knowledge graphs. J. Web Semant. **39**, 47–61 (2016)

14. Kondratyeva, L., Alekseenko, I., Chernov, I., Sverdlov, E.: Data incompleteness may form a hard-to-overcome barrier to decoding life's mechanism. Biology **11**(8), 1208 (2022)

15. Laskey, K.J., Laskey, K.B.: Uncertainty reasoning for the world wide web: Report on the urw3-XG incubator group. URSW **8**, 108–116 (2008)

16. Mihindukulasooriya, N., Rico, M.: Type prediction of RDE knowledge graphs using binary classifiers with structural data. In: Pautasso, C., Sánchez-Figueroa, F., Systä, K., Murillo Rodríguez, J.M. (eds.) ICWE 2018. LNCS, vol. 11153, pp. 279–287. Springer, Cham (2018). https://doi.org/10.1007/978-3-030-03056-8_27

17. Nagy, A., et al.: Identification and correction of abnormal, incomplete and mispredicted proteins in public databases. BMC Bioinform. **9**(1), 1–26 (2008)

18. Nechaev, Y., Corcoglioniti, F., Giuliano, C.: Type prediction combining linked open data and social media. In: Proceedings of the 27th ACM International Conference on Information and Knowledge Management, pp. 1033–1042 (2018). https://doi.org/10.1145/3269206.3271781

19. Paulheim, H., Bizer, C.: Type inference on noisy RDF data. In: Alani, H., et al. (eds.) ISWC 2013. LNCS, vol. 8218, pp. 510–525. Springer, Heidelberg (2013). https://doi.org/10.1007/978-3-642-41335-3_32

20. Riali, I., Fareh, M., Ibnaissa, M.C., Bellil, M.: A semantic-based approach for hepatitis c virus prediction and diagnosis using a fuzzy ontology and a fuzzy bayesian network. J. Intell. Fuzzy Syst. **44**, 1–15 (2022)

21. Ristoski, P., Paulheim, H.: Semantic web in data mining and knowledge discovery: a comprehensive survey. J. Web Semantics **36**, 1–22 (2016). https://doi.org/10.1016/j.websem.2016.01.001

22. Sumba, X., Ortiz, J.: Between the interaction of graph neural networks and semantic web. In: Proceedings of the 2019 NeurIPS Workshop on Graph Representation Learning (2019)

23. Wilcox, C., Djahel, S., Giagos, V.: Identifying the main causes of medical data incompleteness in the smart healthcare era. In: 2021 International Symposium on Networks, Computers and Communications (ISNCC), pp. 1–6. IEEE (2021)

24. Zhang, M.L., Zhou, Z.H.: A review on multi-label learning algorithms. IEEE Trans. Knowl. Data Eng. **26**(8), 1819–1837 (2013). https://doi.org/10.1109/TKDE.2013.39

25. Zhang, X., Lin, E., Pi, S.: Predicting object types in linked data by text classification. In: 2017 Fifth International Conference on Advanced Cloud and Big Data (CBD), pp. 391–396. IEEE (2017). https://doi.org/10.1109/CBD.2017.74

Author Index

E. Ziemba et al. (Eds.): FedCSIS-AIST 2022/ISM 2022, LNBIP 471, p. 233, 2023.
https://doi.org/10.1007/978-3-031-29570-6

Printed in the United States
by Baker & Taylor Publisher Services